HOSPITAL AND COMMUNITY PHARMACY

COMPREHENSIVE GUIDE FOR PROFESSIONAL PRACTICE

PROF. S. SHOBHA RANI, DR. A. MURALIDHAR RAO

Made with ❤ on the Notion Press Platform

www.notionpress.com

Contents

Preface

In the rapidly evolving field of pharmacy, the role of pharmacists has significantly expanded beyond the traditional boundaries of dispensing medications. Today, pharmacists are integral to healthcare teams, contributing to patient care through clinical services, medication management, and health promotion activities. This book, Hospital & Community Pharmacy: Principles and Practices, is designed to equip pharmacy students and practitioners with the comprehensive knowledge and skills required to excel in both hospital and community pharmacy settings.

The genesis of this book stems from the observed challenges faced by students in accessing consolidated and comprehensive reference materials. Many students have struggled to find all the necessary information in one place, often having to refer to multiple books and articles. This fragmented approach can hinder learning and the practical application of knowledge. To address this gap, we have meticulously crafted this book to serve as a single, authoritative resource that covers the breadth and depth of the subject matter.

Our objective is to provide a well-rounded understanding of the principles and practices that underpin hospital and community pharmacy. We have organized the content into ten detailed chapters, each focusing on key aspects of the field:

Introduction to Hospitals and Hospital Pharmacy
Hospital Pharmacy Management
Hospital Formulary and Drug Procurement
Education and Training in Hospital Pharmacy
Community Pharmacy Practice
Management of Community Pharmacy
Prescription Handling and Minor Ailments
Medication Counseling and Adherence
Health Promotion in Community Pharmacy
Research and Home Medicines Review Programs

Each chapter is designed to delve deeply into specific topics, ensuring that complex information is presented in an accessible and digestible manner. We have included numerous subtopics and detailed discussions to facilitate a thorough understanding and to aid in the practical application of knowledge.

Our aim is not only to educate but also to inspire pharmacy students and practitioners to continually strive for excellence in their professional roles. We emphasize the importance of lifelong learning and the need for pharmacists to stay updated with the latest advancements in the field. Through this book, we hope to foster a deeper appreciation of the critical role that pharmacists play in healthcare and to prepare our readers to meet the challenges of contemporary pharmacy practice.

We would like to express our gratitude to all the colleagues, students, and professionals who have contributed to the development of this book. Their insights and feedback have been invaluable. We also acknowledge the support of our families and institutions, without whom this endeavor would not have been possible.

We hope that this book will serve as a valuable resource for pharmacy students, educators, and practitioners, providing them with the knowledge and confidence to excel in their careers.

Prof. S. Shobha Rani
Dr. Muralidhar Rao Akkaladevi

Hospital & Community Pharmacy

Comprehensive Guide for Professional Practice

BY

DR. S. SHOBHA RANI

Professor and Head ,CPS, UCESTH

JNTUH, Kukatpally, Hyderabad

&

DR. MURALIDHAR RAO AKKALADEVI

Professor and Principal St.Mary's College of Pharmacy, Secunderabad

Published By

Notion Press Media Pvt Ltd, #7, Red Cross Road,

Egmore, Chennai, Tamil Nadu 600008

HOSPITAL & COMMUNITY PHARMACY

Email ID: publish@notionpress.com

Notion Press, Inc.
800, West EI Camino Real #180,
California USA 94040

CHAPTER ONE

Introduction to Hospitals and Hospital Pharmacy

1.1 Definition and Classification of Hospitals

1.1.1 Definition of Hospitals

A **hospital** is a comprehensive healthcare institution designed to provide extensive medical and surgical treatment, as well as nursing care, to individuals who are acutely ill or injured. Hospitals play a critical role in the healthcare system by offering a wide range of services that address the needs of patients requiring immediate and specialized care. They are equipped with sophisticated diagnostic tools, advanced medical technologies, and highly trained medical professionals, including doctors, nurses, and specialists, to ensure optimal patient outcomes.

Hospitals are distinguished from other healthcare facilities by their ability to offer continuous patient care, typically on a 24/7 basis, and to handle a variety of complex medical conditions and emergencies. Unlike outpatient clinics or primary care centers, which provide routine medical services and preventative care, hospitals are capable of admitting patients for overnight stays and prolonged treatment. This capacity for inpatient care allows hospitals to manage severe and life-threatening conditions, perform intricate surgical procedures, and provide intensive care unit (ICU) services for critically ill patients.

Hospitals also differ from specialized care facilities, such as rehabilitation centers or long-term care facilities, which focus on extended care for patients with chronic conditions or those recovering from major surgeries. While these facilities provide essential therapeutic and supportive services, they do not possess the broad range of acute care capabilities found in hospitals.

Additionally, hospitals are often categorized based on their scope of services and the populations they serve. General hospitals provide a wide array of services across multiple medical specialties, including emergency care, surgery, obstetrics, pediatrics, and internal medicine. In contrast, specialty hospitals concentrate on specific areas of medicine, such as cardiology, oncology, or orthopedics, and are staffed with experts in those fields. Teaching hospitals, affiliated with medical schools, not only offer patient care but also serve as training grounds for medical students, residents, and fellows, fostering an environment of continuous education and research.

The intricate organization of hospitals encompasses various departments and units, each dedicated to specific aspects of patient care, such as radiology, pathology, and pharmacy services. This complexity ensures that patients receive comprehensive and coordinated care tailored to their unique medical needs.

1.1.2 Types of Hospitals

1.1.2.1 General Hospitals

General hospitals are healthcare facilities that provide a broad range of medical services to address the diverse health needs of the community. These hospitals are equipped to treat various medical conditions and offer services across multiple specialties, making them the cornerstone of comprehensive healthcare delivery.

Services Offered: General hospitals typically have departments for emergency care, internal medicine, surgery, obstetrics and gynecology, pediatrics, and psychiatry, among others. The emergency department is a critical component, providing immediate care for acute injuries, illnesses, and other medical emergencies. Internal medicine focuses on the prevention, diagnosis, and treatment of adult diseases, while the surgical department performs both routine and complex surgical procedures. Obstetrics and gynecology departments manage reproductive health, childbirth, and related surgical procedures. Pediatric departments provide medical care for infants, children, and adolescents, addressing both acute and chronic conditions. Psychiatry departments offer mental health services, including diagnosis, treatment, and counseling for mental health disorders.

General hospitals also feature diagnostic imaging services such as X-rays, CT scans, MRI, and ultrasound, which are essential for accurate diagnosis and treatment planning. Pathology laboratories within these hospitals conduct various tests on blood, tissue, and other bodily fluids to aid in the diagnosis of diseases. Additionally, general hospitals may offer rehabilitation services, including physical therapy, occupational therapy, and speech therapy, to assist patients in recovering from surgeries, injuries, or chronic conditions.

Patient Demographics: General hospitals serve a wide demographic, providing care for patients of all ages, from newborns to the elderly. The patient population includes individuals with acute illnesses and injuries, those requiring surgical interventions, patients with chronic conditions needing ongoing management, pregnant women, and individuals seeking preventive care and routine check-ups. The broad scope of services means that general hospitals must be prepared to handle a diverse array of medical conditions and patient needs.

General hospitals play a vital role in the healthcare system by offering a wide range of services that cater to the diverse needs of the community. Their ability to provide comprehensive care across various specialties ensures that patients receive timely and effective treatment for a multitude of health concerns.

1.1.2 Types of Hospitals

1.1.2.2 Specialty Hospitals

Specialty hospitals are healthcare institutions that concentrate on a specific area of medicine, offering advanced and specialized care for particular types of diseases or medical conditions. These hospitals are equipped with highly specialized medical technology and staffed by healthcare professionals who are experts in their respective fields. The focus on specific medical disciplines allows specialty hospitals to provide a higher level of expertise and more comprehensive care for complex medical issues.

Focus on Specific Medical Fields: Specialty hospitals are dedicated to treating conditions related to a particular medical specialty. For example, a **cardiology hospital** focuses on the diagnosis, treatment, and prevention of heart diseases and disorders. These hospitals are equipped with advanced cardiac care units, catheterization labs, and cardiac surgery facilities. They offer services such as coronary artery bypass grafting (CABG), angioplasty, heart transplants, and management of heart failure and arrhythmias.

An **oncology hospital**, on the other hand, specializes in the treatment of cancer. These hospitals provide a range of services including chemotherapy, radiation therapy, surgical oncology, and palliative care. They often have dedicated cancer research centers and offer clinical trials for new cancer treatments. Oncology hospitals are equipped with state-of-the-art diagnostic tools such as PET scans, MRI, and CT scans, which are crucial for accurate cancer diagnosis and staging.

Other examples of specialty hospitals include **neurology hospitals**, which focus on neurological disorders such as stroke, epilepsy, Parkinson's disease, and multiple sclerosis; **orthopedic hospitals**, which specialize in the treatment of musculoskeletal conditions including fractures, joint replacements, and sports injuries; and **pediatric hospitals**, which provide specialized care for infants, children, and adolescents.

Specialty hospitals often collaborate with general hospitals and other healthcare providers to ensure that patients receive comprehensive care. They may also serve as centers of excellence, providing education and training for healthcare professionals and conducting cutting-edge research to advance medical knowledge in their specialty areas.

By focusing on specific medical fields, specialty hospitals are able to deliver highly specialized and effective treatments, improving patient outcomes and advancing the standards of care within their disciplines. This specialized approach allows for the development of targeted treatment protocols, utilization of advanced technologies, and implementation of innovative therapeutic techniques, all of which contribute to the overall improvement of healthcare services in their respective fields.

1.1.2 Types of Hospitals

1.1.2.3 Teaching Hospitals

Teaching hospitals are unique healthcare institutions affiliated with medical schools, playing a dual role in providing patient care and serving as educational centers for medical students, residents, fellows, and other healthcare professionals. These hospitals are integral to the medical education system and are essential for training the next generation of healthcare providers.

Affiliation with Medical Schools: Teaching hospitals maintain close ties with medical schools, which allows them to integrate clinical education with academic instruction. This affiliation provides medical students with the opportunity to apply their theoretical knowledge in a practical, real-world setting under the supervision of experienced physicians. The collaboration between teaching hospitals and medical schools ensures that students receive a comprehensive education that includes both classroom learning and hands-on clinical experience.

These hospitals often serve as the primary clinical training sites for medical schools, hosting students during their clinical rotations in various specialties such as internal medicine, surgery, pediatrics, obstetrics and gynecology, and psychiatry. The affiliation also extends to nursing schools, pharmacy schools, and other allied health programs, making teaching hospitals multidisciplinary training grounds.

Role in Education and Training: The primary role of teaching hospitals in education and training is to provide a rigorous and immersive learning environment for healthcare students and professionals. They offer a structured curriculum that includes clinical rotations, internships, and residency programs, where trainees gain practical experience by working directly with patients under the guidance of experienced mentors.

Residents and fellows in teaching hospitals undergo specialized training in their chosen fields, participating in patient care, surgical procedures, and advanced diagnostics. This hands-on experience is critical for developing clinical skills, decision-making abilities, and professional competence. Teaching hospitals also provide opportunities for continuing medical education and professional development for practicing physicians, nurses, and other healthcare providers.

In addition to clinical training, teaching hospitals are often involved in medical research and innovation. They conduct clinical trials, explore new treatment modalities, and contribute to the advancement of medical science. This research component not only enhances the educational experience for students and trainees but also leads to improved patient care and outcomes.

Teaching hospitals are equipped with advanced medical technology and resources that support both patient care and education. They offer a wide range of specialized services and have departments dedicated to various medical fields, providing a diverse learning environment. The presence of a large and varied patient population exposes trainees to a broad spectrum of medical conditions and treatments, enriching their clinical education.

Through their affiliation with medical schools and their commitment to education and training, teaching hospitals play a vital role in shaping the future of healthcare. They ensure that medical professionals are well-prepared to meet the challenges of modern medicine, contribute to the advancement of medical knowledge, and provide high-quality care to patients.

1.1.2 Types of Hospitals

1.1.2.4 Non-Teaching Hospitals

Non-teaching hospitals are healthcare facilities that primarily focus on providing patient care rather than serving as educational centers for medical students and residents. Unlike teaching hospitals, which have an academic affiliation and a significant role in the education and training of future healthcare professionals, non-teaching hospitals are dedicated to delivering efficient and high-quality medical services to their patients.

Primary Focus on Patient Care: The central mission of non-teaching hospitals is to offer comprehensive medical treatment and care to the community. These hospitals are staffed by healthcare professionals who concentrate solely on patient care, ensuring that all resources and efforts are directed towards diagnosing, treating, and managing various health conditions. The absence of a teaching component allows non-teaching hospitals to streamline their operations and focus exclusively on clinical services.

Non-teaching hospitals provide a wide range of medical services, including emergency care, inpatient and outpatient services, surgical procedures, maternity care, and specialized treatments for chronic and acute conditions. They are equipped with the necessary medical technologies and facilities to handle diverse healthcare needs, from routine check-ups to complex surgeries.

In non-teaching hospitals, the healthcare team, including doctors, nurses, and support staff, is dedicated to patient care without the additional responsibilities of supervising and mentoring students and residents. This can lead to a more consistent and uninterrupted delivery of care, as the medical staff's primary objective is to ensure the well-being and recovery of their patients.

Non-teaching hospitals may also have fewer administrative and bureaucratic layers compared to teaching hospitals, which can result in more efficient patient care processes. The streamlined focus on patient care allows these hospitals to potentially offer shorter wait times for treatments and more personalized care experiences for patients.

While non-teaching hospitals may not be involved in formal medical education or research, they still play a crucial role in the healthcare system. They often serve as essential healthcare providers in their communities, especially in areas where access to teaching hospitals may be limited. Non-teaching hospitals ensure that patients receive timely and effective medical attention, contributing significantly to public health and wellness.

1.1.2 Types of Hospitals

1.1.2.5 Private vs. Public Hospitals

Private and public hospitals represent two distinct models of healthcare facilities that differ primarily in their funding sources, service models, and accessibility. Understanding the differences between these two types of hospitals is essential for comprehending the broader healthcare landscape and the range of services available to patients.

Funding Sources:

Private Hospitals: Private hospitals are funded through a combination of private investments, patient fees, and health insurance payments. These hospitals often operate as for-profit entities, although some are non-profit organizations. The revenue generated from patient care services, including consultations, surgeries, and diagnostic tests, is reinvested into the hospital to enhance facilities, technologies, and patient care services. Private hospitals may also receive funding from private donors, philanthropic organizations, and corporate partnerships.

Public Hospitals: Public hospitals are funded primarily through government allocations, taxes, and public health insurance programs. These hospitals are typically owned and operated by government entities, such as federal, state, or local governments. Public hospitals are designed to provide accessible healthcare to the general population, including underserved and low-income communities. Funding is often supplemented by grants, subsidies, and specific public health programs aimed at addressing particular health issues or demographic needs.

Service Models:

Private Hospitals: The service model of private hospitals is often characterized by shorter wait times, advanced medical technologies, and a higher level of personalized care. Private hospitals tend to offer a wider range of specialized services and elective procedures that may not be available in public hospitals. They often emphasize comfort and convenience, providing amenities such as private rooms, gourmet meals, and concierge services. The emphasis on patient satisfaction and high-quality care is driven by the competitive nature of the private healthcare market.

Public Hospitals: Public hospitals focus on providing essential healthcare services to the broadest possible segment of the population. Their service model prioritizes accessibility, equity, and comprehensive care. Public hospitals offer emergency services, inpatient and outpatient care, preventive services, and community health programs. They play a critical role in public health, particularly in responding to epidemics, disasters, and other public health emergencies. Public hospitals may have longer wait times and fewer amenities compared to private hospitals, but they are crucial for ensuring that all individuals have access to necessary medical care regardless of their financial situation.

Access and Affordability:

Private Hospitals: Access to private hospitals is often determined by a patient's ability to pay or their health insurance coverage. While private hospitals may offer superior amenities and shorter wait times, the cost of care can be significantly higher. This model can sometimes lead to disparities in access to high-quality healthcare based on economic status.

Public Hospitals: Public hospitals aim to provide healthcare services to everyone, regardless of their ability to pay. They often serve as safety-net providers for low-income, uninsured, and vulnerable populations. Public hospitals may offer sliding scale fees based on income and are more likely to provide uncompensated care. This inclusive approach helps mitigate health disparities and ensures that essential health services are available to all members of the community.

In summary, private and public hospitals play complementary roles in the healthcare system. Private hospitals cater to patients seeking specialized services, advanced treatments, and personalized care, often at a higher cost. Public hospitals ensure that essential healthcare services are accessible to everyone, particularly those who are economically disadvantaged or living in underserved areas. Both types of hospitals are essential for a balanced and effective healthcare system, each addressing different aspects of patient care and public health needs.

1.2 Organizational Structure of Hospitals

1.2.1 Hierarchical Structure

Explanation of the Typical Hierarchy in Hospitals: The organizational structure of hospitals is designed to ensure efficient management, clear lines of authority, and effective communication among staff members. A typical hospital hierarchy is a multi-tiered structure that delineates the roles and responsibilities of various personnel, ranging from top-level executives to frontline healthcare workers. This hierarchical system allows for streamlined operations, accountability, and coordinated patient care.

At the top of the hierarchy is the **Board of Directors** or **Trustees**, responsible for overarching governance, strategic planning, and policy-making. They ensure that the hospital adheres to legal and ethical standards, secures funding, and aligns with the overall mission and vision of the organization. The board appoints the hospital's Chief Executive Officer (CEO) and evaluates the hospital's performance.

Key Positions and Their Roles:

Chief Executive Officer (CEO): The CEO is the highest-ranking executive in the hospital, responsible for overall management and administration. The CEO implements the policies set by the Board of Directors, oversees daily operations, and ensures that the hospital meets its strategic goals. They liaise with department heads, represent the hospital in external affairs, and are accountable for financial performance, patient care quality, and regulatory compliance.

Chief Medical Officer (CMO): The CMO is responsible for the medical staff and clinical services. They oversee the quality of medical care, implement clinical policies, and ensure compliance with medical regulations. The CMO works closely with department heads to coordinate patient care, address clinical issues, and promote best practices in medicine.

Chief Nursing Officer (CNO): The CNO oversees nursing services and ensures the delivery of high-quality patient care. They manage nursing staff, develop nursing policies, and coordinate with other departments to integrate nursing practices into overall patient care. The CNO plays a critical role in workforce planning, staff development, and maintaining nursing standards.

Chief Financial Officer (CFO): The CFO is responsible for the financial health of the hospital. They manage budgeting, financial planning, revenue cycle management, and financial reporting. The CFO ensures that the hospital operates within its financial means, optimizes resource allocation, and adheres to financial regulations.

Chief Operating Officer (COO): The COO oversees the daily operations of the hospital, including administrative and support services. They ensure that the hospital runs smoothly, facilities are maintained, and non-clinical staff are effectively managed. The COO focuses on operational efficiency, patient flow, and service delivery.

Department Heads/Directors: Each clinical and non-clinical department within the hospital is headed by a Director or Head. These departments may include Surgery, Emergency Medicine, Cardiology, Pediatrics, Radiology, Laboratory Services, Pharmacy, Human Resources, and Information Technology. Department heads are responsible for managing their respective areas, implementing policies, and ensuring that their departments meet the hospital's standards and objectives.

Medical Staff: The medical staff comprises physicians, surgeons, specialists, and other healthcare providers who deliver direct patient care. They diagnose and treat patients, perform medical procedures, and collaborate with other healthcare professionals to provide comprehensive care.

Nursing Staff: Nurses play a vital role in patient care, providing bedside care, administering medications, and assisting with medical procedures. The nursing hierarchy includes Nurse Managers, Registered Nurses (RNs), Licensed Practical Nurses (LPNs), and Certified Nursing Assistants (CNAs). Nurse Managers oversee nursing units, ensuring that nursing care is delivered effectively and efficiently.

Support Staff: Hospitals also employ various support staff who contribute to the overall functioning of the facility. This group includes administrative assistants, maintenance workers, housekeeping staff, dietary workers, and security personnel. Each of these roles is essential to maintaining a safe, clean, and well-functioning environment for patients and staff.

In conclusion, the hierarchical structure of hospitals is designed to promote effective management, clear communication, and high-quality patient care. Each level of the hierarchy has distinct roles and responsibilities that contribute to the hospital's overall mission of delivering comprehensive and efficient healthcare services.

1.2 Organizational Structure of Hospitals

1.2.2 Roles and Responsibilities of Various Departments

1.2.2.1 Medical Department

The **Medical Department** is central to any hospital, encompassing a wide array of healthcare professionals, including doctors, surgeons, and specialists. This department is responsible for diagnosing, treating, and managing patient health issues, ensuring that patients receive comprehensive and high-quality medical care.

Doctors: Doctors, also known as physicians, are the primary healthcare providers within the medical department. They conduct patient assessments, diagnose illnesses, develop treatment plans, and monitor patient progress. Doctors often specialize in various fields such as internal medicine, pediatrics, geriatrics, and more. Their responsibilities include performing physical exams, ordering and interpreting diagnostic tests, prescribing medications, and providing preventive care advice. In hospitals, doctors may be categorized into attending physicians, who have completed their training and oversee patient care, and resident physicians, who are still undergoing specialized training.

Surgeons: Surgeons are specialized doctors who perform surgical procedures to treat diseases, injuries, and deformities. They are trained in preoperative, operative, and postoperative care. Surgeons may specialize in areas such as general surgery, orthopedic surgery, neurosurgery, cardiovascular surgery, and more. Their responsibilities include evaluating patients for surgery, conducting operations, and managing post-surgical care to ensure proper recovery. Surgeons work closely with anesthesiologists, surgical nurses, and other operating room staff to ensure patient safety and successful surgical outcomes.

Specialists: Specialists are doctors who have advanced training and expertise in specific areas of medicine. Examples include cardiologists, oncologists, neurologists, and endocrinologists. Specialists provide in-depth knowledge and advanced treatment options for complex medical conditions. Their roles involve conducting specialized diagnostic tests, interpreting results, performing advanced procedures, and collaborating with other healthcare providers to manage patient care. Specialists often lead multidisciplinary teams to provide comprehensive care tailored to the specific needs of patients with complex or chronic conditions.

In addition to their clinical duties, doctors, surgeons, and specialists in the medical department are often involved in medical education and research. They may teach medical students, residents, and fellows, contributing to the next generation of healthcare professionals. Many also engage in clinical research to advance medical knowledge, develop new treatments, and improve patient care practices.

The medical department operates in close collaboration with other hospital departments, such as nursing, pharmacy, radiology, and laboratory services, to provide integrated and holistic patient care. Effective communication and teamwork among these professionals are crucial for delivering high-quality healthcare and achieving positive patient outcomes.

1.2 Organizational Structure of Hospitals

1.2.2 Roles and Responsibilities of Various Departments

1.2.2.2 Nursing Department

The **Nursing Department** is integral to the healthcare system, playing a crucial role in patient care, support, and recovery. This department comprises various levels of nursing staff, each with distinct roles and responsibilities that ensure comprehensive and continuous patient care.

Roles of Nurses:

Registered Nurses (RNs): Registered Nurses are the backbone of the nursing department. They provide direct patient care, administer medications, and perform treatments and procedures. RNs are responsible for monitoring patient health, recording vital signs, and updating medical records. They play a critical role in patient education, offering guidance on managing illnesses and post-discharge care. RNs work in various hospital settings, including emergency rooms, intensive care units, operating rooms, and general wards. They collaborate with doctors and other healthcare professionals to develop and implement patient care plans.

Licensed Practical Nurses (LPNs): LPNs, also known as Licensed Vocational Nurses (LVNs) in some regions, provide basic medical care under the supervision of RNs and doctors. Their duties include checking vital signs, administering basic treatments, assisting with personal hygiene, and providing comfort to patients. LPNs are essential in maintaining patient well-being, offering supportive care, and ensuring that patient needs are met promptly.

Certified Nursing Assistants (CNAs): CNAs provide essential support to RNs and LPNs by assisting with daily patient care activities. Their responsibilities include helping patients with bathing, dressing, eating, and mobility. CNAs also take and record vital signs, assist with medical equipment, and report any changes in a patient's condition to the nursing staff. They are crucial in ensuring that patients receive compassionate and attentive care.

Nurse Managers: Nurse Managers oversee specific units or departments within the hospital. They are responsible for staffing, budgeting, and ensuring that nursing care meets the highest standards. Nurse Managers also handle administrative duties, coordinate with other departments, and address any issues that arise within their units. Their leadership ensures that the nursing staff is well-supported and that patient care is efficiently managed.

Roles of Nurse Practitioners:

Nurse Practitioners (NPs): NPs are advanced practice registered nurses with additional education and training, often holding a master's or doctoral degree in nursing. They have the authority to diagnose and treat medical conditions, prescribe medications, and perform procedures. NPs can work independently or in collaboration with physicians, providing primary and specialty care. Their roles include conducting physical exams, ordering and interpreting diagnostic tests, managing chronic diseases, and offering preventive healthcare services. NPs often serve as primary care providers, especially in underserved areas where access to healthcare may be limited.

Clinical Nurse Specialists (CNSs): CNSs are NPs who specialize in specific areas of healthcare, such as oncology, pediatrics, or critical care. They provide expert advice and support to nursing staff, develop and implement evidence-based practices, and improve patient outcomes through specialized knowledge. CNSs also engage in research, education, and policy development within their specialty areas.

The Nursing Department operates collaboratively with other departments, ensuring that patient care is holistic and coordinated. Nurses play a pivotal role in patient advocacy, ensuring that patient needs and concerns are addressed. Their continuous presence and direct interaction with patients make them vital in detecting early signs of complications, providing emotional support, and fostering a healing environment.

Overall, the roles and responsibilities within the Nursing Department are diverse and essential to the effective functioning of a hospital. Nurses and nurse practitioners are at the forefront of patient care, delivering critical services that contribute to patient recovery, health, and well-being. Their dedication and expertise ensure that patients receive comprehensive, compassionate, and high-quality care.

1.2 Organizational Structure of Hospitals

1.2.2 Roles and Responsibilities of Various Departments

1.2.2.3 Administrative Department

The **Administrative Department** plays a pivotal role in the overall functioning and efficiency of a hospital. This department is responsible for the non-clinical operations of the hospital, ensuring that the institution runs smoothly and effectively. The key functions of the Administrative Department include hospital administration, financial management, human resources, facilities management, and patient services.

Hospital Administration and Management:

Hospital Administrators: Hospital administrators are at the helm of the administrative department, overseeing the day-to-day operations of the hospital. Their responsibilities include strategic planning, policy formulation, and implementation of hospital-wide procedures. Administrators work to ensure compliance with healthcare regulations and standards, maintain accreditation, and manage risk. They also focus on improving patient care quality, enhancing operational efficiency, and fostering a positive workplace culture.

Financial Management: Financial management is a critical aspect of hospital administration. This involves budgeting, financial planning, and oversight of revenue cycles. Administrators ensure that the hospital remains financially stable by managing costs, optimizing revenue, and ensuring accurate billing and coding practices. They also oversee funding allocation for various departments, capital expenditures, and financial reporting. Effective financial management ensures that the hospital can provide high-quality care while remaining economically sustainable.

Human Resources: The human resources (HR) function within the administrative department is responsible for recruiting, hiring, training, and managing hospital staff. HR professionals ensure that the hospital attracts and retains skilled healthcare professionals, provides ongoing training and development, and maintains employee satisfaction. They also handle employee relations, benefits administration, performance evaluations, and compliance with labor laws and regulations. A well-functioning HR department is essential for maintaining a motivated and competent workforce.

Facilities Management: Facilities management involves maintaining the physical infrastructure of the hospital. This includes overseeing the maintenance of buildings, equipment, and grounds to ensure a safe and functional environment for patients, staff, and visitors. Facilities managers are responsible for ensuring that the hospital complies with health and safety regulations, managing waste disposal, and overseeing housekeeping and security services. Proper facilities management is crucial for preventing disruptions in hospital operations and ensuring patient safety.

Patient Services: Patient services encompass a range of functions aimed at enhancing the patient experience. This includes admissions and discharge processes, patient registration, medical records management, and customer service. Administrators work to streamline these processes to reduce wait times, improve communication, and ensure that patients have access to necessary information and support. They also handle patient complaints and feedback, working to resolve issues and improve service delivery.

Information Technology (IT): The IT function within the administrative department manages the hospital's information systems and technology infrastructure. This includes maintaining electronic health records (EHRs), managing hospital databases, ensuring cybersecurity, and supporting telehealth services. IT professionals work to integrate technology into healthcare delivery, improve data accuracy, and enhance the efficiency of hospital operations.

Marketing and Public Relations: The administrative department is also responsible for marketing and public relations activities. This includes promoting the hospital's services, managing the hospital's public image, and engaging with the community. Administrators develop marketing strategies, manage media relations, and oversee communication with stakeholders. Effective marketing and public relations efforts help attract patients, build the hospital's reputation, and foster community trust.

In summary, the Administrative Department is essential for ensuring that a hospital operates efficiently and effectively. Hospital administrators and managers oversee a wide range of functions, from financial management to human resources, facilities management, patient services, IT, and marketing. Their work supports the clinical staff, enhances patient care, and ensures that the hospital meets its strategic goals. The success of a hospital largely depends on the competence and efficiency of its administrative department, which provides the necessary support for clinical operations and patient care.

1.2 Organizational Structure of Hospitals

1.2.2 Roles and Responsibilities of Various Departments

1.2.2.4 Support Services

The **Support Services** department is crucial in providing the necessary diagnostic and ancillary services that support the core clinical functions of a hospital. This department encompasses a variety of specialized units that play a significant role in patient diagnosis, treatment, and overall care. Key components of support services include laboratory services, radiology, and other diagnostic services, each contributing uniquely to patient care.

Laboratory Services:

Laboratory Services are vital for diagnosing and monitoring diseases. They perform a wide array of tests on patient samples, such as blood, urine, and tissue. These tests are essential for detecting abnormalities, diagnosing conditions, and guiding treatment decisions. Laboratory services are typically divided into several specialized areas:

- **Hematology:** This section deals with the study of blood, blood-forming organs, and blood diseases. Hematology labs conduct tests like complete blood counts (CBC), coagulation studies, and blood typing.
- **Clinical Chemistry:** This area focuses on the chemical analysis of bodily fluids. Tests include measuring glucose, electrolytes, enzymes, hormones, and other substances to detect metabolic and endocrine disorders.
- **Microbiology:** Microbiology labs identify infectious agents such as bacteria, viruses, fungi, and parasites. They perform cultures, sensitivity testing, and molecular diagnostics to guide antimicrobial therapy.
- **Pathology:** Pathologists examine tissues and cells to diagnose diseases, including cancer. They perform biopsies, cytology tests, and autopsies to provide comprehensive diagnostic information.
- **Immunology:** This section analyzes immune system components and functions, conducting tests for allergies, autoimmune diseases, and immune deficiencies.

Radiology Services:

Radiology Services use imaging technologies to diagnose and sometimes treat diseases. Radiology departments are equipped with advanced imaging modalities that provide detailed views of the body's internal structures. Key areas within radiology include:

- **Diagnostic Radiology:** This involves the use of X-rays, CT scans, and fluoroscopy to visualize bones, organs, and tissues. These imaging techniques are essential for diagnosing fractures, infections, tumors, and other conditions.
- **Magnetic Resonance Imaging (MRI):** MRI uses strong magnetic fields and radio waves to produce detailed images of soft tissues, such as the brain, spinal cord, and joints. It is particularly useful for detecting abnormalities in these areas.
- **Ultrasound:** Ultrasound uses high-frequency sound waves to create images of internal organs and tissues. It is commonly used in obstetrics to monitor fetal development, as well as to examine organs like the liver, kidneys, and heart.
- **Nuclear Medicine:** This specialty involves the use of small amounts of radioactive materials to diagnose and treat diseases. Techniques like PET scans and SPECT imaging are used to assess organ function and detect

abnormalities.

- **Interventional Radiology:** Interventional radiologists use imaging guidance to perform minimally invasive procedures, such as angioplasty, stent placement, and biopsies. These procedures often serve as alternatives to traditional surgery.

Other Diagnostic Services:

Other Diagnostic Services include various specialized areas that support patient care through diagnostic testing and therapeutic interventions. These services encompass:

- **Cardiology Services:** Cardiology departments perform diagnostic tests such as electrocardiograms (ECGs), echocardiograms, stress tests, and cardiac catheterization. These tests are critical for diagnosing and managing heart diseases.
- **Respiratory Therapy:** Respiratory therapists provide care for patients with breathing disorders. They perform diagnostic tests like pulmonary function tests (PFTs) and administer treatments such as oxygen therapy and mechanical ventilation.
- **Physical Therapy:** Physical therapists assess and treat patients with physical impairments or disabilities. They develop individualized treatment plans to improve mobility, strength, and function through exercises, manual therapy, and other interventions.
- **Pharmacy Services:** Hospital pharmacies manage the procurement, preparation, and dispensing of medications. Pharmacists provide clinical support by ensuring appropriate medication use, monitoring for drug interactions, and educating patients and healthcare providers.
- **Dietary Services:** Dietitians and nutritionists develop dietary plans for patients based on their medical conditions and nutritional needs. They provide counseling, manage special diets, and ensure that patients receive adequate nutrition.

The Support Services department is integral to the hospital's mission of providing comprehensive patient care. By delivering accurate diagnostic information and specialized treatments, support services enhance the ability of clinical staff to diagnose, treat, and manage patient conditions effectively. These services operate collaboratively with other hospital departments to ensure a holistic approach to healthcare, ultimately improving patient outcomes and satisfaction.

1.2 Organizational Structure of Hospitals

1.2.2 Roles and Responsibilities of Various Departments

1.2.2.5 Ancillary Services

The **Ancillary Services** department provides essential support to the primary clinical services, ensuring comprehensive patient care. This department encompasses various specialized services that contribute significantly to patient treatment, recovery, and overall well-being. Key components of ancillary services include pharmacy, dietary, and rehabilitation services.

Pharmacy Services:

The **Pharmacy Services** department is a crucial component of ancillary services, responsible for managing medication therapy and ensuring the safe and effective use of pharmaceuticals. Hospital pharmacies are involved in the procurement, preparation, dispensing, and monitoring of medications.

- **Procurement and Inventory Management:** Hospital pharmacies are responsible for the procurement of medications and maintaining an adequate inventory. This involves negotiating with suppliers, managing drug shortages, and ensuring the availability of essential medications.
- **Medication Preparation and Dispensing:** Pharmacists and pharmacy technicians prepare and dispense medications to inpatients and outpatients. This includes compounding sterile and non-sterile medications, preparing intravenous (IV) admixtures, and ensuring accurate dispensing practices.
- **Clinical Pharmacy Services:** Clinical pharmacists work directly with healthcare teams to optimize medication therapy. They conduct medication therapy management, monitor for drug interactions and adverse effects, provide drug information, and participate in patient care rounds.
- **Patient Education and Counseling:** Pharmacists provide education and counseling to patients about their medications, including proper use, potential side effects, and adherence strategies. This is particularly important for patients with complex medication regimens or chronic conditions.

Dietary Services:

Dietary Services play a vital role in patient care by addressing nutritional needs and promoting healthy eating habits. Dietitians and nutritionists work closely with healthcare providers to develop and implement individualized dietary plans for patients.

- **Nutritional Assessment:** Dietitians assess the nutritional status of patients through comprehensive evaluations, including dietary history, medical conditions, and laboratory results. This helps identify patients at nutritional risk and develop appropriate interventions.
- **Individualized Dietary Plans:** Based on the nutritional assessment, dietitians create personalized dietary plans that meet the specific needs of patients. This includes special diets for conditions such as diabetes, hypertension, renal disease, and malnutrition.
- **Nutritional Counseling and Education:** Dietitians provide counseling and education to patients and their families about healthy eating habits, dietary modifications, and managing specific dietary restrictions. This empowers patients to make informed food choices and improve their nutritional status.
- **Meal Planning and Food Services:** The dietary services department collaborates with food service staff to ensure that hospital meals meet the nutritional requirements of patients. This includes planning menus, overseeing food preparation, and ensuring food safety and hygiene.

Rehabilitation Services:

Rehabilitation Services focus on helping patients recover from injuries, surgeries, and medical conditions that affect their physical and functional abilities. Rehabilitation professionals, including physical therapists, occupational therapists, and speech-language pathologists, provide specialized therapeutic interventions.

- **Physical Therapy:** Physical therapists assess and treat patients with physical impairments, disabilities, or pain. They develop individualized treatment plans that include exercises, manual therapy, and modalities such as ultrasound and electrical stimulation. The goal is to improve mobility, strength, balance, and overall physical function.
- **Occupational Therapy:** Occupational therapists help patients regain independence in daily activities. They assess the patient's ability to perform tasks such as dressing, bathing, and eating, and provide

interventions to improve functional skills. This may include adaptive equipment training, home safety assessments, and cognitive rehabilitation.

- **Speech-Language Pathology:** Speech-language pathologists assess and treat patients with communication and swallowing disorders. They provide therapy for speech, language, voice, and cognitive-communication issues, as well as interventions for dysphagia (swallowing difficulties).
- **Multidisciplinary Approach:** Rehabilitation services often involve a multidisciplinary approach, where different rehabilitation professionals collaborate to address the comprehensive needs of the patient. This ensures a holistic and coordinated plan of care that maximizes patient outcomes.

The Ancillary Services department is essential for supporting the overall mission of the hospital to provide high-quality, patient-centered care. Pharmacy, dietary, and rehabilitation services each play a critical role in the health and recovery of patients, ensuring that all aspects of their well-being are addressed. Through collaboration with other hospital departments, ancillary services contribute to a seamless and effective healthcare experience, ultimately enhancing patient outcomes and satisfaction.

1.3 Hospital Pharmacy

1.3.1 Definition and Importance

Comprehensive Definition of Hospital Pharmacy:

Hospital pharmacy is a specialized field of pharmacy practice that is integrated within the hospital environment. It encompasses the procurement, storage, preparation, distribution, and monitoring of medications for inpatients and outpatients. Hospital pharmacies are equipped to handle a wide range of pharmaceutical needs, from dispensing routine medications to compounding sterile preparations, such as intravenous (IV) admixtures and parenteral nutrition solutions. Pharmacists working in hospital pharmacies are involved in various clinical and administrative roles, contributing to the overall healthcare delivery system within the hospital.

Hospital pharmacies are distinct from retail or community pharmacies in that they operate within the hospital's framework, collaborating closely with other healthcare professionals to ensure optimal patient care. This collaboration often includes participating in multidisciplinary rounds, providing drug information and education, and managing medication therapy for individual patients. The scope of hospital pharmacy practice includes clinical pharmacy services, which involve direct patient care activities such as medication therapy management, therapeutic drug monitoring, and adverse drug reaction monitoring.

Importance in Patient Care and Hospital Operations:

The **importance of hospital pharmacy** in patient care and hospital operations cannot be overstated. Hospital pharmacists play a critical role in ensuring the safe, effective, and rational use of medications, which is fundamental to achieving positive patient outcomes. Several key aspects highlight the significance of hospital pharmacy:

1. **Medication Safety:** Hospital pharmacists are pivotal in preventing medication errors, ensuring accurate medication dispensing, and monitoring for potential drug interactions and adverse effects. They implement and oversee medication safety protocols and use advanced technologies such as computerized physician order entry (CPOE) and automated dispensing cabinets (ADCs) to enhance accuracy and efficiency.

2. **Clinical Pharmacy Services:** By providing clinical pharmacy services, hospital pharmacists directly contribute to patient care. They assess medication regimens, recommend adjustments based on clinical parameters, and educate patients and healthcare providers about proper medication use. This helps in optimizing therapeutic outcomes and minimizing the risks associated with pharmacotherapy.

3. **Medication Management:** Effective medication management within the hospital is crucial for operational efficiency and patient safety. Hospital pharmacists are responsible for managing the hospital formulary, conducting drug utilization reviews, and implementing evidence-based therapeutic guidelines. They also play a role in inventory control, ensuring the availability of essential medications while minimizing waste.

4. **Interdisciplinary Collaboration:** Hospital pharmacists collaborate with physicians, nurses, and other healthcare professionals to provide comprehensive care. Their expertise in pharmacotherapy allows them to offer valuable insights during clinical rounds, contribute to treatment plans, and support the overall healthcare team in decision-making processes.

5. **Patient Education and Counseling:** Educating patients about their medications, including proper administration, potential side effects, and adherence strategies, is a key responsibility of hospital pharmacists. This education helps patients understand their treatment regimens, promotes adherence, and reduces the likelihood of medication-related problems after discharge.

6. **Regulatory Compliance:** Hospital pharmacies must comply with various regulatory requirements to ensure the safe and legal handling of medications. Pharmacists are responsible for maintaining proper documentation, adhering to storage and dispensing regulations, and ensuring that all pharmacy operations meet the standards set by accrediting bodies such as the Joint Commission and the National Accreditation Board for Hospitals & Healthcare Providers (NABH).

7. **Research and Innovation:** Hospital pharmacists are often involved in clinical research, contributing to the development of new therapies and improving existing treatment protocols. Their participation in research activities helps advance the field of pharmacotherapy and enhances the quality of care provided to patients.

In summary, hospital pharmacy is an integral part of the hospital ecosystem, providing essential services that support patient care and hospital operations. Through their expertise in medication management, safety, and clinical services, hospital pharmacists ensure that patients receive the most appropriate and effective pharmacological interventions, ultimately improving health outcomes and enhancing the overall quality of care.

1.3 Hospital Pharmacy

1.3.2 Relationship with Other Departments

1.3.2.1 Collaboration with Medical Department

The **relationship between the hospital pharmacy and the medical department** is critical for ensuring effective and safe patient care. This collaboration primarily revolves around medication management and therapeutic consultations, which are essential components of the healthcare delivery system within a hospital.

Medication Management:

Medication management involves the selection, procurement, prescribing, dispensing, administration, and monitoring of medications. Hospital pharmacists work closely with physicians to develop and implement medication management protocols that optimize therapeutic outcomes and minimize risks. This collaboration includes:

- **Formulary Management:** Pharmacists and physicians collaborate to create and maintain the hospital formulary, which is a list of approved medications for use within the hospital. This ensures that the most effective, safe, and cost-efficient medications are available for patient care.
- **Therapeutic Drug Monitoring:** Pharmacists assist physicians in monitoring drug levels for medications with narrow therapeutic indices, such as anticoagulants, antibiotics, and immunosuppressants. By measuring drug concentrations in the blood, pharmacists help adjust dosages to achieve optimal therapeutic effects while avoiding toxicity.
- **Medication Reconciliation:** At various points of care, such as admission, transfer, and discharge, pharmacists work with medical staff to perform medication reconciliation. This process involves comparing a patient's medication orders to all of the medications they have been taking to identify and resolve discrepancies, thereby preventing medication errors.
- **Adverse Drug Reaction (ADR) Monitoring:** Pharmacists monitor patients for adverse drug reactions and work with physicians to manage these reactions. They provide recommendations for alternative therapies and report ADRs to relevant authorities, contributing to the safety and efficacy of pharmacotherapy.

Therapeutic Consultations:

Therapeutic consultations are an integral part of the collaboration between pharmacists and physicians. Pharmacists provide expert advice on medication therapy, helping physicians make informed decisions regarding drug selection, dosing, and administration. Key aspects of therapeutic consultations include:

- **Drug Information Services:** Pharmacists serve as a valuable resource for drug information, providing evidence-based answers to physicians' queries about medication use, side effects, interactions, and contraindications. This helps in making informed clinical decisions and tailoring treatments to individual patient needs.

- **Clinical Rounds Participation:** Pharmacists often participate in clinical rounds with medical teams, offering their expertise in pharmacotherapy. During rounds, they review patient cases, suggest medication adjustments, and provide recommendations for optimizing drug therapy based on the latest clinical guidelines and evidence.
- **Protocol and Guideline Development:** Pharmacists collaborate with physicians to develop clinical protocols and treatment guidelines for various medical conditions. These standardized protocols help ensure consistent and effective treatment across the hospital, improving patient outcomes and streamlining care processes.
- **Education and Training:** Pharmacists play a key role in educating medical staff about new medications, therapeutic guidelines, and best practices in medication management. They conduct in-service training sessions, workshops, and seminars to keep physicians updated on advancements in pharmacotherapy and medication safety practices.

The collaboration between hospital pharmacists and the medical department enhances the quality of patient care by ensuring that medication therapies are safe, effective, and evidence-based. This integrated approach to healthcare delivery fosters a multidisciplinary environment where pharmacists and physicians work together to achieve the best possible outcomes for patients. Through their specialized knowledge and skills, hospital pharmacists contribute significantly to the optimization of medication use and the overall success of the medical department's therapeutic goals.

1.3 Hospital Pharmacy

1.3.2 Relationship with Other Departments

1.3.2.2 Collaboration with Nursing Department

Administration of Medications:

The collaboration between the **hospital pharmacy and the nursing department** is fundamental to ensuring the accurate and safe administration of medications to patients. Nurses are responsible for the direct administration of medications, and pharmacists play a crucial role in supporting this process. This collaboration includes several key activities:

- **Medication Preparation and Verification:** Pharmacists prepare and verify medications before they are administered by nurses. This involves checking for the correct drug, dosage, route of administration, and timing, as well as ensuring the medication is compatible with the patient's other treatments and medical conditions. By providing properly labeled and packaged medications, pharmacists help reduce the risk of medication errors.

- **Order Review and Clarification:** Pharmacists review medication orders written by physicians to ensure they are complete, accurate, and appropriate for the patient's condition. If there are any questions or discrepancies, pharmacists communicate with nurses and physicians to clarify orders before administration, ensuring that patients receive the correct medications.

- **Medication Administration Records (MAR):** Pharmacists help maintain accurate and up-to-date MARs, which are essential tools for nurses to track medication administration. This collaboration ensures that all medication-related information is clearly documented and accessible, facilitating safe and effective administration.

- **Intravenous (IV) Therapy:** Pharmacists collaborate with nurses in the preparation and administration of IV medications. This includes compounding sterile IV admixtures, providing guidelines for infusion rates, and monitoring for potential complications. Pharmacists also educate nurses on the proper handling and administration of IV drugs, ensuring patient safety.

Patient Education:

Pharmacists and nurses work together to educate patients about their medications, which is crucial for promoting medication adherence and ensuring patients understand their treatment regimens. This collaborative effort includes:

- **Medication Counseling:** Pharmacists provide detailed medication counseling to patients, explaining the purpose, dosage, administration, and potential side effects of each medication. Nurses reinforce this information during their interactions with patients, answering questions and providing additional support as needed.

- **Discharge Planning:** As part of the discharge process, pharmacists and nurses collaborate to create comprehensive medication plans for patients leaving the hospital. Pharmacists ensure that patients receive clear instructions and necessary supplies for their medications, while nurses provide additional education on how to take the medications correctly at home.

- **Patient Education Materials:** Pharmacists develop educational materials such as patient information leaflets and medication guides, which nurses distribute to patients. These materials provide valuable information about medications, helping patients understand their treatment and adhere to their prescribed regimens.
- **Managing Side Effects and Adverse Reactions:** Pharmacists and nurses monitor patients for side effects and adverse drug reactions, providing timely interventions and education. Pharmacists offer guidance on managing side effects, while nurses monitor patients' responses and provide ongoing support and education.
- **Chronic Disease Management:** In managing chronic diseases such as diabetes, hypertension, and asthma, pharmacists and nurses collaborate to educate patients on the long-term use of medications, lifestyle modifications, and self-monitoring techniques. This integrated approach helps patients manage their conditions effectively and prevents complications.

The collaboration between hospital pharmacists and the nursing department enhances the overall quality of patient care by ensuring that medications are administered safely and effectively. By working together, pharmacists and nurses provide comprehensive education and support to patients, promoting medication adherence and improving health outcomes. This teamwork fosters a patient-centered approach to healthcare, where both pharmacists and nurses contribute their expertise to achieve the best possible therapeutic results for patients.

1.3 Hospital Pharmacy

1.3.2 Relationship with Other Departments

1.3.2.3 Collaboration with Administrative Department

Budgeting and Inventory Management:

The **collaboration between the hospital pharmacy and the administrative department** is essential for effective budgeting and inventory management, ensuring that the pharmacy operates efficiently and that patients have access to the necessary medications. This collaboration encompasses several critical areas:

Budgeting:

- **Financial Planning:** Pharmacists work with the administrative department to develop and manage the pharmacy's budget. This involves forecasting medication expenses, considering factors such as anticipated patient volume, drug prices, and new therapeutic options. Accurate financial planning ensures that the pharmacy has the resources needed to provide optimal patient care.
- **Cost Control:** To manage costs effectively, pharmacists and administrators collaborate on cost-control strategies, such as negotiating drug prices with suppliers, participating in group purchasing organizations, and seeking out cost-effective therapeutic alternatives. These efforts help to reduce expenses while maintaining the quality of care.
- **Resource Allocation:** The administrative department relies on pharmacists' expertise to allocate resources efficiently within the pharmacy. This includes decisions about staffing levels, technology investments, and facility upgrades. By working together, pharmacists and administrators ensure that resources are used optimally to support patient care and operational needs.
- **Financial Reporting:** Pharmacists provide regular financial reports to the administrative department, detailing medication expenditures, revenue from pharmacy services, and cost-saving initiatives. These reports help administrators monitor the pharmacy's financial performance and make informed decisions about future investments and budget adjustments.

Inventory Management:

- **Procurement and Supplier Relations:** Pharmacists collaborate with the administrative department to establish relationships with reliable suppliers and manage procurement processes. This includes negotiating contracts, ensuring timely delivery of medications, and maintaining adequate stock levels. Effective supplier management helps prevent medication shortages and ensures that the pharmacy can meet patient needs.
- **Inventory Control:** Pharmacists and administrators work together to implement inventory control systems that track medication stock levels, usage patterns, and expiration dates. This collaboration helps to minimize waste, reduce carrying costs, and ensure that medications are

available when needed. Techniques such as just-in-time inventory and automated inventory systems are often employed to enhance efficiency.

- **Formulary Management:** The administrative department supports pharmacists in maintaining the hospital formulary, a list of approved medications. Pharmacists regularly review and update the formulary based on clinical guidelines, therapeutic effectiveness, and cost considerations. By collaborating on formulary management, pharmacists and administrators ensure that the hospital provides safe, effective, and affordable medications.

- **Regulatory Compliance:** Pharmacists ensure that the pharmacy adheres to regulatory requirements for medication storage, handling, and disposal. They work with the administrative department to maintain compliance with local, state, and federal regulations, including those set by agencies such as the Food and Drug Administration (FDA) and the Drug Enforcement Administration (DEA). This collaboration helps avoid legal issues and ensures patient safety.

- **Technology and Automation:** The administrative department invests in technology and automation to support pharmacy operations. Pharmacists provide input on the selection and implementation of systems such as electronic health records (EHRs), computerized physician order entry (CPOE), and automated dispensing cabinets (ADCs). These technologies improve efficiency, accuracy, and safety in medication management.

- **Data Analytics:** Pharmacists and administrators use data analytics to monitor inventory levels, track medication usage, and identify trends. By analyzing data, they can make informed decisions about inventory management, identify opportunities for cost savings, and improve patient care outcomes.

The collaboration between the hospital pharmacy and the administrative department is vital for effective budgeting and inventory management. Through financial planning, cost control, procurement, inventory control, and compliance efforts, pharmacists and administrators ensure that the pharmacy operates efficiently and provides high-quality care to patients. This partnership helps to optimize resource use, reduce costs, and maintain the availability of essential medications, ultimately contributing to the hospital's overall success.

1.3 Hospital Pharmacy

1.3.3 Organizational Structure of Hospital Pharmacy

Roles within the Hospital Pharmacy:

The **organizational structure of a hospital pharmacy** is designed to ensure efficient management, optimal patient care, and effective communication within the pharmacy and with other departments. The structure typically includes various roles, each with specific responsibilities:

- **Chief Pharmacist:** The Chief Pharmacist, also known as the Pharmacy Director, is the highest-ranking pharmacist in the hospital. This individual oversees the entire pharmacy department, including administrative and clinical functions. Responsibilities include strategic planning, budgeting, policy development, regulatory compliance, and overall management of pharmacy operations. The Chief Pharmacist also represents the pharmacy in hospital-wide committees and collaborates with other department heads to ensure integrated patient care.

- **Staff Pharmacists:** Staff Pharmacists are responsible for the direct provision of pharmaceutical care to patients. Their duties include dispensing medications, verifying prescriptions, providing medication counseling, monitoring patient therapy, and participating in multidisciplinary healthcare teams. Staff Pharmacists also play a critical role in clinical services, such as therapeutic drug monitoring, medication reconciliation, and adverse drug reaction management.

- **Clinical Pharmacists:** Clinical Pharmacists specialize in specific areas of patient care, such as oncology, cardiology, or infectious diseases. They work closely with physicians and other healthcare providers to develop and manage patient-specific medication therapy plans. Clinical Pharmacists conduct patient assessments, provide drug information, and educate healthcare staff and patients on medication use and safety.

- **Pharmacy Technicians:** Pharmacy Technicians assist pharmacists in various tasks, including preparing and dispensing medications, managing inventory, and maintaining medication records. They are trained to handle routine technical functions, allowing pharmacists to focus on clinical and patient care activities. Pharmacy Technicians also support the preparation of intravenous admixtures, unit-dose medications, and other pharmaceutical preparations.

- **Pharmacy Interns:** Pharmacy Interns are students in the process of completing their pharmacy education. They work under the supervision of licensed pharmacists, gaining practical experience in various aspects of pharmacy practice. Interns participate in dispensing, compounding, patient counseling, and clinical services, applying their academic knowledge to real-world situations.

- **Support Staff:** Support Staff in the pharmacy includes administrative assistants, billing specialists, and clerical staff. These individuals handle non-clinical tasks such as scheduling, billing, and record-keeping, ensuring smooth and efficient pharmacy operations.

Reporting Lines and Hierarchy:

The **hierarchical structure** within the hospital pharmacy defines clear reporting lines and ensures accountability and effective communication. The typical hierarchy is as follows:

- **Chief Pharmacist:** At the top of the hierarchy, the Chief Pharmacist reports directly to the hospital administration, such as the Chief Medical Officer (CMO) or the Chief Executive Officer (CEO). The Chief Pharmacist oversees all pharmacy operations and is responsible for the overall performance of the department.
- **Assistant or Deputy Chief Pharmacist:** In larger hospitals, there may be one or more Assistant or Deputy Chief Pharmacists who report to the Chief Pharmacist. These individuals manage specific areas such as clinical services, operations, or administrative functions, ensuring that all aspects of the pharmacy are effectively coordinated.
- **Clinical Pharmacists and Pharmacy Managers:** Clinical Pharmacists and Pharmacy Managers report to the Chief Pharmacist or their deputies. Clinical Pharmacists are responsible for specialized patient care areas, while Pharmacy Managers oversee operational aspects such as inventory management, staff scheduling, and quality assurance.
- **Staff Pharmacists:** Staff Pharmacists report to Pharmacy Managers or directly to the Chief Pharmacist, depending on the hospital's size and structure. They are responsible for day-to-day pharmaceutical care and dispensing activities.
- **Pharmacy Technicians:** Pharmacy Technicians report to Staff Pharmacists or Pharmacy Managers. They support pharmacists in technical tasks and ensure the efficient operation of the pharmacy.
- **Pharmacy Interns:** Pharmacy Interns report to their assigned preceptors, who are typically Staff or Clinical Pharmacists. Interns receive guidance and supervision as they gain practical experience in

various pharmacy functions.

- **Support Staff:** Support Staff report to the administrative leaders within the pharmacy, such as the Pharmacy Manager or an Administrative Coordinator. They handle administrative and clerical tasks to support pharmacy operations.

The **organizational structure of the hospital pharmacy** ensures that all team members understand their roles and responsibilities, promoting a cohesive and efficient working environment. Clear reporting lines facilitate communication, decision-making, and accountability, ultimately enhancing the quality of patient care provided by the pharmacy department.

1.3 Hospital Pharmacy

1.3.4 Legal Requirements for Hospital Pharmacy

Regulations and Compliance Standards:

Hospital pharmacies operate under strict regulations and compliance standards to ensure the safety and efficacy of medication use and to protect patient welfare. These regulations are established by various governmental and professional bodies, including the Food and Drug Administration (FDA), the Drug Enforcement Administration (DEA), state boards of pharmacy, and accreditation organizations such as The Joint Commission (TJC) and the National Accreditation Board for Hospitals & Healthcare Providers (NABH).

Key regulatory requirements include:

- **Controlled Substances Management:** The DEA sets forth specific guidelines for the storage, handling, dispensing, and documentation of controlled substances to prevent misuse and diversion. Hospital pharmacies must maintain accurate records and conduct regular audits to ensure compliance.
- **Medication Storage and Handling:** The FDA and state boards of pharmacy establish standards for the proper storage and handling of medications, including temperature control, security measures, and inventory management. Compliance with these standards ensures medication integrity and patient safety.
- **Labeling and Packaging:** Regulations require that medications be labeled and packaged according to specific guidelines, including clear identification of the drug, dosage, administration instructions, expiration dates, and warnings. These requirements help prevent

medication errors and ensure proper use.

- **Dispensing Practices:** Hospital pharmacies must adhere to standards for prescription verification, compounding, and dispensing to ensure that medications are prepared and delivered safely and accurately. This includes verifying patient information, checking for drug interactions, and following aseptic techniques for sterile preparations.

Licensing and Accreditation Processes:

Hospital pharmacies must obtain and maintain various licenses and accreditations to operate legally and demonstrate their commitment to high-quality care. These processes involve rigorous evaluation and ongoing compliance with established standards.

- **Licensing:** State boards of pharmacy issue licenses to hospital pharmacies, which must be renewed periodically. The licensing process involves an application, inspection, and review of the pharmacy's compliance with state laws and regulations. Pharmacists and pharmacy technicians also need individual licenses to practice.
- **Accreditation:** Accreditation by organizations such as TJC and NABH is a voluntary process that signifies a hospital pharmacy's adherence to high standards of care. Accreditation involves a thorough evaluation of the pharmacy's operations, including medication management, patient safety practices, and quality improvement initiatives. Accredited pharmacies must undergo regular reviews and demonstrate continuous compliance with accreditation standards.

Ethical Considerations and Patient Safety Protocols:

Hospital pharmacies are guided by ethical principles and patient safety protocols that ensure the delivery of safe, effective, and patient-centered care. These considerations are integral to the pharmacy's mission and daily operations.

- **Ethical Considerations:** Pharmacists are bound by a code of ethics that emphasizes professionalism, integrity, and respect for patient autonomy. Ethical considerations include maintaining patient confidentiality, obtaining informed consent for medication use, avoiding conflicts of interest, and providing unbiased, evidence-based information to patients and healthcare providers.

- **Patient Safety Protocols:** Patient safety is a primary concern in hospital pharmacy practice. Protocols and practices designed to enhance safety include:

  - **Medication Reconciliation:** Ensuring accurate and complete medication information is transferred at all points of care, reducing the risk of errors and adverse drug events.
  - **Adverse Drug Event (ADE) Monitoring:** Implementing systems to detect, report, and analyze ADEs, allowing for timely interventions and improvements in medication safety practices.
  - **Pharmacovigilance:** Monitoring the safety of medications through post-marketing surveillance and reporting adverse reactions to regulatory authorities, contributing to the overall safety profile of drugs.
  - **Patient Education:** Providing comprehensive counseling and education to patients about their medications, including proper use, potential side effects, and the importance of adherence, empowering patients to manage their health effectively.

By adhering to these legal requirements, regulations, and ethical principles, hospital pharmacies ensure they operate within the law, provide high-quality care, and prioritize patient safety. This framework not only enhances the pharmacy's operational integrity but also fosters trust and confidence among patients and healthcare professionals.

Chapter 2: Hospital Pharmacy Management 2.1 Workload Statistics and Infrastructural Requirements • 2.1.1 Measuring and Managing Workload • 2.1.1.1 Methods to Measure Workload • Quantitative metrics (prescriptions filled, patient interactions) • Qualitative assessments (staff feedback, service quality)

Hospital Pharmacy Management

2.1 Workload Statistics and Infrastructural Requirements

2.1.1 Measuring and Managing Workload

2.1.1.1 Methods to Measure Workload

Quantitative Metrics (Prescriptions Filled, Patient Interactions):

Measuring the workload in a hospital pharmacy involves various quantitative metrics that provide objective data on the volume of work handled by the pharmacy staff. One of the primary metrics is the number of prescriptions filled. This includes not only the total count of prescriptions but also the types, such as oral medications, intravenous admixtures, and compounded preparations. Tracking these figures over time helps identify trends, peak periods, and resource allocation needs.

Another critical quantitative measure is the number of patient interactions. This encompasses consultations with patients, medication counseling sessions, and participation in multidisciplinary healthcare teams. Patient interactions are essential for ensuring proper medication use, adherence, and addressing any concerns or side effects. Recording the frequency and nature of these interactions helps assess the demand for clinical pharmacy services and the effectiveness of patient communication strategies.

Quantitative metrics also include the time taken for specific tasks, such as prescription processing, medication compounding, and inventory management. Time studies and process mapping can identify bottlenecks and areas for improvement, enabling the pharmacy to streamline operations and enhance efficiency. These metrics are crucial for staffing decisions, workload distribution, and justifying the need for additional resources or technological investments.

Qualitative Assessments (Staff Feedback, Service Quality):

In addition to quantitative data, qualitative assessments play a vital role in understanding the workload and its impact on staff and service quality. Staff feedback is a valuable source of information about the working conditions, job satisfaction, and potential stressors within the pharmacy. Regular surveys, interviews, and focus group discussions can provide insights into the challenges faced by the staff, their perceptions of workload, and suggestions for improvements.

Qualitative assessments also involve evaluating the quality of services provided by the pharmacy. This includes patient satisfaction surveys, which gather feedback on the patients' experiences with the pharmacy services, including the clarity of information provided, the professionalism of the staff, and the overall efficiency of the service. High patient satisfaction scores indicate that the pharmacy is meeting its service quality goals, while lower scores highlight areas needing attention.

Service quality can also be assessed through peer reviews and audits conducted by external bodies or internal quality assurance teams. These evaluations consider various aspects of pharmacy operations, such as adherence to protocols, accuracy of medication dispensing, and compliance with regulatory standards. The findings from these reviews help identify best practices, areas for improvement, and opportunities for staff development.

Combining quantitative metrics with qualitative assessments provides a comprehensive view of the workload in a hospital pharmacy. This integrated approach enables pharmacy managers to make informed decisions about resource allocation, process optimization, and staff training, ultimately enhancing the efficiency and effectiveness of pharmacy services. By continuously monitoring and managing workload through these methods, hospital pharmacies can maintain high standards of patient care and operational excellence.

2.1.1 Measuring and Managing Workload

2.1.1.2 Tools and Techniques for Workload Management

Scheduling Software:

Scheduling software is an essential tool for managing workload in a hospital pharmacy. These systems help automate the scheduling process, ensuring that the right number of staff members are available at the right times to meet the pharmacy's needs. The software can take into account various factors such as peak hours, staff availability, and skill levels, creating optimized schedules that enhance productivity and reduce downtime.

Advanced scheduling software can also handle shift swaps, vacation requests, and overtime management, making it easier to accommodate staff preferences and maintain work-life balance. Additionally, these systems often come with features for tracking hours worked, generating reports, and ensuring compliance with labor regulations. By using scheduling software, pharmacy managers can ensure adequate staffing levels, minimize scheduling conflicts, and improve overall operational efficiency.

Resource Allocation Strategies:

Effective resource allocation is crucial for managing workload in a hospital pharmacy. This involves strategically distributing tasks and responsibilities among the pharmacy staff to ensure that all areas of the pharmacy operate smoothly and efficiently. One common strategy is task delegation, where specific tasks are assigned to staff members based on their expertise and experience. For instance, experienced pharmacists may handle complex medication therapy management, while pharmacy technicians might focus on prescription filling and inventory management.

Cross-training staff is another valuable resource allocation strategy. By training employees to perform multiple roles within the pharmacy, managers can create a more flexible workforce that can adapt to changing workload demands. Cross-trained staff can fill in for absent colleagues, assist during peak periods, and contribute to various aspects of pharmacy operations, enhancing overall resilience and continuity.

Implementing a workload distribution matrix can help visualize and plan resource allocation. This tool maps out the various tasks and responsibilities within the pharmacy, the time required for each, and the staff members assigned to them. By regularly reviewing and updating the matrix, managers can identify imbalances, anticipate workload spikes, and make proactive adjustments to maintain optimal staffing levels.

Furthermore, lean management principles can be applied to streamline workflows and eliminate inefficiencies. Techniques such as process mapping, value stream analysis, and the 5S methodology (Sort, Set in order,

Shine, Standardize, Sustain) can help identify and eliminate waste, standardize procedures, and create a more organized and efficient work environment.

Combining these tools and techniques allows hospital pharmacies to manage their workload effectively, ensuring that resources are used optimally, staff are engaged and productive, and patient care is delivered at the highest standards. This integrated approach to workload management not only improves operational efficiency but also enhances job satisfaction and reduces burnout among pharmacy staff.

2.1 Workload Statistics and Infrastructural Requirements

2.1.1 Measuring and Managing Workload

2.1.1.2 Tools and Techniques for Workload Management

Scheduling Software:

Scheduling software is an essential tool for managing workload in a hospital pharmacy. These systems help automate the scheduling process, ensuring that the right number of staff members are available at the right times to meet the pharmacy's needs. The software can take into account various factors such as peak hours, staff availability, and skill levels, creating optimized schedules that enhance productivity and reduce downtime.

Advanced scheduling software can also handle shift swaps, vacation requests, and overtime management, making it easier to accommodate staff preferences and maintain work-life balance. Additionally, these systems often come with features for tracking hours worked, generating reports, and ensuring compliance with labor regulations. By using scheduling software, pharmacy managers can ensure adequate staffing levels, minimize scheduling conflicts, and improve overall operational efficiency.

Resource Allocation Strategies:

Effective resource allocation is crucial for managing workload in a hospital pharmacy. This involves strategically distributing tasks and responsibilities among the pharmacy staff to ensure that all areas of the pharmacy operate smoothly and efficiently. One common strategy is task delegation, where specific tasks are assigned to staff members based on their expertise and experience. For instance, experienced pharmacists may handle complex medication therapy management, while pharmacy technicians might focus on prescription filling and inventory management.

Cross-training staff is another valuable resource allocation strategy. By training employees to perform multiple roles within the pharmacy, managers can create a more flexible workforce that can adapt to changing workload demands. Cross-trained staff can fill in for absent colleagues, assist during peak periods, and contribute to various aspects of pharmacy operations, enhancing overall resilience and continuity.

Implementing a workload distribution matrix can help visualize and plan resource allocation. This tool maps out the various tasks and responsibilities within the pharmacy, the time required for each, and the staff members assigned to them. By regularly reviewing and updating the matrix, managers can identify imbalances, anticipate workload spikes, and make proactive adjustments to maintain optimal staffing levels.

Furthermore, lean management principles can be applied to streamline workflows and eliminate inefficiencies. Techniques such as process mapping, value stream analysis, and the 5S methodology (Sort, Set in order, Shine, Standardize, Sustain) can help identify and eliminate waste, standardize procedures, and create a more organized and efficient work environment.

Combining these tools and techniques allows hospital pharmacies to manage their workload effectively, ensuring that resources are used optimally, staff are engaged and productive, and patient care is delivered at the highest standards. This integrated approach to workload management not only improves operational efficiency but also enhances job satisfaction and reduces burnout among pharmacy staff.

2.1.1 Measuring and Managing Workload

2.1.1.3 Impact of Workload on Staff and Patient Care

Effects of High Workload on Staff Morale and Patient Outcomes:

High workload in a hospital pharmacy can significantly impact both staff morale and patient outcomes. When pharmacy staff are overburdened, they often experience increased stress, burnout, and job dissatisfaction. This can lead to higher turnover rates, as overworked employees may seek less demanding positions elsewhere. The constant pressure to meet high demands can also result in decreased motivation and engagement, further exacerbating the problem.

Stress and burnout among pharmacy staff can have a direct effect on their performance. Errors in medication dispensing, patient counseling, and inventory management become more likely under stressful conditions. This not only compromises the quality of care but also endangers patient safety.

For instance, incorrect medication or dosage errors can lead to adverse drug reactions, prolonged hospital stays, or even fatalities. Additionally, the time constraints imposed by a heavy workload can limit pharmacists' ability to provide thorough patient counseling, reducing the overall effectiveness of treatment and patient adherence to medication regimens.

Patient outcomes are closely tied to the quality of care provided by the pharmacy staff. When pharmacists and technicians are overwhelmed, the risk of medication errors increases, which can result in negative health outcomes for patients. Furthermore, high workload conditions can lead to longer wait times for medication dispensing and consultations, causing patient frustration and potentially delaying treatment. In the long term, this can erode patient trust in the healthcare system and reduce their willingness to seek medical help.

To mitigate these issues, it is crucial to implement strategies that manage workload effectively. This includes hiring sufficient staff to meet demand, providing adequate training and support, and ensuring a balanced distribution of tasks. Additionally, fostering a positive work environment that recognizes and addresses the challenges faced by pharmacy staff can help maintain high morale and job satisfaction. Regular feedback sessions, professional development opportunities, and wellness programs are essential components of a supportive workplace.

By addressing the impact of high workload on staff and patient care, hospital pharmacies can enhance their service quality, ensure patient safety, and create a more sustainable and satisfying work environment for their employees. This holistic approach to workload management ultimately leads to better health outcomes for patients and a more resilient healthcare system.

2.1.2 Infrastructure Needs for Efficient Operations

2.1.2.1 Physical Layout of the Pharmacy

Design Considerations for Workflow Efficiency:

The physical layout of a hospital pharmacy is a critical factor in ensuring workflow efficiency and effective operations. A well-designed pharmacy layout minimizes unnecessary movement, reduces the risk of errors, and enhances the overall productivity of the pharmacy staff. Key design considerations include the strategic placement of workstations, storage areas, and equipment to facilitate a smooth flow of activities.

For instance, the dispensing area should be centrally located with easy access to the medication storage and patient consultation areas. This reduces the time spent walking between these key zones, allowing pharmacists to focus more on patient care and medication management. Adequate space should be provided for each workstation to accommodate multiple staff members working simultaneously without crowding, ensuring a seamless and efficient workflow.

Space Allocation for Different Functions (Dispensing, Compounding):

In addition to the overall layout, specific space allocations for various functions within the pharmacy are essential for efficient operations. The dispensing area should be designed to handle high volumes of prescriptions with ease. This includes having ample counter space for preparing medications, a secure area for storing controlled substances, and sufficient shelving for organizing medications by type and frequency of use.

The compounding area requires special attention to ensure compliance with safety and cleanliness standards. It should be equipped with proper ventilation, laminar airflow hoods, and containment systems to protect both the staff and the integrity of the medications being prepared. Adequate space must be provided for compounding equipment, raw materials, and work surfaces to facilitate accurate and efficient preparation of compounded medications.

Additional areas to consider include a patient consultation space that ensures privacy and comfort, an office space for administrative tasks, and a designated area for receiving and storing inventory. Each of these spaces should be designed with the specific needs of the pharmacy in mind, balancing functionality, safety, and efficiency.

By focusing on these design considerations and space allocations, hospital pharmacies can create an environment that supports efficient operations, enhances staff productivity, and ultimately improves patient care.

2.1.2 Infrastructure Needs for Efficient Operations

2.1.2.2 Technological Infrastructure

Importance of Modern IT Systems (Electronic Health Records, Automated Dispensing Systems):

The incorporation of modern IT systems is crucial for the efficient operation of hospital pharmacies. These technologies streamline various processes, improve accuracy, and enhance the overall quality of patient care. Key components of this technological infrastructure include electronic health records (EHRs) and automated dispensing systems.

Electronic Health Records (EHRs) are essential tools that enable seamless communication and information sharing among healthcare providers. EHRs provide pharmacists with real-time access to comprehensive patient data, including medical history, current medications, and allergy information. This accessibility facilitates better-informed decision-making, ensuring that pharmacists can accurately review prescriptions and identify potential drug interactions or contraindications. The use of EHRs also reduces paperwork and administrative burdens, allowing pharmacists to allocate more time to direct patient care.

Automated Dispensing Systems (ADS) significantly enhance the efficiency and accuracy of medication dispensing processes. These systems automate the storage, dispensing, and tracking of medications, minimizing the risk of human error. Automated systems can accurately count and label medications, ensuring precise dosages and reducing the likelihood of dispensing errors. Additionally, ADS can streamline inventory management by keeping track of medication stock levels and expiration dates, prompting timely reordering and reducing wastage.

The integration of modern IT systems also supports better compliance with regulatory standards and improves patient safety. For example, barcoding technology can be used in conjunction with ADS to verify that the correct medication is dispensed and administered to the right patient. This technology provides an additional layer of safety, particularly in busy hospital settings where the risk of errors is higher.

Moreover, modern IT systems enable advanced analytics and reporting capabilities. Data collected through EHRs and ADS can be analyzed to identify trends, monitor performance, and implement quality improvement initiatives. These insights can help hospital pharmacies optimize their operations, enhance patient outcomes, and support evidence-based practice.

Investing in modern technological infrastructure is not only beneficial for operational efficiency but also essential for meeting the evolving demands of healthcare delivery. As hospital pharmacies continue to adopt and integrate these advanced systems, they can expect to see improvements in workflow efficiency, patient safety, and overall quality of care.

2.1.2 Infrastructure Needs for Efficient Operations

2.1.2.3 Equipment and Supplies

Essential Equipment for Hospital Pharmacies:

Hospital pharmacies require a wide range of equipment to ensure efficient and accurate medication preparation, dispensing, and patient care. Essential equipment includes:

- **Dispensing Cabinets and Shelving:** These are crucial for the organized storage of medications, allowing for easy access and inventory management. Automated dispensing cabinets (ADCs) are particularly useful for storing and dispensing medications in a controlled manner, reducing the risk of errors and theft.
- **Compounding Equipment:** For pharmacies involved in compounding medications, specialized equipment such as laminar airflow hoods, biological safety cabinets, and compounding isolators are essential. These devices ensure a sterile environment, preventing contamination and ensuring the safety of compounded medications.
- **Refrigeration Units:** Many medications require specific temperature conditions for storage. Hospital pharmacies must have reliable refrigeration units and freezers to store temperature-sensitive medications, such as vaccines and biologics.
- **Automated Dispensing Machines:** These machines streamline the dispensing process by automating the selection, packaging, and labeling of medications. This reduces manual errors and enhances efficiency, especially in high-volume settings.
- **Infusion Pumps and IV Preparation Equipment:** Infusion pumps are essential for accurately delivering intravenous medications. IV preparation areas should be equipped with clean rooms or aseptic compounding areas to ensure the safe and sterile preparation of IV medications.
- **Labeling and Packaging Machines:** Accurate labeling is critical to patient safety. Automated labeling machines ensure that each medication is correctly labeled with patient information, dosage instructions, and other essential details.

Maintenance and Regular Updates of Pharmacy Infrastructure:
Maintaining the pharmacy's equipment and infrastructure is crucial to ensure continuous and safe operations. Regular maintenance schedules should be established for all equipment to prevent breakdowns and extend their lifespan. This includes routine checks, cleaning, calibration, and servicing of machines and devices.

- **Preventive Maintenance:** Implementing a preventive maintenance program helps identify potential issues before they lead to equipment failure. This proactive approach minimizes downtime and ensures that the pharmacy can operate efficiently without unexpected interruptions.
- **Upgrading Equipment:** Staying updated with technological advancements is essential for maintaining the efficiency and safety of pharmacy operations. Periodically upgrading equipment to newer models with enhanced features can improve workflow, accuracy, and patient safety. For example, upgrading to the latest automated dispensing systems can enhance inventory management and reduce medication errors.
- **Compliance and Safety Checks:** Regular compliance checks should be conducted to ensure that all equipment meets regulatory standards and safety guidelines. This includes ensuring that all refrigeration units are functioning correctly and that compounding equipment is operating within the required sterility standards.
- **Training and Competency:** Staff should be trained on the proper use and maintenance of all equipment. Regular competency assessments ensure that pharmacy personnel are proficient in operating and troubleshooting equipment, further enhancing the efficiency and safety of the pharmacy environment.

By prioritizing the maintenance and regular updates of pharmacy infrastructure, hospital pharmacies can ensure reliable and efficient operations, ultimately leading to better patient outcomes and higher standards of care.

2.2 Budgeting for Hospital Pharmacy

2.2.1 Budget Planning and Management
2.2.1.1 Budget Planning Process
Steps Involved in Creating a Pharmacy Budget:
Creating an effective pharmacy budget involves a systematic process that ensures all financial aspects are accounted for, enabling the pharmacy to operate efficiently while meeting its financial goals. The budget planning process typically includes the following steps:

1. **Assessment of Current Financial Status:** Begin by reviewing the pharmacy's current financial status, including income, expenses, and financial performance over the past year. This helps identify trends, areas of overspending, and opportunities for cost savings.
2. **Setting Financial Goals:** Establish clear financial goals for the upcoming budget period. These goals may include increasing revenue, reducing costs, investing in new technology, or expanding services.
3. **Forecasting Revenue:** Project the pharmacy's expected revenue based on historical data, current trends, and any anticipated changes in services or patient volume. This involves estimating income from prescription sales, consulting services, and other revenue streams.
4. **Estimating Expenses:** Identify and estimate all potential expenses the pharmacy will incur. This includes both fixed costs (e.g., salaries, rent) and variable costs (e.g., drug costs, supplies). Accurate expense estimation is crucial for realistic budget planning.
5. **Allocating Resources:** Allocate the available financial resources to various expense categories based on priorities and goals. Ensure that essential areas such as salaries, drug procurement, and equipment maintenance receive adequate funding.
6. **Contingency Planning:** Include a contingency fund in the budget to cover unexpected expenses or emergencies. This helps ensure financial stability and continuity of operations in case of unforeseen events.
7. **Review and Approval:** Present the draft budget to the relevant stakeholders, such as the hospital administration or finance committee, for review and approval. This step may involve revisions and adjustments based on feedback.
8. **Implementation and Monitoring:** Once approved, implement the budget and establish mechanisms for ongoing monitoring and review. Regularly compare actual financial performance against the budget to identify variances and take corrective actions as needed.

Identifying Key Budget Components (Salaries, Drug Costs, Equipment):

Creating a comprehensive pharmacy budget requires identifying and categorizing all key components that contribute to the pharmacy's expenses. The primary budget components typically include:

1. **Salaries and Wages:** This is often the largest expense category and includes the salaries and wages of all pharmacy staff, including pharmacists, pharmacy technicians, administrative personnel, and support staff. Benefits, overtime pay, and bonuses should also be considered.

2. **Drug Costs:** Medication costs constitute a significant portion of the pharmacy budget. This includes the purchase of prescription drugs, over-the-counter medications, and any compounding ingredients. It's essential to forecast drug prices accurately and account for potential price fluctuations.

3. **Equipment and Supplies:** Allocate funds for the purchase, maintenance, and replacement of pharmacy equipment. This includes dispensing cabinets, compounding equipment, refrigeration units, and automated dispensing systems. Additionally, budget for routine supplies such as labels, packaging materials, and safety equipment.

4. **Facility Costs:** These include expenses related to the physical space of the pharmacy, such as rent, utilities, and maintenance. Ensuring a well-maintained and functional facility is crucial for efficient operations.

5. **IT and Technological Investments:** Budget for the implementation and maintenance of information technology systems, such as electronic health records, pharmacy management software, and automated dispensing machines. Investing in modern technology can improve efficiency and patient safety.

6. **Training and Development:** Allocate funds for the ongoing training and professional development of pharmacy staff. This includes continuing education, certification programs, and attendance at industry conferences.

7. **Regulatory and Compliance Costs:** Ensure that the budget includes expenses related to regulatory compliance, such as licensing fees, accreditation costs, and compliance with safety and quality standards.

8. **Miscellaneous Expenses:** Account for other expenses that may arise, such as marketing, insurance, and administrative costs. Including a miscellaneous category helps cover any unexpected or minor expenses that may not fit into other categories.

By meticulously planning and managing the budget, hospital pharmacies can ensure financial stability, optimize resource allocation, and support the delivery of high-quality patient care.

2.2 Budgeting for Hospital Pharmacy

2.2.1 Budget Planning and Management
2.2.1.2 Managing the Pharmacy Budget
Strategies for Cost Control and Financial Efficiency:

Effective management of the pharmacy budget involves implementing strategies that control costs and promote financial efficiency while maintaining high standards of patient care. Key strategies include:

1. **Cost-Benefit Analysis:** Regularly perform cost-benefit analyses to evaluate the financial impact of new initiatives, technologies, or processes. This helps determine whether potential investments will provide sufficient benefits to justify the costs.
2. **Negotiating with Suppliers:** Engage in strategic negotiations with drug and equipment suppliers to secure better pricing, discounts, and favorable payment terms. Building strong relationships with suppliers can lead to long-term cost savings.
3. **Bulk Purchasing:** Where feasible, purchase medications and supplies in bulk to benefit from volume discounts. Coordinating with other departments or hospitals for group purchasing can also enhance buying power and reduce costs.
4. **Inventory Management:** Implement robust inventory management practices to minimize waste, reduce overstocking, and avoid stockouts. Techniques such as just-in-time inventory, regular audits, and automated inventory systems can enhance efficiency.
5. **Generic and Formulary Drugs:** Promote the use of generic drugs and formulary-approved medications to lower drug costs. Educating staff and patients about the efficacy and safety of generics can increase their acceptance and use.
6. **Energy and Resource Efficiency:** Optimize the use of energy and other resources within the pharmacy. Implement energy-efficient lighting, heating, and cooling systems, and encourage practices that reduce waste, such as recycling and reusing materials.
7. **Staff Productivity:** Enhance staff productivity through training, process improvements, and the use of technology. Efficient workflows and task delegation can reduce labor costs and improve service quality.

8. **Regular Financial Reviews:** Conduct regular financial reviews to assess budget performance, identify variances, and implement corrective actions. Frequent monitoring helps detect issues early and maintain budget alignment.

9. **Cost-Effective Technology:** Invest in cost-effective technology solutions that streamline operations and improve accuracy, such as automated dispensing systems and electronic health records. These technologies can reduce labor costs and medication errors.

10. **Outsourcing Non-Core Functions:** Consider outsourcing non-core functions, such as housekeeping or certain administrative tasks, to external providers who can perform them more cost-effectively.

Monitoring and Adjusting the Budget as Needed:

Continuous monitoring and periodic adjustment of the pharmacy budget are crucial to ensuring financial stability and responsiveness to changing circumstances. Key practices include:

1. **Monthly Financial Reports:** Generate detailed monthly financial reports to track income, expenses, and budget adherence. These reports should highlight variances and provide insights into the financial health of the pharmacy.

2. **Key Performance Indicators (KPIs):** Establish and monitor KPIs related to financial performance, such as cost per prescription, inventory turnover rates, and labor costs. KPIs provide measurable benchmarks for assessing efficiency and effectiveness.

3. **Variance Analysis:** Regularly conduct variance analysis to compare actual financial performance against the budget. Identify the root causes of significant variances and take corrective actions to address them.

4. **Flexible Budgeting:** Adopt a flexible budgeting approach that allows for adjustments in response to unforeseen events or changes in the operating environment. This ensures the budget remains relevant and achievable.

5. **Stakeholder Involvement:** Involve key stakeholders, including pharmacy staff, department heads, and finance personnel, in the budgeting process and financial reviews. Their input and buy-in are essential for successful budget management.

6. **Forecasting Adjustments:** Update financial forecasts periodically based on current performance data and anticipated changes. Adjust budget

allocations as necessary to reflect updated revenue projections and expense requirements.

7. **Cost Control Initiatives:** Implement and track specific cost control initiatives aimed at reducing expenses or increasing efficiency. Regularly review the progress and impact of these initiatives to ensure they are delivering the desired results.

8. **Risk Management:** Identify potential financial risks and develop mitigation strategies to minimize their impact. This includes maintaining a contingency fund and having plans in place for addressing unexpected expenses or revenue shortfalls.

By employing these strategies, hospital pharmacies can effectively manage their budgets, control costs, and ensure financial efficiency while continuing to provide high-quality care to patients.

2.2 Budgeting for Hospital Pharmacy

2.2.1 Budget Planning and Management
2.2.1.3 Financial Reporting and Accountability
Importance of Transparent Financial Reporting:

Transparent financial reporting is critical for the effective management and accountability of a hospital pharmacy. It ensures that all financial activities are accurately documented, accessible, and understandable to stakeholders, including hospital administrators, regulatory bodies, and the pharmacy team. Transparent reporting promotes trust, facilitates informed decision-making, and helps identify areas for financial improvement. It also aids in detecting and preventing fraud, waste, and abuse within the pharmacy operations. Moreover, clear and transparent financial reports enable the hospital to demonstrate financial responsibility and compliance with legal and regulatory requirements.

Regular Audits and Compliance Checks:

Regular audits and compliance checks are essential components of financial accountability in hospital pharmacy management. These processes involve systematic reviews of financial records, transactions, and operations to ensure accuracy, integrity, and adherence to established policies and regulations.

1. **Internal Audits:** Conducted by the hospital's internal audit team, these audits focus on verifying the accuracy of financial records, evaluating internal controls, and ensuring compliance with hospital policies. Internal audits help identify discrepancies, inefficiencies, and areas for improvement in financial management practices.

2. **External Audits:** Performed by independent auditing firms, external audits provide an objective assessment of the pharmacy's financial statements and operations. They offer an unbiased evaluation of financial health and compliance with industry standards and regulatory requirements. External audits enhance credibility and reassure stakeholders of the pharmacy's financial integrity.

3. **Regulatory Compliance Checks:** These checks ensure that the pharmacy complies with all relevant laws, regulations, and guidelines set by governmental and accrediting bodies. Compliance checks may include reviewing licensing and accreditation status, verifying adherence to drug procurement and distribution regulations, and ensuring proper documentation of financial transactions.

4. **Continuous Monitoring:** Implementing continuous monitoring systems allows for real-time tracking of financial activities and quick identification of anomalies or irregularities. Automated tools and software can facilitate continuous monitoring by flagging potential issues and generating regular reports for review.

5. **Corrective Actions:** Based on audit findings and compliance checks, it is crucial to implement corrective actions promptly. Addressing identified issues, improving internal controls, and updating policies and procedures help mitigate risks and enhance financial management.

6. **Stakeholder Communication:** Regularly communicating audit results and compliance status to stakeholders, including hospital management, staff, and external entities, fosters transparency and accountability. Clear communication ensures that everyone is informed about the pharmacy's financial performance and any corrective measures being taken.

By prioritizing transparent financial reporting and conducting regular audits and compliance checks, hospital pharmacies can maintain financial integrity, ensure accountability, and support the overall financial health and sustainability of the hospital.

2.3 Hospital Drug Policy

2.3.1 Pharmacy & Therapeutics Committee
2.3.1.1 Composition and Roles
Key Members of the Committee:

The Pharmacy & Therapeutics (P&T) Committee is a critical component of hospital drug policy management, comprising a multidisciplinary team of healthcare professionals. The committee typically includes:

1. **Pharmacists:** Clinical and staff pharmacists bring expertise in pharmacology, therapeutics, and medication management. They play a central role in evaluating drug efficacy, safety, and cost-effectiveness.
2. **Physicians:** Specialists and general practitioners contribute their clinical knowledge and experience. They provide insights into disease management and therapeutic strategies, ensuring that the formulary meets the diverse needs of the patient population.
3. **Nurses:** Representing the nursing staff, they offer perspectives on medication administration and patient care, ensuring that nursing considerations are integrated into formulary decisions.
4. **Hospital Administrators:** These members provide a broader organizational perspective, focusing on budgetary constraints, regulatory compliance, and overall hospital policy.
5. **Other Healthcare Professionals:** Depending on the hospital's needs, the committee may also include dietitians, social workers, and laboratory technicians, who contribute their specialized knowledge to the decision-making process.

Primary Functions:

The P&T Committee has several essential functions aimed at optimizing medication use within the hospital:

1. **Drug Formulary Management:** One of the primary responsibilities of the P&T Committee is to develop and maintain the hospital's drug formulary. This involves selecting medications based on their efficacy, safety, cost-effectiveness, and therapeutic need. The committee regularly reviews and updates the formulary to reflect new evidence, clinical guidelines, and market availability.

2. **Therapeutic Guidelines Development:** The committee establishes therapeutic guidelines and protocols for the use of medications within the hospital. These guidelines are evidence-based and aim to standardize treatment approaches, improve patient outcomes, and ensure the rational use of drugs. The development process includes reviewing current literature, evaluating clinical trial data, and incorporating best practices.

3. **Medication Use Evaluation (MUE):** The P&T Committee conducts MUE programs to assess the appropriateness, safety, and effectiveness of medication use. These evaluations help identify areas for improvement in prescribing practices, medication administration, and patient adherence.

4. **Adverse Drug Reaction (ADR) Monitoring:** The committee oversees the hospital's ADR monitoring and reporting system. It reviews ADR reports, identifies trends, and recommends actions to prevent future occurrences. This function is crucial for enhancing patient safety and minimizing medication-related risks.

5. **Drug Shortage Management:** In cases of drug shortages, the P&T Committee develops strategies to manage limited supplies, including identifying alternative therapies and ensuring equitable distribution of available medications.

6. **Education and Training:** The committee provides education and training to healthcare staff on formulary changes, therapeutic guidelines, and best practices in medication use. This ensures that all staff members are informed and competent in their roles related to drug therapy.

7. **Regulatory Compliance:** The P&T Committee ensures that the hospital's medication management practices comply with regulatory requirements and accreditation standards. This includes adherence to guidelines from bodies such as the National Accreditation Board for Hospitals & Healthcare Providers (NABH) and other relevant authorities.

By incorporating diverse expertise and focusing on evidence-based practices, the P&T Committee plays a pivotal role in enhancing the quality and safety of medication use in hospitals. Its functions ensure that the hospital's drug policy aligns with clinical needs, regulatory standards, and financial constraints, ultimately contributing to improved patient care.

2.3.1.2 Decision-Making Process

How the Committee Makes and Implements Decisions:

The decision-making process of the Pharmacy & Therapeutics (P&T) Committee is systematic and structured to ensure that policies are evidence-based, transparent, and aligned with the hospital's goals. The process typically involves the following steps:

1. **Issue Identification:** Committee members identify issues or areas needing policy development or revision. This can stem from various sources, including new drug approvals, clinical practice updates, adverse event reports, and feedback from healthcare providers.
2. **Gathering Evidence:** The committee collects relevant data and evidence to inform their decisions. This includes clinical trial results, meta-analyses, practice guidelines, pharmacoeconomic studies, and real-world evidence. The aim is to gather comprehensive information that covers the safety, efficacy, and cost-effectiveness of the medications under consideration.
3. **Evaluation and Discussion:** Committee members critically evaluate the gathered evidence. This involves reviewing clinical data, comparing therapeutic alternatives, and considering the hospital's specific patient population and resources. Discussions are collaborative, with each member providing insights from their area of expertise.
4. **Formulating Recommendations:** Based on the evaluation, the committee formulates recommendations. These recommendations can include adding or removing drugs from the formulary, updating therapeutic guidelines, implementing new safety protocols, or addressing identified medication use issues.
5. **Drafting Policies:** Once recommendations are agreed upon, the committee drafts detailed policies and guidelines. These documents outline the rationale behind decisions, the intended outcomes, and specific instructions for implementation. They also specify monitoring and evaluation mechanisms to assess the impact of the new policies.
6. **Approval and Endorsement:** The drafted policies are presented to higher hospital administration or relevant governing bodies for approval. This step ensures that policies align with broader hospital goals and regulatory requirements.
7. **Implementation:** Upon approval, the committee oversees the implementation of the new policies. This includes disseminating information to relevant departments, providing necessary training, updating documentation and IT systems, and ensuring that all healthcare

providers are aware of the changes.

8. **Monitoring and Review:** After implementation, the committee continuously monitors the impact of the new policies. This involves collecting data on medication use, patient outcomes, and compliance with the guidelines. Periodic reviews are conducted to assess the effectiveness of the policies and make necessary adjustments.

Role of Evidence-Based Medicine in Policy Development:

Evidence-based medicine (EBM) is central to the P&T Committee's decision-making process. EBM involves integrating clinical expertise with the best available research evidence and patient values to make informed decisions about patient care. In the context of the P&T Committee, EBM ensures that policies are grounded in scientifically validated information and that they reflect the latest advancements in medical research.

1. **Systematic Review of Literature:** The committee relies on systematic reviews and meta-analyses to gather high-quality evidence. These reviews synthesize data from multiple studies, providing a comprehensive overview of the efficacy and safety of medications.

2. **Clinical Guidelines:** The committee references established clinical guidelines from reputable organizations such as the World Health Organization (WHO), the National Institute for Health and Care Excellence (NICE), and specialty-specific professional societies. These guidelines provide evidence-based recommendations for the treatment and management of various conditions.

3. **Risk-Benefit Analysis:** Evidence-based medicine involves conducting a risk-benefit analysis to determine the overall value of a medication or therapeutic intervention. The committee evaluates the potential benefits in terms of patient outcomes against the risks, such as adverse effects and cost implications.

4. **Pharmacoeconomic Evaluations:** Cost-effectiveness and budget impact analyses are integral to EBM. The committee assesses the economic implications of their decisions, ensuring that the hospital can provide the best possible care within its financial constraints.

5. **Patient-Centered Considerations:** EBM also emphasizes the importance of patient preferences and values. The committee considers factors such as patient adherence, quality of life, and acceptability of treatments in their decision-making process.

By adhering to the principles of evidence-based medicine, the P&T Committee ensures that their decisions are scientifically sound, patient-centered, and aligned with the hospital's commitment to high-quality care. This approach enhances the credibility of their policies and fosters trust among healthcare providers and patients.

2.3.2 Infection Control Committee

2.3.2.1 Importance of Infection Control

Role of Pharmacy in Preventing Healthcare-Associated Infections:

Infection control is a critical aspect of hospital management, aiming to prevent healthcare-associated infections (HAIs) which are infections that patients acquire while receiving treatment for medical or surgical conditions. These infections can lead to severe health complications, prolonged hospital stays, increased healthcare costs, and even mortality. The Infection Control Committee (ICC) is responsible for developing and implementing strategies to minimize the risk of HAIs.

The pharmacy department plays a vital role in infection control by ensuring the appropriate use of antimicrobial agents, contributing to the formulation of infection control policies, and educating healthcare staff on best practices. The pharmacy's involvement in infection control can be detailed as follows:

1. **Antimicrobial Stewardship:** Pharmacists are integral to antimicrobial stewardship programs, which aim to optimize the use of antibiotics to combat antibiotic resistance and reduce the incidence of HAIs. This involves selecting the appropriate antibiotic, dosing, route of administration, and duration of therapy. Pharmacists review antibiotic prescriptions, provide recommendations to clinicians, and ensure that antibiotic use aligns with established guidelines.

2. **Formulary Management:** The pharmacy oversees the hospital formulary, ensuring that it includes effective antimicrobial agents while minimizing the use of broad-spectrum antibiotics that contribute to resistance. Pharmacists work with the ICC to evaluate new antimicrobial agents and make evidence-based decisions on their inclusion in the formulary.

3. **Infection Control Policies:** Pharmacists collaborate with the ICC to develop and implement infection control policies and protocols. This includes guidelines for hand hygiene, sterilization of equipment, isolation procedures, and the management of infectious diseases.

Pharmacists provide input on the proper storage and handling of medications to prevent contamination.

4. **Education and Training:** Pharmacists educate healthcare providers on infection control practices, the rational use of antibiotics, and the risks associated with improper antibiotic use. They conduct training sessions on aseptic techniques, hand hygiene, and the management of drug-resistant infections. By raising awareness and providing knowledge, pharmacists help ensure that all staff adhere to infection control protocols.

5. **Surveillance and Reporting:** The pharmacy contributes to the surveillance of HAIs by monitoring antibiotic usage patterns and resistance trends. Pharmacists analyze data on antibiotic prescribing and resistance, identify potential outbreaks, and report findings to the ICC. This information is used to adjust infection control strategies and improve patient outcomes.

6. **Patient Care and Counseling:** Pharmacists play a direct role in patient care by counseling patients on the proper use of antibiotics, potential side effects, and the importance of adherence to prescribed treatments. They educate patients on measures to prevent infections, such as vaccination, hygiene practices, and wound care.

7. **Sterile Compounding:** Hospital pharmacies often prepare sterile medications, including intravenous antibiotics. Pharmacists ensure that these medications are compounded under strict aseptic conditions to prevent contamination and infection. They follow guidelines for the preparation, storage, and administration of sterile products to maintain their safety and efficacy.

8. **Collaboration with Other Departments:** Pharmacists work closely with other departments, such as nursing and surgery, to ensure that infection control measures are consistently applied. They participate in multidisciplinary rounds and infection control audits, providing expertise on medication-related aspects of infection prevention.

2.3.2 Infection Control Committee
2.3.2.2 Strategies for Infection Control
Guidelines for Antibiotic Stewardship:
Antibiotic stewardship programs (ASPs) are designed to optimize the use of antibiotics to combat antibiotic resistance, reduce healthcare-associated infections (HAIs), and improve patient outcomes. Effective

stewardship involves a multidisciplinary approach, including pharmacists, physicians, microbiologists, and infection control specialists. Key strategies for antibiotic stewardship include:

1. **Appropriate Antibiotic Selection:** Pharmacists and clinicians collaborate to select the most appropriate antibiotic based on the infection type, patient characteristics, and local resistance patterns. This includes choosing the narrowest spectrum antibiotic that effectively treats the infection to minimize the impact on normal flora and reduce the risk of resistance development.

2. **Optimal Dosing and Duration:** Ensuring that antibiotics are prescribed at the correct dose and for the appropriate duration is crucial. Pharmacists review prescriptions to adjust dosing based on factors such as patient age, weight, renal function, and severity of infection. Shortening the duration of antibiotic therapy when appropriate helps reduce the risk of resistance and adverse effects.

3. **Formulary Restrictions:** Limiting the use of certain broad-spectrum or high-risk antibiotics to specific indications or requiring approval from an infectious disease specialist can help control inappropriate use. This strategy ensures that these powerful antibiotics are reserved for cases where they are truly needed.

4. **Education and Training:** Continuous education for healthcare providers on the principles of antibiotic stewardship and the risks of antibiotic resistance is essential. Training programs should cover guidelines for prescribing antibiotics, the importance of culture and sensitivity testing, and the consequences of overuse and misuse of antibiotics.

5. **Monitoring and Feedback:** Regular audits of antibiotic use and feedback to prescribers help identify patterns of inappropriate use and areas for improvement. Pharmacists play a key role in reviewing antibiotic prescriptions, providing recommendations, and implementing corrective actions.

6. **Clinical Pathways and Guidelines:** Developing and implementing evidence-based clinical pathways and treatment guidelines for common infections ensure standardized and effective antibiotic use. These guidelines are regularly updated based on the latest evidence and resistance data.

7. **Rapid Diagnostic Testing:** Utilizing rapid diagnostic tests to identify pathogens and their resistance patterns allows for targeted therapy,

reducing the use of broad-spectrum antibiotics. This approach helps in early de-escalation of therapy and minimizes unnecessary antibiotic exposure.

8. **Pharmacist-Led Interventions:** Pharmacists can lead various interventions, such as dose optimization, IV to oral switch programs, and therapeutic drug monitoring, to ensure effective and safe antibiotic use. Their expertise in pharmacokinetics and pharmacodynamics is crucial for managing complex cases.

Hygiene and Sanitation Protocols:

Maintaining high standards of hygiene and sanitation is fundamental to preventing HAIs. Effective protocols involve rigorous cleaning and disinfection practices, hand hygiene compliance, and adherence to aseptic techniques. Key strategies include:

1. **Hand Hygiene:** Ensuring that all healthcare workers adhere to hand hygiene protocols is one of the most effective ways to prevent the spread of infections. Hand hygiene practices include using alcohol-based hand rubs or washing with soap and water before and after patient contact, before performing aseptic tasks, and after exposure to bodily fluids.

2. **Environmental Cleaning:** Regular cleaning and disinfection of hospital surfaces, equipment, and patient care areas are essential. This includes high-touch surfaces such as bed rails, doorknobs, and medical equipment. Using appropriate disinfectants and following standardized cleaning protocols help eliminate pathogens.

3. **Sterilization of Medical Equipment:** Proper sterilization and disinfection of medical instruments and devices prevent the transmission of infectious agents. Autoclaving, chemical disinfection, and single-use disposable instruments are some methods used to ensure the sterility of medical equipment.

4. **Isolation Precautions:** Implementing isolation precautions for patients with known or suspected infections helps prevent cross-contamination. This includes using personal protective equipment (PPE), dedicated equipment, and separate rooms or areas for infected patients.

5. **Aseptic Techniques:** Adherence to aseptic techniques during medical procedures, such as catheter insertion, wound care, and surgeries, minimizes the risk of introducing infections. Training healthcare workers in aseptic practices and regularly monitoring compliance is

crucial.

6. **Waste Management:** Proper disposal of medical waste, including sharps, infectious waste, and pharmaceutical waste, is vital for infection control. Hospitals must follow guidelines for segregating, handling, and disposing of waste to prevent contamination and spread of infections.

7. **Antimicrobial Surfaces and Coatings:** Using antimicrobial surfaces and coatings in high-risk areas can reduce microbial load and transmission. This includes coatings on medical devices, bed rails, and other frequently touched surfaces.

8. **Staff Education and Compliance Monitoring:** Regular training sessions for healthcare workers on hygiene and sanitation protocols, coupled with monitoring and feedback systems, ensure compliance. Staff should be aware of the importance of infection control measures and the role they play in preventing HAIs.

Implementing these strategies effectively requires a coordinated effort among all hospital departments, with strong leadership and commitment to infection control principles. The pharmacy, in collaboration with the ICC, ensures that these protocols are followed, contributing to a safer healthcare environment for patients and staff.

2.3.3 Research & Ethics Committee

2.3.3.1 Role of the Research & Ethics Committee:

The Research & Ethics Committee (REC) plays a pivotal role in overseeing clinical research involving medications within a hospital setting. This committee ensures that all research activities are conducted ethically, safeguarding the rights, safety, and well-being of participants. The REC is composed of a diverse group of professionals, including clinicians, pharmacists, ethicists, and community representatives, who collectively bring a broad perspective to the review process.

The primary function of the REC is to review and monitor research proposals to ensure they adhere to ethical standards and regulatory requirements. This involves a thorough examination of study protocols, informed consent documents, and the potential risks and benefits to participants. By ensuring that ethical standards are maintained, the REC promotes public trust in clinical research and protects participants from harm.

In addition to reviewing new research proposals, the REC is responsible for ongoing oversight of approved studies. This includes monitoring progress reports, reviewing any adverse events or protocol deviations, and ensuring that any modifications to the study are ethically justified. The committee also provides guidance and support to researchers, helping them navigate ethical challenges and maintain high standards of conduct throughout their studies.

2.3.3.2 Approval Process for Research:

Obtaining ethical approval for clinical research is a rigorous process designed to ensure that studies are conducted responsibly and with respect for participants' rights. The approval process involves several key steps:

1. **Submission of Research Proposal:** Researchers must submit a detailed research proposal to the REC for review. This proposal typically includes the study protocol, objectives, methodology, participant recruitment strategies, and informed consent documents. The proposal should also outline the potential risks and benefits of the study, as well as measures to minimize harm and protect participants' confidentiality.

2. **Initial Review:** Upon receipt of the research proposal, the REC conducts an initial review to assess the study's ethical implications. This involves evaluating the scientific validity of the study, the adequacy of the informed consent process, and the potential risks and benefits to participants. The REC also considers the qualifications and experience of the research team to ensure they are capable of conducting the study safely and ethically.

3. **Ethical Deliberation:** The committee engages in thorough ethical deliberation, discussing the potential impacts of the study on participants and the wider community. Key considerations include the study's risk-benefit ratio, the appropriateness of the participant population, and the adequacy of measures to ensure informed consent and confidentiality. The REC may request additional information or revisions to the proposal to address any ethical concerns.

4. **Decision Making:** Based on the review and deliberation, the REC makes a decision regarding the study's approval. Possible outcomes include full approval, conditional approval (requiring modifications or additional safeguards), or rejection. The decision is communicated to the researchers, along with detailed feedback and any required changes.

5. **Ongoing Monitoring:** For approved studies, the REC maintains ongoing oversight to ensure continued compliance with ethical standards. Researchers are required to submit regular progress reports, report any

adverse events or protocol deviations, and seek approval for any proposed changes to the study. The REC may conduct audits or site visits to verify compliance and address any ethical issues that arise during the study.

6. **Final Reporting:** Upon completion of the study, researchers must submit a final report to the REC, summarizing the study's outcomes, any ethical issues encountered, and how they were addressed. This final report allows the REC to evaluate the study's overall ethical conduct and contribute to the knowledge base for future research.

By adhering to this structured approval process, the REC ensures that clinical research is conducted ethically, protecting participants' rights and well-being while advancing scientific knowledge in a responsible manner.

2.3.4 NABH Guidelines for Medicine Management

2.3.4.1 Overview of NABH

Introduction to the National Accreditation Board for Hospitals & Healthcare Providers (NABH):

The National Accreditation Board for Hospitals & Healthcare Providers (NABH) is a constituent board of the Quality Council of India (QCI), established to promote high standards of healthcare in India. NABH provides accreditation to hospitals and healthcare providers that meet its rigorous standards for quality and patient safety. The accreditation process involves a comprehensive evaluation of the hospital's services, facilities, and practices, ensuring they adhere to national and international standards. NABH accreditation is recognized as a mark of excellence in healthcare, indicating that an institution is committed to maintaining high standards of care, continuous improvement, and patient safety.

2.3.4.2 Key Medicine Management Guidelines

Compliance Requirements for Medication Safety:

NABH's guidelines for medicine management emphasize the importance of medication safety across all stages of the medication use process. Key compliance requirements include:

1. **Patient Identification:** Ensuring accurate patient identification to prevent medication errors. This involves using at least two patient identifiers (e.g., name and date of birth) before administering any medication.

2. **Medication Reconciliation:** Implementing processes to reconcile medications at all transition points of care (admission, transfer, discharge) to prevent discrepancies and ensure continuity of care.

3. **High-Alert Medications:** Establishing protocols for the safe handling of high-alert medications, which have a higher risk of causing significant harm if used inappropriately. This includes clear labeling, double-checking processes, and staff education.

4. **Adverse Drug Event (ADE) Reporting:** Creating a system for reporting and analyzing ADEs to identify trends, implement preventive measures, and improve medication safety practices.

Standards for Storage, Prescribing, and Dispensing Practices:

NABH outlines specific standards for the storage, prescribing, and dispensing of medications to ensure their safety and efficacy:

1. **Storage:**

- Medications must be stored in a secure, organized, and clean environment, with controlled access to prevent unauthorized use.
- Temperature-sensitive medications should be stored in refrigeration units with temperature monitoring systems to maintain their stability and efficacy.
- Separate storage areas for high-alert medications, controlled substances, and hazardous drugs to minimize the risk of errors and contamination.

1. **Prescribing:**

- Prescriptions must be clear, legible, and complete, including the patient's name, medication name, dosage, route, frequency, and duration.
- Electronic prescribing systems (e-prescribing) are encouraged to reduce errors associated with handwritten prescriptions and enhance tracking and monitoring.
- Protocols for prescribing antibiotics to promote judicious use and prevent the development of antibiotic resistance.

3. **Dispensing:**

- Pharmacists must verify the accuracy and appropriateness of each prescription before dispensing, ensuring it aligns with clinical guidelines and patient-specific factors.
- Implementing barcode scanning and automated dispensing systems to enhance accuracy and efficiency in the dispensing process.
- Providing clear and comprehensive labeling on dispensed medications, including instructions for use, potential side effects, and storage requirements.

2.3.4.3 Implementing NABH Guidelines

Steps for Aligning Hospital Pharmacy Practices with NABH Standards:

1. **Gap Analysis:** Conduct a thorough gap analysis to compare current pharmacy practices with NABH standards. Identify areas requiring improvement and develop an action plan to address these gaps.
2. **Policy Development:** Develop and update policies and procedures to align with NABH guidelines. Ensure these documents are comprehensive, clearly written, and accessible to all staff members.
3. **Staff Training and Education:** Provide regular training sessions for pharmacy staff and other healthcare providers on NABH standards and best practices for medication management. Emphasize the importance of adherence to protocols and continuous education.
4. **Quality Improvement Initiatives:** Implement quality improvement initiatives to enhance medication safety and efficiency. This may include adopting new technologies, streamlining processes, and encouraging a culture of safety and accountability.
5. **Monitoring and Auditing:** Establish a robust system for monitoring compliance with NABH standards. Conduct regular internal audits to assess adherence to guidelines and identify areas for further improvement.
6. **Patient Education:** Develop educational materials and counseling programs to inform patients about their medications, proper usage, and potential risks. Engaging patients in their care can improve adherence and outcomes.
7. **Collaboration with Other Departments:** Foster collaboration with other hospital departments, such as nursing, administration, and quality assurance, to ensure a multidisciplinary approach to implementing

NABH guidelines.

8. **Documentation and Reporting:** Maintain accurate and comprehensive documentation of all medication management activities, including adverse events, interventions, and compliance efforts. Regularly report these findings to hospital leadership and the NABH.

By following these steps, hospital pharmacies can successfully align their practices with NABH standards, enhancing medication safety, improving patient outcomes, and achieving excellence in healthcare delivery.

CHAPTER THREE

Hospital Formulary and Drug Procurement

3.1 Hospital Formulary Guidelines and Development

3.1.1 Introduction to Hospital Formulary

3.1.1.1 Definition and Purpose

Definition of a Hospital Formulary:

A **hospital formulary** is a continually updated list of medications and related information, representing the clinical judgment of pharmacists, physicians, and other healthcare experts. This list is intended to ensure the availability of medications that are most effective and safe to meet the healthcare needs of patients within a hospital. The formulary includes information about medication selection, prescribing guidelines, therapeutic indications, dosing, potential side effects, and cost-effectiveness.

Importance and Objectives in Clinical Settings:

The hospital formulary serves several critical purposes and objectives in clinical settings:

1. **Standardization of Medication Use:** The formulary standardizes the medications used within the hospital, promoting consistency in prescribing practices. This helps reduce variability in patient care and ensures that all patients receive the most effective and safest treatments based on current clinical evidence.

2. **Improved Patient Safety:** By carefully selecting medications based on efficacy, safety, and quality, the formulary helps minimize the risk of adverse drug reactions and medication errors. Clear guidelines and protocols associated with the formulary aid healthcare providers in

making informed prescribing decisions.

3. **Cost-Effectiveness:** The formulary promotes the use of cost-effective medications, balancing clinical benefits with economic considerations. By including generic medications and implementing therapeutic interchange policies, the formulary helps manage healthcare costs without compromising patient care.

4. **Streamlined Inventory Management:** A well-maintained formulary simplifies inventory management by reducing the number of different medications stocked. This leads to more efficient procurement, storage, and distribution processes, ensuring that essential medications are always available when needed.

5. **Enhanced Therapeutic Outcomes:** By focusing on medications with proven efficacy and safety profiles, the formulary aims to enhance therapeutic outcomes for patients. This includes providing guidance on optimal dosing, administration routes, and monitoring requirements to achieve the best possible clinical results.

6. **Education and Training:** The formulary serves as an educational tool for healthcare providers, offering comprehensive information on medication use. It supports ongoing education and training efforts, ensuring that staff are knowledgeable about the medications they prescribe and administer.

7. **Regulatory Compliance:** The formulary helps ensure compliance with regulatory standards and guidelines set by healthcare authorities and accreditation bodies. By adhering to these standards, hospitals can maintain high-quality care and avoid potential legal and regulatory issues.

8. **Facilitation of Evidence-Based Practice:** The formulary is developed based on current clinical evidence and best practices. It encourages the use of evidence-based treatments, supporting healthcare providers in delivering high-quality, scientifically grounded care to patients.

In summary, a hospital formulary is an essential tool for optimizing medication use within a hospital. It plays a crucial role in standardizing care, enhancing patient safety, controlling costs, and ensuring the effective management of medication therapy. Through its comprehensive and dynamic nature, the formulary supports the overall mission of the hospital to provide safe, effective, and patient-centered care.

3.1.1.2 Benefits of a Hospital Formulary

Improved Patient Care:

A hospital formulary significantly enhances patient care by providing a curated list of medications that are evaluated for their efficacy, safety, and clinical appropriateness. This systematic approach to medication selection and use offers several key benefits:

1. **Consistency and Standardization:** The formulary ensures that medications used within the hospital are standardized, leading to consistent treatment protocols across different departments and among various healthcare providers. This consistency reduces variability in patient care and helps ensure that all patients receive the most effective treatments based on the best available evidence.
2. **Enhanced Medication Safety:** By including only those medications that have been rigorously evaluated for their safety profiles, the formulary minimizes the risk of adverse drug reactions and interactions. Clear guidelines on medication use, dosing, and monitoring further enhance safety, ensuring that healthcare providers administer medications correctly and effectively.
3. **Evidence-Based Practice:** The formulary supports evidence-based practice by incorporating medications that are backed by robust clinical data and expert recommendations. This promotes the use of proven therapies, improving clinical outcomes and ensuring that patients receive the highest standard of care.
4. **Patient Education and Compliance:** The formulary includes comprehensive information about medications, which can be used to educate patients about their treatments. When patients understand their medications, including how to take them correctly and what side effects to expect, they are more likely to adhere to their treatment regimens, leading to better health outcomes.
5. **Interdisciplinary Collaboration:** The development and maintenance of the formulary involve collaboration among pharmacists, physicians, and other healthcare professionals. This interdisciplinary approach fosters a cohesive healthcare team that works together to optimize patient care.

Cost-Effectiveness and Inventory Management:

A hospital formulary also brings significant financial and operational benefits through cost-effective medication use and streamlined inventory management:

1. **Cost Control:** By selecting cost-effective medications, including generics, the formulary helps control drug expenditures without compromising the quality of care. The use of therapeutic interchange policies, where appropriate, allows for the substitution of less expensive but equally effective medications, further reducing costs.

2. **Budget Optimization:** The formulary helps hospitals manage their budgets more effectively by forecasting drug expenditures and allocating resources efficiently. This financial planning ensures that the hospital can maintain a sustainable and predictable budget for pharmaceuticals.

3. **Efficient Inventory Management:** A well-maintained formulary simplifies inventory management by reducing the variety of medications that need to be stocked. This leads to more efficient procurement, storage, and distribution processes. By focusing on a core list of approved medications, the pharmacy can maintain adequate stock levels and reduce waste due to expired or unused medications.

4. **Minimized Waste:** With a standardized list of medications, hospitals can minimize waste associated with overstocking or underutilizing certain drugs. This efficiency not only reduces costs but also ensures that essential medications are always available for patient care.

5. **Streamlined Procurement Processes:** The formulary facilitates better relationships with suppliers and more effective negotiations for bulk purchasing or discounts. Consistent ordering patterns based on formulary requirements can lead to better pricing and terms from suppliers.

6. **Regulatory Compliance and Reporting:** The formulary helps ensure compliance with regulatory requirements regarding medication use and management. Accurate record-keeping and reporting facilitated by a formulary system help meet legal and accreditation standards, avoiding potential fines and enhancing overall compliance.

7. **Reduction in Medication Errors:** By providing clear guidelines and standardized practices for medication prescribing, dispensing, and administration, the formulary reduces the likelihood of medication errors. This not only improves patient safety but also reduces costs associated with adverse drug events and their subsequent treatments.

In conclusion, the benefits of a hospital formulary extend beyond clinical advantages to include significant financial and operational efficiencies. By improving patient care, enhancing safety, controlling costs, and streamlining inventory management, the formulary supports the hospital's mission to deliver high-quality, cost-effective healthcare.

3.1.2 Steps to Develop a Hospital Formulary

3.1.2.1 Formulary Committee Formation

Composition of the Committee (Pharmacists, Physicians, Administrators):

The first and most crucial step in developing a hospital formulary is the formation of a dedicated formulary committee. This committee is responsible for the selection, evaluation, and continuous review of the medications included in the formulary. A well-rounded and multidisciplinary committee ensures diverse perspectives and comprehensive decision-making. The typical composition of this committee includes:

1. **Pharmacists:** Pharmacists play a central role in the formulary committee due to their expertise in pharmacology, therapeutics, and medication management. They provide insights into the safety profiles, efficacy, and cost-effectiveness of medications. Pharmacists are also instrumental in developing guidelines for the appropriate use of medications and in educating other healthcare providers about formulary decisions.

2. **Physicians:** Physicians from various specialties are essential members of the formulary committee. Their clinical expertise and firsthand experience with patient care allow them to evaluate the therapeutic benefits of medications and their relevance to different medical conditions. Physicians also help in prioritizing medications that address the most prevalent and critical health issues within the hospital.

3. **Nurses:** Nurses contribute valuable insights into the practical aspects of medication administration and patient care. They help ensure that the selected medications are user-friendly and feasible for day-to-day clinical practice. Their input on patient education and compliance is also crucial for formulary decisions.

4. **Administrators:** Hospital administrators bring a strategic and operational perspective to the formulary committee. They focus on the financial implications of formulary decisions, ensuring that the selected medications align with the hospital's budgetary constraints and procurement policies. Administrators also help in addressing regulatory compliance and organizational goals.

5. **Clinical Pharmacologists:** These specialists provide in-depth knowledge of drug actions, interactions, and pharmacokinetics. Their expertise is vital for assessing the scientific evidence supporting the use of specific medications and for addressing complex therapeutic issues.

6. **Infection Control Specialists:** These professionals are particularly important when evaluating antibiotics and other anti-infective agents. Their input helps in developing strategies for antimicrobial stewardship and infection control, which are critical for patient safety and public health.

7. **Patient Safety Officers:** Ensuring patient safety is a primary goal of the formulary committee. Patient safety officers help in identifying potential risks associated with medications and in developing protocols to mitigate these risks.

8. **Health Economists:** In some settings, health economists may be included to provide a thorough analysis of the cost-effectiveness of medications. Their input helps balance clinical benefits with financial sustainability.

The committee meets regularly to review new medications, assess existing formulary items, and address any issues related to medication use within the hospital. The collaborative effort of these diverse professionals ensures that the formulary is comprehensive, evidence-based, and aligned with the hospital's mission to provide safe, effective, and cost-efficient patient care.

3.1.2.2 Criteria for Drug Selection

Clinical Efficacy, Safety, Cost, and Availability:

Selecting drugs for a hospital formulary involves a systematic evaluation of various criteria to ensure that the chosen medications meet the clinical needs of the patient population while also considering safety, cost-effectiveness, and availability. The primary criteria for drug selection include:

Clinical Efficacy: The clinical efficacy of a drug is one of the most important factors in its selection. This criterion assesses the ability of the medication to produce the desired therapeutic effect in the target population. Clinical efficacy is determined through rigorous analysis of clinical trial data, peer-reviewed studies, and real-world evidence. Drugs that demonstrate superior outcomes in terms of symptom relief, disease management, or cure rates are prioritized. Additionally, comparisons with existing treatment options help establish the relative efficacy of new drugs.

Safety: Patient safety is paramount in drug selection. The safety profile of a medication includes its side effects, adverse reactions, contraindications, and potential interactions with other drugs. The formulary committee evaluates data from clinical trials, post-marketing surveillance, and pharmacovigilance reports to assess the risk-to-benefit ratio of each drug. Medications with a high incidence of severe adverse effects or those that pose significant risks to vulnerable patient groups may be excluded or used with caution. Safety monitoring plans and protocols for managing adverse reactions are also considered in the selection process.

Cost: Cost is a critical factor in formulary management, especially in resource-limited settings. The committee performs a cost-benefit analysis to ensure that the selected drugs provide maximum therapeutic value for the expenditure. This analysis includes the direct costs of the medication, such as purchase price and administration costs, as well as indirect costs, such as potential savings from reduced hospital stays or fewer complications. The goal is to balance high-quality patient care with financial sustainability. Bulk purchasing, generic alternatives, and negotiated pricing with suppliers are strategies used to manage costs.

Availability: The availability of a drug refers to its consistent supply and ease of access. The formulary committee considers the reliability of manufacturers and suppliers, the potential for shortages, and the logistics of storage and distribution within the hospital. Drugs that are prone to frequent shortages or that require complex storage conditions may pose challenges to their inclusion in the formulary. Ensuring a stable and continuous supply of essential medications is crucial for uninterrupted patient care.

In addition to these primary criteria, the committee also evaluates other factors such as:

- **Pharmacokinetics and Pharmacodynamics:** Understanding how the drug is absorbed, distributed, metabolized, and excreted, and its mechanism of action.
- **Patient Compliance:** Assessing the ease of administration, dosage forms, and the likelihood of patient adherence to the medication regimen.
- **Therapeutic Guidelines and Standards:** Aligning drug selection with national and international clinical guidelines and standards of care.

- **Formulary Integration:** Considering how the new drug fits into the existing formulary and its potential impact on the use of other formulary medications.

By systematically evaluating these criteria, the formulary committee ensures that the selected drugs are safe, effective, affordable, and readily available, ultimately contributing to optimal patient outcomes and efficient hospital operations.

3.1.2.3 Formulary Maintenance

Regular Review and Updates:

Maintaining a hospital formulary is an ongoing process that requires regular review and updates to ensure that it continues to meet the evolving needs of patients and keeps pace with advances in medical science. The formulary committee is responsible for periodically evaluating the current list of medications to determine if any changes are necessary. This evaluation typically occurs on a quarterly or biannual basis but can be more frequent if there are significant developments in drug therapy or new clinical guidelines.

During these reviews, the committee assesses several factors, including:

- **Clinical Efficacy and Safety:** Re-evaluating the therapeutic benefits and safety profiles of existing formulary drugs in light of new research findings, clinical trial results, and pharmacovigilance data.
- **Usage Patterns:** Analyzing prescribing trends, patient outcomes, and feedback from healthcare providers to identify underutilized or overutilized medications.
- **Cost-effectiveness:** Reviewing cost data to ensure that the formulary remains financially sustainable, considering changes in drug pricing, the availability of generics, and new cost-saving opportunities.
- **Regulatory Changes:** Keeping abreast of updates from regulatory authorities, such as the FDA or EMA, which may affect the approval status, labeling, or recommended use of specific drugs.

Incorporating New Drugs and Removing Outdated Ones:

The dynamic nature of medical practice necessitates the regular incorporation of new drugs and the removal of outdated ones from the formulary. This process involves several key steps:

- **Introduction of New Drugs:** When new medications become available, the formulary committee conducts a thorough evaluation to determine their suitability for inclusion. This evaluation considers clinical trial data, safety profiles, comparative effectiveness, and cost. The committee may also solicit input from specialists and primary care providers to gauge the potential impact on patient care.
- **Pilot Programs:** Before full integration into the formulary, new drugs may be introduced through pilot programs to assess their real-world effectiveness and safety in the hospital setting. Feedback from these programs helps inform the final decision on formulary inclusion.
- **Removal of Outdated Drugs:** Drugs that no longer meet the necessary criteria for clinical efficacy, safety, or cost-effectiveness may be removed from the formulary. This includes medications that have been superseded by newer, more effective treatments, those with safety concerns, or those that are no longer available due to manufacturing discontinuation.
- **Communication and Implementation:** Once decisions are made, the formulary committee communicates the changes to all relevant stakeholders, including physicians, pharmacists, and nurses. Training sessions and informational materials may be provided to ensure smooth implementation of new formulary drugs and to educate staff on the reasons behind the removal of outdated medications.
- **Monitoring and Feedback:** After changes are implemented, the committee monitors the impact on patient care and solicits feedback from healthcare providers to identify any issues or areas for further improvement.

By maintaining a systematic and proactive approach to formulary maintenance, hospitals can ensure that their formulary remains up-to-date, safe, and aligned with the best practices in patient care. This ongoing process helps to optimize therapeutic outcomes, improve patient safety, and manage healthcare costs effectively.

3.2 Developing Therapeutic Guidelines

3.2.1 Introduction to Therapeutic Guidelines

3.2.1.1 Definition and Importance

Therapeutic guidelines are systematically developed statements that assist healthcare providers in making decisions about appropriate healthcare for specific clinical conditions. These guidelines are grounded in evidence-based medicine and are designed to offer recommendations on diagnosis, management, and treatment protocols. The primary purpose of therapeutic guidelines is to improve the quality of care by providing a standardized approach to patient management, which is especially crucial in complex clinical settings like hospitals.

Therapeutic guidelines are essential for several reasons. Firstly, they synthesize vast amounts of clinical research and expert opinion into a practical format that can be readily used by healthcare providers. This helps to bridge the gap between research and practice, ensuring that patients receive care that is based on the best available evidence. Secondly, they facilitate the implementation of best practices, reducing variability in patient care and minimizing the risk of errors. By providing clear and concise recommendations, therapeutic guidelines help clinicians make informed decisions quickly and confidently, which is critical in high-pressure environments such as emergency departments and intensive care units.

3.2.1.2 Role in Standardizing Treatment

The standardization of treatment is a key role of therapeutic guidelines, ensuring that all patients receive consistent and high-quality care regardless of where they are treated or who their healthcare provider is. By outlining specific diagnostic and treatment protocols, these guidelines help to ensure that all healthcare professionals are working from the same playbook, which enhances the coordination of care and improves patient outcomes.

Standardization of treatment through therapeutic guidelines offers several benefits:

- **Consistency in Care:** By adhering to the same set of guidelines, healthcare providers can deliver a uniform standard of care, which is particularly important in large healthcare systems with multiple providers. This consistency reduces discrepancies in treatment approaches and helps to ensure that patients receive the same level of care, whether they are treated in a rural clinic or a metropolitan hospital.

- **Quality Improvement:** Therapeutic guidelines are regularly updated to reflect the latest research and clinical advancements. This ongoing revision process ensures that the guidelines represent the current best practices, contributing to continuous quality improvement in patient care. Healthcare providers can rely on these guidelines to keep their practice current and aligned with the most effective and safe treatment strategies.

- **Reduction of Errors:** Clear guidelines help to reduce the risk of medical errors by providing specific instructions for the diagnosis and treatment of various conditions. This is particularly important for less experienced healthcare providers who may benefit from the structured approach provided by the guidelines. By following standardized protocols, the likelihood of errors due to omissions or incorrect decisions is minimized.

- **Enhanced Patient Safety:** AStandardized treatment protocols include safety checks and balance measures that are designed to protect patients. For instance, guidelines for medication management may include recommendations for monitoring for adverse effects, dosage adjustments based on patient characteristics, and interactions with other medications. These safety measures help to prevent complications and improve overall patient safety.

- **Efficient Use of Resources:** Therapeutic guidelines help to optimize the use of healthcare resources by recommending the most effective and efficient treatment options. This can lead to cost savings for healthcare systems by reducing unnecessary tests, treatments, and hospitalizations. Additionally, by streamlining the treatment process, guidelines can help to reduce the length of hospital stays and improve the overall efficiency of healthcare delivery.

3.2.2 Evidence-Based Practices
3.2.2.1 Importance of Evidence-Based Medicine
Incorporating Clinical Research and Data into Guidelines:

Evidence-based medicine (EBM) is the cornerstone of modern clinical practice, emphasizing the use of the best available research evidence to guide healthcare decisions. The importance of EBM in developing therapeutic guidelines lies in its systematic approach to evaluating and applying clinical research and data to patient care. By incorporating findings from high-quality studies, EBM ensures that therapeutic guidelines reflect the most effective and safest treatment options.

Incorporating clinical research and data into therapeutic guidelines involves several key steps:

1. **Systematic Literature Review:** A thorough review of the existing medical literature is conducted to gather relevant studies, including

randomized controlled trials (RCTs), observational studies, and clinical practice guidelines from reputable sources.

2. **Critical Appraisal:** The quality of the evidence is assessed using standardized tools and criteria, such as the GRADE (Grading of Recommendations, Assessment, Development, and Evaluations) system. This appraisal helps determine the strength and reliability of the findings.

3. **Synthesis of Evidence:** Data from multiple studies are synthesized to provide a comprehensive view of the evidence. Meta-analyses and systematic reviews are particularly valuable in this step as they combine results from several studies to increase the overall power and reliability of the conclusions.

4. **Integration into Guidelines:** The synthesized evidence is then integrated into the therapeutic guidelines, providing clear, actionable recommendations for clinicians. These recommendations are often accompanied by grading or levels of evidence to indicate the strength of the underlying research.

By grounding guidelines in robust clinical evidence, EBM ensures that healthcare providers have access to the most current and reliable information, leading to improved patient outcomes and more consistent care.

3.2.2.2 Developing Evidence-Based Guidelines
Steps for Creating Guidelines Based on Scientific Evidence:

1. **Identify Clinical Questions:** The first step in developing evidence-based guidelines is to identify the key clinical questions that need to be addressed. These questions should be specific, focused, and relevant to clinical practice, such as "What is the most effective treatment for hypertension in adults?"

2. **Formulate Search Strategy:** Develop a comprehensive search strategy to find relevant studies. This involves defining inclusion and exclusion criteria, selecting appropriate databases (e.g., PubMed, Cochrane Library), and using specific search terms to capture all pertinent literature.

3. **Conduct Systematic Review:** Perform a systematic review of the literature based on the formulated search strategy. This includes screening titles and abstracts, reviewing full-text articles, and selecting

studies that meet the predefined criteria.

4. **Appraise the Evidence:** Critically appraise the selected studies to assess their quality, validity, and applicability. Tools such as the GRADE system or the Cochrane Risk of Bias tool can be used to evaluate the strength of the evidence.

5. **Synthesize Findings:** Synthesize the evidence from the appraised studies to develop a comprehensive understanding of the clinical question. This may involve statistical analysis and meta-analyses to combine data from multiple studies and derive overall conclusions.

6. **Develop Recommendations:** Based on the synthesized evidence, formulate clear, actionable recommendations. These recommendations should be practical and feasible for implementation in clinical practice. Each recommendation should be accompanied by the level of evidence and strength of the recommendation.

7. **Peer Review and Public Consultation:** Draft guidelines are often subjected to peer review and public consultation to gather feedback from other experts and stakeholders. This step helps ensure the guidelines' credibility, accuracy, and acceptance in the medical community.

8. **Finalization and Dissemination:** After incorporating feedback, the guidelines are finalized and disseminated to healthcare providers through various channels, such as professional organizations, journals, and online platforms. Educational programs and training sessions may also be conducted to promote guideline implementation.

Role of Clinical Trials, Meta-Analyses, and Expert Consensus:

1. **Clinical Trials:** Randomized controlled trials (RCTs) are the gold standard for evaluating the efficacy and safety of interventions. Well-conducted RCTs provide high-quality evidence that forms the foundation of many clinical guidelines. When multiple RCTs on a specific topic are available, they offer robust data that can significantly influence guideline recommendations.

2. **Meta-Analyses:** Meta-analyses aggregate data from several studies, increasing the statistical power and providing a more precise estimate of treatment effects. This approach is particularly useful when individual studies have conflicting results or when small sample sizes limit the reliability of findings. Meta-analyses help reconcile these differences and provide a clearer picture of the overall evidence.

3. **Expert Consensus:** In areas where high-quality evidence is lacking or where clinical trials are not feasible, expert consensus plays a crucial role. Panels of experienced clinicians and researchers review the available evidence and use their clinical judgment to develop recommendations. Consensus statements are particularly valuable for emerging therapies, rare conditions, or complex clinical scenarios where data may be sparse.

By integrating clinical trials, meta-analyses, and expert consensus, evidence-based guidelines provide comprehensive, reliable, and practical recommendations for healthcare providers, ultimately improving patient care and outcomes.

3.3 Drug Procurement Process

3.3.1 Introduction to Drug Procurement

3.3.1.1 Importance of Efficient Procurement

Efficient drug procurement is crucial for the uninterrupted functioning of healthcare facilities, ensuring that necessary medications are available when patients need them. This process involves the acquisition of drugs from manufacturers or suppliers, adhering to quality standards, and managing costs effectively. The timely availability of medications is vital for maintaining optimal patient care and safety. Without an efficient procurement system, hospitals may face drug shortages, leading to treatment delays, compromised patient outcomes, and increased healthcare costs. Moreover, efficient procurement helps in maintaining a balanced inventory, reducing wastage, and ensuring that expired or obsolete drugs are minimized. By streamlining procurement processes, healthcare facilities can achieve better financial management, negotiate favorable terms with suppliers, and enhance overall operational efficiency. This is particularly important in high-demand scenarios such as pandemics or emergencies, where the rapid acquisition and distribution of medications can significantly impact public health outcomes.

3.3.1.2 Challenges in Drug Procurement

Drug procurement processes face several challenges that can hinder the efficient supply of medications. Common issues include:

1. **Supply Chain Disruptions:** Factors such as natural disasters, political instability, and pandemics can disrupt the supply chain, leading to delays or shortages in drug availability. These disruptions can be exacerbated

by dependency on a limited number of suppliers or geographical regions for critical medications.

2. **Quality Control:** Ensuring that procured drugs meet stringent quality standards is a significant challenge. Counterfeit or substandard medications can enter the supply chain, posing serious risks to patient safety. Effective quality control measures and regulatory compliance are essential to mitigate this risk.

3. **Cost Management:** Balancing cost-efficiency with the need for high-quality medications is a persistent challenge. Budget constraints may force healthcare facilities to compromise on the quality or quantity of drugs procured. Additionally, fluctuating drug prices and inflation can impact budget planning and financial stability.

4. **Regulatory Compliance:** Navigating complex regulatory requirements and ensuring compliance with local and international standards can be cumbersome. Non-compliance can result in legal penalties, supply chain disruptions, and compromised patient safety.

5. **Inventory Management:** Maintaining an optimal inventory level is challenging, as both overstocking and understocking have adverse effects. Overstocking leads to increased storage costs and potential wastage of expired drugs, while understocking can result in drug shortages and treatment delays.

6. **Vendor Reliability:** Identifying and partnering with reliable vendors is crucial. Inconsistent or unreliable suppliers can lead to supply chain disruptions and quality issues. Establishing strong relationships with trustworthy vendors and conducting regular performance evaluations are essential for a robust procurement process.

Addressing these challenges requires a strategic approach, incorporating advanced procurement practices, technology integration, and robust risk management strategies. Effective communication and collaboration with stakeholders, including suppliers, regulatory bodies, and healthcare professionals, are vital for overcoming these hurdles and ensuring the efficient procurement of drugs.

3.3.2 Vendor Selection and Contracting

3.3.2.1 Criteria for Vendor Selection

Quality, Reliability, Cost, and Compliance:

Selecting the right vendors is crucial for ensuring a consistent supply of high-quality medications. The key criteria for vendor selection include:

1. **Quality:** Vendors must supply medications that meet stringent quality standards. This involves verifying the vendor's manufacturing processes, quality control measures, and adherence to Good Manufacturing Practices (GMP). Certification from recognized bodies, such as the FDA or WHO, is also a critical indicator of quality.
2. **Reliability:** The vendor's track record in delivering products on time and in full is essential. Reliable vendors ensure that there are no disruptions in the supply chain, which is vital for maintaining uninterrupted patient care. Historical performance, references from other clients, and capacity to handle large orders are considered during the evaluation.
3. **Cost:** While quality and reliability are paramount, cost is also a significant factor. The procurement team must balance affordability with quality, seeking vendors that offer competitive pricing without compromising on the quality of the products. Cost analysis should include not just the price of the medications but also shipping, handling, and any additional fees.
4. **Compliance:** Vendors must comply with all relevant regulatory requirements and standards. This includes adherence to local and international laws governing the manufacture, distribution, and sale of medications. Compliance with environmental and ethical standards is also increasingly important.

3.3.2.2 Contracting with Vendors
Negotiation and Formalizing Agreements:
Negotiating and formalizing agreements with vendors involves several steps to ensure mutually beneficial terms and clear expectations:

1. **Negotiation:** Engage in detailed negotiations to agree on pricing, payment terms, delivery schedules, and quality standards. Effective negotiation requires understanding market conditions, the vendor's position, and leveraging volume purchasing to secure better terms.
2. **Contract Formalization:** Once terms are agreed upon, formalize the agreement through a detailed contract. The contract should clearly outline all terms and conditions, including the scope of supply, pricing, delivery schedules, quality assurance measures, compliance with regulations, and penalties for non-compliance.
3. **Legal Review:** Have the contract reviewed by legal experts to ensure that it protects the interests of the hospital and complies with all relevant

laws and regulations. This review helps mitigate risks and prevents potential legal issues.

Ensuring Adherence to Contract Terms:

1. **Monitoring Performance:** Regularly monitor the vendor's performance against the contract terms. This includes tracking delivery times, product quality, and adherence to agreed pricing. Establish key performance indicators (KPIs) to objectively assess vendor performance.
2. **Communication:** Maintain open lines of communication with vendors to address any issues promptly. Regular meetings and updates help ensure that both parties are aligned and any potential problems are resolved quickly.
3. **Compliance Audits:** Conduct periodic audits to ensure that vendors comply with the contract terms, including regulatory and quality standards. These audits help identify areas for improvement and ensure ongoing compliance.

3.3.3 Inventory Control Methods
3.3.3.1 Types of Inventory Control
Just-in-Time (JIT), Economic Order Quantity (EOQ), ABC Analysis:

1. **Just-in-Time (JIT):** This inventory management method aims to minimize inventory levels by ordering supplies only as needed. JIT reduces storage costs and minimizes waste due to expiration but requires precise coordination with vendors to prevent stockouts.
2. **Economic Order Quantity (EOQ):** EOQ is a mathematical model that determines the optimal order quantity that minimizes total inventory costs, including ordering and holding costs. This method helps balance the cost of ordering with the cost of holding inventory, ensuring cost-effective inventory management.
3. **ABC Analysis:** This technique categorizes inventory into three classes based on their importance:

   - **A-items:** High-value items with low frequency of use. These require tight control and accurate records.

- **B-items:** Moderate-value items with moderate frequency of use. These require routine control.
- **C-items:** Low-value items with high frequency of use. These require simpler controls and can be ordered in bulk.

3.3.3.2 Implementing Inventory Control
Monitoring Stock Levels and Reordering:

1. **Stock Monitoring:** Implement systems to continuously monitor stock levels. Automated inventory management systems can provide real-time data on inventory levels, usage rates, and reorder points, ensuring timely reordering.
2. **Reordering:** Set reorder points and safety stock levels for each medication to ensure that new orders are placed before stock levels become critically low. Automated systems can generate reorder alerts when stock falls below the predefined levels.

Minimizing Wastage and Stockouts:

1. **Regular Audits:** Conduct regular audits to verify physical inventory against records. This helps identify discrepancies, prevent stockouts, and reduce wastage due to expired or excess stock.
2. **Demand Forecasting:** Use historical data and predictive analytics to forecast demand accurately. This helps in maintaining optimal inventory levels, reducing both stockouts and overstock situations.
3. **Supplier Collaboration:** Work closely with suppliers to ensure reliable delivery schedules and address any supply chain issues promptly. Collaborative planning with suppliers can help in adjusting order quantities based on changing demand patterns.

By implementing these inventory control methods, hospitals can achieve a balance between having sufficient stock to meet patient needs and minimizing the costs associated with holding and managing inventory. This leads to improved operational efficiency, cost savings, and better patient care outcomes.

3.4 Drug Distribution Systems
3.4.1 Introduction to Drug Distribution Systems
3.4.1.1 Importance of Efficient Distribution:

Efficient drug distribution systems are vital in hospitals to ensure the correct and timely delivery of medications to patients. An efficient system reduces the risk of medication errors, enhances patient safety, and ensures that patients receive their medications exactly when needed. This is particularly crucial in a hospital setting where delays or mistakes in medication administration can have serious or even life-threatening consequences. Additionally, efficient distribution systems streamline pharmacy operations, improve workflow, reduce waste, and optimize the use of resources. This, in turn, can lead to significant cost savings and improved overall healthcare outcomes.

3.4.1.2 Types of Drug Distribution Systems:

Overview of Different Systems Used in Hospitals:

Hospitals utilize various drug distribution systems to meet their specific needs. These systems vary in complexity and suitability depending on the size of the hospital, the volume of medications dispensed, and the specific requirements of different departments. The primary drug distribution systems used in hospitals include:

1. **Unit Dose System:**

    - **Definition:** The unit dose system involves dispensing medications in single-use, individually packaged doses. Each dose is labeled with the drug name, dosage, and administration instructions.
    - **Benefits:** This system enhances patient safety by reducing medication errors, simplifies the medication administration process for nurses, and allows for better inventory control and tracking.
    - **Challenges:** The unit dose system can be labor-intensive and may require additional packaging equipment and space.

1. **Centralized Distribution System:**

    - **Definition:** In a centralized distribution system, medications are prepared and dispensed from a central pharmacy location within the hospital. This system often involves automated dispensing machines and centralized inventory management.
    - **Benefits:** Centralized systems can improve efficiency, reduce medication wastage, and provide better oversight of medication dispensing.

- **Challenges:** Centralized systems may require significant initial investment in technology and infrastructure. Additionally, they rely on effective communication and coordination between the central pharmacy and patient care units.

3. **Decentralized Distribution System:**

- **Definition:** In a decentralized distribution system, satellite pharmacies are located within various patient care units or departments. Medications are dispensed directly from these satellite locations.
- **Benefits:** Decentralized systems provide quicker access to medications, reduce the turnaround time for medication orders, and can improve responsiveness to patient needs.
- **Challenges:** Managing multiple satellite locations can be complex and may require additional staffing and resources. Inventory control and coordination between central and satellite pharmacies are critical.

4. **Automated Dispensing Cabinets (ADCs):**

- **Definition:** ADCs are secure, computerized cabinets located within patient care units. They store and dispense medications electronically, tracking each transaction.
- **Benefits:** ADCs enhance medication security, reduce the risk of diversion, and improve accountability and tracking of medication use. They also support just-in-time inventory management.
- **Challenges:** The implementation and maintenance of ADCs can be costly. Training staff to use these systems effectively is essential to maximize their benefits.

5. **Robotic Dispensing Systems:**

- **Definition:** These advanced systems utilize robotics to automate the dispensing of medications. Robots can fill prescriptions, package unit doses, and manage inventory.
- **Benefits:** Robotic systems can significantly reduce medication errors, enhance efficiency, and free up pharmacy staff to focus on clinical tasks. They also improve the accuracy and speed of medication

dispensing.

- **Challenges:** The high initial cost of robotic systems and the need for specialized maintenance can be barriers to implementation. Integration with existing pharmacy information systems is also necessary.

6. **Floor Stock System:**

- **Definition:** In a floor stock system, commonly used medications are stored in bulk on each patient care unit. Nurses or other healthcare providers access these medications as needed.
- **Benefits:** This system provides immediate access to frequently used medications and reduces the need for frequent pharmacy orders.
- **Challenges:** Floor stock systems can lead to inventory management issues, increased risk of medication errors, and higher potential for drug diversion. Proper protocols and monitoring are essential to mitigate these risks.

Each of these drug distribution systems has its advantages and challenges. Hospitals often use a combination of systems tailored to their specific needs and operational requirements. The goal is to achieve a balance between efficiency, safety, and cost-effectiveness while ensuring that patients receive the highest quality of care.

3.4.2 Centralized vs Decentralized Systems

3.4.2.1 Centralized Distribution

Benefits and Limitations:

Benefits:

1. **Efficiency and Control:** Centralized distribution systems enable streamlined operations, allowing for better oversight and management of medication inventory. Centralized control helps in maintaining consistent standards and protocols across the hospital.
2. **Cost-Effectiveness:** Centralized systems often lead to cost savings through bulk purchasing, reduced wastage, and optimized staffing. By consolidating resources in one location, hospitals can achieve economies of scale.
3. **Enhanced Security:** Centralized distribution reduces the risk of medication diversion and theft, as access to medications is restricted to

a central location with stringent security measures.

4. **Improved Accuracy:** Automated dispensing systems and centralized inventory management can reduce medication errors, ensuring that the right medications are dispensed in the correct doses.

Limitations:

1. **Turnaround Time:** Centralized distribution may result in longer turnaround times for medication delivery, especially in large hospitals or those with multiple floors and units. This can delay patient care in urgent situations.
2. **Communication:** Effective communication and coordination between the central pharmacy and patient care units are crucial. Miscommunication can lead to delays and errors in medication delivery.
3. **Infrastructure Costs:** Implementing a centralized system requires significant investment in technology, infrastructure, and training. Maintenance costs can also be high.
4. **Dependency on Technology:** Centralized systems often rely heavily on technology. Any technological failures or downtimes can disrupt the entire medication distribution process.

3.4.2.2 Decentralized Distribution
Benefits and Limitations:
Benefits:

1. **Reduced Turnaround Time:** Decentralized distribution systems enable quicker access to medications, as they are stored closer to patient care units. This can significantly reduce the time required to administer medications, improving patient care.
2. **Enhanced Responsiveness:** Immediate availability of medications in satellite pharmacies or automated dispensing cabinets allows healthcare providers to respond rapidly to patient needs and emergencies.
3. **Increased Flexibility:** Decentralized systems can be tailored to the specific needs of different departments or units within the hospital, providing customized solutions for diverse patient populations.
4. **Improved Communication:** Proximity to patient care units fosters better communication and collaboration between pharmacy staff and healthcare providers, enhancing overall workflow and coordination.

Limitations:

1. **Inventory Management:** Managing inventory across multiple decentralized locations can be challenging. It requires robust systems to track medication usage, prevent stockouts, and minimize wastage.
2. **Resource Allocation:** Decentralized systems may require additional staffing and resources to manage multiple locations effectively. This can lead to higher operational costs.
3. **Risk of Diversion:** With medications stored in various locations, there is an increased risk of diversion and theft. Implementing stringent security measures and regular audits is essential.
4. **Consistency and Standardization:** Ensuring consistent practices and standards across multiple decentralized locations can be difficult. Regular training and monitoring are necessary to maintain quality and safety.

3.4.2.3 Hybrid Models

Combining Elements of Both Systems for Optimal Efficiency:

Hybrid models incorporate elements of both centralized and decentralized distribution systems to achieve optimal efficiency and flexibility. These models aim to leverage the strengths of each system while mitigating their respective limitations.

Benefits:

1. **Enhanced Efficiency:** Hybrid models can centralize inventory management and bulk purchasing while decentralizing the actual dispensing of medications. This ensures cost-effectiveness and better control over inventory.
2. **Improved Responsiveness:** By strategically placing automated dispensing cabinets or satellite pharmacies in high-demand areas, hybrid models reduce turnaround times and enhance responsiveness to patient needs.
3. **Flexibility and Customization:** Hybrid systems can be tailored to the unique requirements of different hospital units, providing customized solutions that balance efficiency, cost, and patient care.
4. **Increased Redundancy:** Having both centralized and decentralized elements adds redundancy to the system, reducing the risk of complete disruption in case of a failure in one part of the system.

Implementation Strategies:

1. **Strategic Placement:** Place decentralized units (such as automated dispensing cabinets) in high-traffic or critical care areas to ensure rapid access to medications, while maintaining a central pharmacy for bulk storage and complex compounding.
2. **Integrated Technology:** Use integrated pharmacy management systems that connect centralized and decentralized units, allowing for real-time inventory tracking, automated reordering, and seamless communication.
3. **Regular Audits and Training:** Conduct regular audits to ensure compliance with standards and protocols across both centralized and decentralized locations. Provide ongoing training to staff to maintain consistency in practices.
4. **Scalability:** Design the hybrid system to be scalable, allowing for adjustments based on changes in patient volume, hospital expansion, or evolving healthcare needs.

By combining the best aspects of centralized and decentralized distribution systems, hybrid models offer a balanced approach that maximizes efficiency, improves patient care, and enhances overall operational effectiveness in hospital pharmacy management.

-

3.5 Intravenous Admixtures and Hospital Waste Management

3.5.1 Intravenous Admixtures

3.5.1.1 Preparation and Safety Protocols

Aseptic Techniques and Guidelines for Preparation:

The preparation of intravenous (IV) admixtures involves combining medications with IV fluids to be administered to patients directly into their bloodstream. Due to the high-risk nature of IV therapy, meticulous aseptic techniques are essential to prevent contamination and ensure patient safety. Key guidelines and aseptic techniques include:

1. **Sterile Environment:** IV admixtures must be prepared in a controlled environment, such as a laminar airflow hood or a cleanroom, designed to minimize the risk of contamination. These environments must comply with stringent standards, such as those outlined in USP Chapter <797>.
2. **Hand Hygiene:** Proper hand hygiene is crucial. Staff must wash their hands thoroughly with antiseptic soap and water before donning sterile

gloves. Hand sanitizers with at least 60% alcohol can be used as an additional measure.

3. **Sterile Attire:** Personnel must wear sterile gowns, gloves, masks, and hair covers to reduce the risk of introducing contaminants into the IV admixtures. Gloves should be disinfected with sterile alcohol regularly during the preparation process.

4. **Disinfection of Surfaces:** All surfaces within the preparation area, including workbenches and equipment, must be disinfected with appropriate cleaning agents before and after each preparation session. Regular cleaning schedules must be adhered to.

5. **Use of Sterile Equipment:** Only sterile equipment, such as syringes, needles, and IV bags, should be used. Single-use, disposable items are preferred to minimize the risk of cross-contamination.

6. **Aseptic Manipulation:** The manipulation of sterile products should be conducted using aseptic techniques. This includes minimizing the exposure of sterile components to the air and using proper techniques to withdraw and inject solutions.

Safety Measures to Prevent Contamination:

Ensuring the sterility of IV admixtures is paramount. Safety measures to prevent contamination include:

1. **Closed Systems:** Whenever possible, use closed-system transfer devices (CSTDs) to reduce the risk of contamination during the transfer of medications.

2. **Sterile Filtration:** Solutions that cannot be sterilized by other means can be passed through a sterile filter to remove potential contaminants.

3. **Labeling and Documentation:** Clearly label all IV admixtures with information including the medication name, concentration, preparation date, expiration date, and preparer's initials. Proper documentation helps trace any issues back to their source.

4. **Regular Training:** Staff should receive regular training on aseptic techniques and infection control practices. Competency assessments should be conducted periodically to ensure adherence to protocols.

5. **Environmental Monitoring:** Regular environmental monitoring should be performed to detect and address any potential contamination sources in the preparation area. This includes air quality testing and surface sampling for microbial contaminants.

3.5.1.2 Quality Assurance

Ensuring the Stability and Efficacy of IV Admixtures:

Quality assurance in the preparation of IV admixtures involves several steps to ensure the stability and efficacy of the medications:

1. **Stability Testing:** Conduct stability testing for all IV admixtures to determine the appropriate storage conditions and shelf life. This testing assesses how the medication interacts with the IV fluid over time and under various conditions.
2. **Compatibility Checks:** Verify the compatibility of the medications with the IV fluids and other drugs to be administered concurrently. Incompatibilities can lead to precipitation, reduced efficacy, or harmful reactions.
3. **Regular Inspections:** Implement regular inspections of prepared IV admixtures to check for particulate matter, discoloration, or any signs of contamination. Inspections should be conducted before administration to the patient.
4. **Batch Testing:** Perform batch testing for compounded IV admixtures, particularly for those prepared in large volumes. Random samples from each batch should be tested for sterility, potency, and particulate contamination.
5. **Temperature Control:** Ensure that IV admixtures are stored and transported at the correct temperatures to maintain their stability. Temperature logs should be maintained to track storage conditions.
6. **Documentation and Traceability:** Maintain detailed records of each IV admixture prepared, including the lot numbers of ingredients, preparation procedures, and quality control checks. This documentation ensures traceability and accountability.
7. **Adherence to Guidelines:** Follow established guidelines and standards, such as those from USP, the American Society of Health-System Pharmacists (ASHP), and other relevant bodies. These guidelines provide comprehensive protocols for ensuring the quality and safety of IV admixtures.

By implementing rigorous preparation protocols and robust quality assurance measures, hospitals can ensure that IV admixtures are safe, effective, and free from contamination, thereby enhancing patient safety and therapeutic outcomes.

3.5.2 Hospital Waste Management
3.5.2.1 Importance of Proper Waste Management
Impact on Health and Environment:

Proper waste management in hospitals is crucial due to its significant impact on both health and the environment. Hospitals generate a wide variety of waste, including infectious, hazardous, and general waste, each requiring specific handling to prevent harm. Mismanagement of hospital waste can lead to severe health risks, such as the spread of infectious diseases, exposure to hazardous chemicals, and injuries from sharps. Moreover, improper disposal methods, such as open burning or unregulated landfilling, can lead to environmental pollution, contaminating soil, water, and air. The release of toxic substances can have long-term detrimental effects on ecosystems and human health. Thus, ensuring effective waste management practices in hospitals is essential to safeguarding public health and protecting the environment.

3.5.2.2 Waste Management Regulations
Overview of Relevant Laws and Guidelines:

Waste management in hospitals is governed by a comprehensive set of laws and guidelines designed to ensure safe and environmentally responsible disposal practices. Key regulations include the Biomedical Waste Management Rules, which mandate the segregation, treatment, and disposal of biomedical waste to minimize health risks. These rules require hospitals to categorize waste into color-coded containers for specific treatment processes, such as autoclaving, incineration, or chemical disinfection. Additionally, guidelines from organizations like the World Health Organization (WHO) and national health authorities provide frameworks for managing hazardous waste, including pharmaceuticals, radioactive materials, and chemicals. Compliance with these regulations ensures that hospitals adhere to safe practices, thereby reducing the risk of contamination and environmental damage.

3.5.2.3 Implementing Waste Management Practices
Segregation, Disposal, and Recycling of Pharmaceutical Waste:

Effective waste management practices in hospitals begin with the segregation of waste at the point of generation. This involves sorting waste into distinct categories, such as infectious waste, hazardous waste, and general waste, using clearly labeled, color-coded containers. Infectious waste, such as used syringes and biological materials, is typically autoclaved or incinerated to destroy pathogens. Hazardous waste, including pharmaceuticals and chemicals, requires specialized treatment to neutralize harmful substances before disposal.

Disposal practices must comply with regulatory requirements to prevent environmental contamination. For instance, pharmaceutical waste should never be disposed of in regular trash or down the drain due to the risk of polluting water sources. Instead, it should be collected in designated containers and treated through methods such as incineration or chemical neutralization.

Recycling is an integral part of waste management, aiming to reduce the volume of waste sent to landfills. Materials such as plastics, paper, and glass can often be recycled if they are not contaminated with hazardous substances. Implementing a recycling program within the hospital can help minimize waste and promote sustainability.

Training and education of hospital staff are essential to ensure proper waste management practices are followed consistently. Regular audits and inspections can help identify areas for improvement and ensure compliance with waste management protocols. By adhering to these practices, hospitals can effectively manage their waste, protect public health, and minimize their environmental footprint.

Chapter 4: Education and Training in Hospital Pharmacy 4.1 Training of Technical Staff • 4.1.1 Orientation Programs • 4.1.1.1 Introduction to Hospital Pharmacy Operations • Overview of roles and responsibilities • Importance of adherence to protocols

Education and Training in Hospital Pharmacy

4.1 Training of Technical Staff

4.1.1 Orientation Programs
4.1.1.1 Introduction to Hospital Pharmacy Operations
Overview of Roles and Responsibilities:

Orientation programs are critical for integrating new technical staff into hospital pharmacy operations. These programs provide a comprehensive introduction to the various roles and responsibilities within the pharmacy, ensuring that new employees understand their specific duties and how they contribute to overall patient care. Technical staff, including pharmacy technicians and assistants, play a vital role in supporting pharmacists by performing tasks such as medication preparation, inventory management, and patient interactions.

During orientation, new staff members are introduced to the organizational structure of the hospital pharmacy, including key personnel and their functions. They learn about the workflow processes, from receiving prescriptions and verifying orders to dispensing medications and handling inventory. This overview helps new employees understand how their role fits into the larger healthcare system and the importance of their contributions to patient safety and effective pharmacy operations.

Importance of Adherence to Protocols:

Adherence to established protocols is essential in hospital pharmacy operations to ensure consistency, accuracy, and safety in medication management. Orientation programs emphasize the critical importance of following these protocols, which are designed to minimize errors, enhance patient outcomes, and comply with regulatory standards.

Protocols cover a wide range of activities, including:

1. **Medication Preparation:** Detailed procedures for compounding, labeling, and packaging medications to ensure that they are prepared accurately and safely.
2. **Inventory Management:** Guidelines for tracking inventory levels, handling drug shortages, and managing expired medications to maintain an adequate supply of necessary drugs.
3. **Safety and Compliance:** Procedures for handling hazardous substances, managing controlled substances, and ensuring compliance with legal and regulatory requirements.
4. **Patient Interaction:** Best practices for interacting with patients, including confidentiality, communication skills, and providing medication counseling when necessary.

By adhering to these protocols, technical staff can help prevent medication errors, ensure the correct and safe administration of drugs, and maintain the high standards of care expected in hospital settings. The orientation program reinforces the importance of vigilance, attention to detail, and a commitment to patient safety in all aspects of pharmacy operations.

4.1.1.2 Initial Training Modules

Basic Skills Required (Dispensing, Compounding, Inventory Management):

Initial training modules for new technical staff in hospital pharmacy focus on imparting the fundamental skills necessary for their roles. These modules cover key areas such as medication dispensing, compounding, and inventory management to ensure that staff are well-prepared to handle their responsibilities effectively.

1. **Dispensing:** Training in dispensing covers the entire process from receiving and interpreting prescriptions to preparing and delivering medications to patients. Staff learn how to:

   - Verify prescription information for accuracy and completeness.
   - Select the correct medications and dosages.

- Label medications appropriately with patient-specific information and usage instructions.
- Provide medications in the appropriate packaging, ensuring safety and compliance with regulatory standards.

1. **Compounding:** Compounding involves preparing customized medications that are not commercially available, tailored to individual patient needs. Training includes:

- Understanding different compounding techniques, such as mixing, reconstituting, and preparing sterile products.
- Using compounding equipment and tools, such as mortar and pestle, balance scales, and aseptic hoods.
- Following precise formulations and protocols to ensure accuracy and consistency.
- Maintaining a sterile environment to prevent contamination, especially when preparing IV admixtures and other sterile products.

3. **Inventory Management:** Effective inventory management is crucial for ensuring that the pharmacy has the necessary medications available at all times. Training in this area includes:

- Tracking inventory levels using inventory management systems.
- Conducting regular stock audits and reconciling discrepancies.
- Managing drug shortages and backorders by coordinating with suppliers.
- Properly storing medications according to manufacturer guidelines to maintain their efficacy and safety.

Safety Protocols and Regulatory Compliance:
Safety protocols and regulatory compliance are paramount in hospital pharmacy operations. Initial training modules emphasize the importance of adhering to these protocols to ensure patient safety and compliance with legal standards.

1. **Safety Protocols:** Training covers a wide range of safety protocols, including:

- **Aseptic Techniques:** Proper procedures for maintaining sterility during the preparation and handling of medications, especially injectable and IV products.
- **Hazardous Materials Handling:** Safe handling and disposal of hazardous drugs and chemicals to prevent exposure and contamination.
- **Emergency Procedures:** Responding to emergencies such as spills, contamination incidents, and adverse reactions, including the use of safety equipment and reporting protocols.

2. **Regulatory Compliance:** Ensuring compliance with relevant laws and guidelines is critical for hospital pharmacies. Training includes:

- **Legal Requirements:** Understanding federal, state, and local regulations governing pharmacy practice, including controlled substances laws and pharmacy licensing requirements.
- **Documentation:** Accurate record-keeping and documentation practices to track medication orders, inventory levels, and patient interactions. This includes maintaining records for controlled substances and ensuring proper documentation for compounding activities.
- **Accreditation Standards:** Familiarity with standards from accrediting organizations such as The Joint Commission (TJC) or the National Association of Boards of Pharmacy (NABP), which set benchmarks for quality and safety in pharmacy practice.

By focusing on these basic skills, safety protocols, and regulatory compliance, initial training modules equip new technical staff with the knowledge and competencies needed to perform their roles effectively and safely. This foundational training is crucial for ensuring that the hospital pharmacy operates smoothly and meets the highest standards of patient care and safety.

sterile compounding, IV admixtures)

4.1.2 Skill Development Programs

4.1.2.1 Advanced Skill Training

Specialized Training (e.g., Sterile Compounding, IV Admixtures):

Skill devclopment programs in hospital pharmacy are designed to provide technical staff with advanced training in specialized areas, enhancing their expertise and ability to handle complex tasks. These programs focus on areas such as sterile compounding and IV admixtures, which require meticulous attention to detail and adherence to stringent safety protocols.

1. **Sterile Compounding:**

   - **Aseptic Technique:** Advanced training in aseptic techniques is critical for sterile compounding. Staff learn how to maintain a sterile environment by working in laminar airflow hoods or cleanrooms, using sterile gloves and gowns, and following strict hand hygiene practices.
   - **Sterile Preparation:** Training covers the preparation of sterile products, including injectable medications, ophthalmic solutions, and other compounded sterile preparations. This includes understanding the principles of sterility, the use of sterile equipment, and techniques to prevent contamination.
   - **Quality Control:** Emphasis is placed on quality control measures, such as sterility testing, particulate matter inspection, and stability testing, to ensure that compounded products are safe and effective.
   - **Documentation and Compliance:** Staff are trained to maintain accurate records of sterile compounding activities, including batch records, sterility test results, and compliance with USP Chapter <797> guidelines.

2. **IV Admixtures:**

   - **Preparation Techniques:** Advanced training in IV admixture preparation includes the accurate measurement, mixing, and dilution of medications to be administered intravenously. This involves understanding the compatibility of different medications and fluids, as well as the appropriate use of infusion devices and equipment.
   - **Safety Protocols:** Ensuring the safety of IV admixtures is paramount. Training focuses on preventing contamination through aseptic techniques, proper labeling of IV bags, and verifying medication orders against patient records.
   - **Handling and Storage:** Staff learn the correct handling and storage of IV admixtures to maintain their stability and efficacy. This includes

temperature control, protection from light, and proper transport methods within the hospital.

- **Administration Guidelines:** Understanding the guidelines for administering IV medications, including infusion rates, monitoring for adverse reactions, and providing patient education on IV therapy.

Benefits of Advanced Skill Training:

- **Enhanced Patient Safety:** Specialized training ensures that technical staff can prepare and handle complex medications safely, reducing the risk of errors and contamination.
- **Improved Efficiency:** Advanced skills enable staff to perform their tasks more efficiently, streamlining pharmacy operations and reducing delays in medication administration.
- **Professional Development:** Skill development programs contribute to the professional growth of technical staff, providing opportunities for career advancement and increased job satisfaction.
- **Compliance and Accreditation:** Adhering to advanced training standards helps the hospital maintain compliance with regulatory and accreditation requirements, ensuring high-quality care and safety for patients.

By investing in advanced skill training, hospitals can equip their technical staff with the expertise needed to manage specialized pharmacy tasks, ultimately enhancing the overall quality and safety of patient care.

4.1.2.2 Continuing Professional Development (CPD)

Workshops, Seminars, and Hands-On Training Sessions:

Continuing Professional Development (CPD) is essential for ensuring that technical staff in hospital pharmacies remain current with the latest advancements in pharmaceutical practice, technology, and regulatory requirements. CPD programs encompass a variety of learning activities designed to enhance skills, knowledge, and professional competence. Key components of CPD include workshops, seminars, and hands-on training sessions.

Workshops:

- **Interactive Learning:** Workshops provide an interactive learning environment where technical staff can engage in discussions, group activities, and case studies. These sessions often focus on practical skills and real-world applications, allowing participants to practice and refine their abilities.

- **Specialized Topics:** Workshops can cover specialized topics such as advanced compounding techniques, medication safety practices, or the implementation of new technologies in pharmacy practice. This targeted approach helps staff develop expertise in specific areas relevant to their roles.
- **Problem-Solving:** Participants work collaboratively to solve problems and address challenges they encounter in their daily practice. This fosters critical thinking and enhances problem-solving skills.

Seminars:

- **Expert Presentations:** Seminars feature presentations by experts in the field, providing insights into recent developments, research findings, and best practices in pharmacy. These sessions keep staff informed about the latest trends and innovations in healthcare.
- **Continuing Education Credits:** Many seminars offer continuing education credits, which are essential for maintaining professional licensure and certification. This incentivizes staff to participate and stay engaged in their professional development.
- **Networking Opportunities:** Seminars provide opportunities for technical staff to network with peers, share experiences, and learn from each other. Building a professional network can lead to collaborative opportunities and career advancement.

Hands-On Training Sessions:

- **Practical Experience:** Hands-on training sessions allow technical staff to apply their knowledge in a controlled environment, practicing skills such as sterile compounding, IV admixture preparation, and the use of pharmacy automation systems.
- **Simulation-Based Learning:** Simulations and practical exercises help staff develop proficiency in performing complex tasks and responding to emergency situations. These sessions often use realistic scenarios to enhance learning and retention.

- **Skill Assessment:** Hands-on training provides an opportunity for skill assessment and feedback. Instructors can evaluate participants' performance, identify areas for improvement, and offer personalized guidance to enhance their competence.

Benefits of CPD Programs:

- **Enhanced Competence:** CPD ensures that technical staff are well-equipped with the latest skills and knowledge, enabling them to perform their roles effectively and safely.
- **Adaptability:** By staying current with advancements in pharmacy practice, staff can adapt to changes in the healthcare environment and implement new practices and technologies efficiently.
- **Improved Patient Care:** Ongoing professional development leads to better patient care outcomes, as staff are more knowledgeable about best practices and safety protocols.
- **Career Advancement:** CPD supports career growth by providing opportunities for learning and professional development, leading to increased job satisfaction and motivation.
- **Regulatory Compliance:** Participation in CPD programs helps ensure compliance with regulatory requirements and accreditation standards, maintaining the hospital's reputation for excellence in healthcare.

4.1.2.3 Performance Evaluation and Feedback

Regular Assessments and Constructive Feedback Mechanisms:

Performance evaluation and feedback are essential components of the professional development of technical staff in hospital pharmacies. Regular assessments and constructive feedback help ensure that staff meet the required standards of practice, identify areas for improvement, and support their ongoing professional growth.

Regular Assessments:

1. **Objective Evaluation:** Regular performance assessments provide an objective measure of an employee's skills, knowledge, and competencies. These evaluations can include:

   - **Skills Assessments:** Practical assessments to evaluate technical abilities in areas such as medication dispensing, compounding, and inventory management.

- **Knowledge Tests:** Written or oral examinations to assess understanding of pharmacy protocols, safety procedures, and regulatory requirements.
- **Performance Metrics:** Analysis of performance metrics such as accuracy in medication preparation, efficiency in task completion, and adherence to safety standards.

2. **Performance Reviews:** Structured performance reviews conducted by supervisors or managers provide a comprehensive evaluation of an employee's performance over a specific period. These reviews typically cover:

- **Work Quality:** Assessment of the accuracy, consistency, and reliability of the employee's work.
- **Work Ethic:** Evaluation of the employee's dedication, punctuality, and professionalism.
- **Teamwork and Communication:** Assessment of the employee's ability to work effectively with colleagues, communicate clearly, and contribute to a positive work environment.

Constructive Feedback Mechanisms:

1. **Feedback Sessions:** Regular one-on-one feedback sessions between employees and their supervisors provide an opportunity for open communication. These sessions should focus on:

- **Strengths and Achievements:** Highlighting the employee's strengths and recognizing their accomplishments to motivate and encourage continued excellence.
- **Areas for Improvement:** Identifying specific areas where the employee can improve, providing clear examples and actionable suggestions for enhancement.

2. **360-Degree Feedback:** This comprehensive feedback method involves collecting input from multiple sources, including peers, supervisors, and subordinates. 360-degree feedback provides a well-rounded view of an employee's performance and behavior, highlighting areas for growth

from different perspectives.

3. **Continuous Feedback:** Implementing a culture of continuous feedback, where employees receive regular, informal feedback on their performance, helps them make timely adjustments and improvements. This can be facilitated through:

- **Daily Check-Ins:** Brief, informal check-ins to discuss progress, address concerns, and provide immediate feedback.
- **Mentorship Programs:** Pairing employees with mentors who provide ongoing guidance, support, and feedback.

4. **Written Feedback:** Providing written feedback in performance reviews and assessments ensures that employees have a documented record of their performance, goals, and areas for improvement. This written feedback serves as a reference for future evaluations and development plans.

Benefits of Performance Evaluation and Feedback:

1. **Improved Performance:** Regular assessments and constructive feedback help employees identify and address performance gaps, leading to improved job performance and higher quality of care.
2. **Professional Growth:** Feedback mechanisms support the professional growth and development of employees by highlighting opportunities for learning and skill enhancement.
3. **Employee Engagement:** Constructive feedback fosters a supportive work environment, enhancing employee engagement, motivation, and job satisfaction.
4. **Goal Setting:** Performance evaluations help set clear, achievable goals for employees, aligning their efforts with the hospital's objectives and standards.
5. **Accountability:** Regular assessments and feedback mechanisms promote accountability, ensuring that employees adhere to established protocols and maintain high standards of practice.

4.2 Continuing Education for Pharmacists
4.2.1 Importance of Lifelong Learning
4.2.1.1 Keeping Up with Advances in Pharmacy Practice

Importance of Staying Updated with the Latest Research and Guidelines:

The field of pharmacy is continuously evolving, with new research, medications, technologies, and guidelines emerging regularly. Lifelong learning is crucial for pharmacists to stay updated with these advancements to provide the highest quality of care to their patients. By keeping abreast of the latest research and guidelines, pharmacists can:

1. **Improve Patient Outcomes:** Staying informed about the latest evidence-based practices ensures that pharmacists can recommend the most effective treatments, leading to better patient outcomes. This includes understanding new drug therapies, interactions, and contraindications.
2. **Ensure Safety and Compliance:** Updated knowledge helps pharmacists ensure that they are compliant with the latest regulatory requirements and safety standards, reducing the risk of medication errors and adverse events.
3. **Adopt New Technologies:** Advances in technology, such as electronic health records (EHRs), telepharmacy, and automated dispensing systems, require pharmacists to continuously update their technical skills. Familiarity with these technologies enhances efficiency and accuracy in pharmacy practice.
4. **Adapt to Changing Healthcare Landscape:** Healthcare is dynamic, with changes in disease prevalence, treatment protocols, and healthcare policies. Lifelong learning enables pharmacists to adapt to these changes and continue to meet the needs of their patients effectively.
5. **Contribute to Research and Innovation:** Pharmacists who engage in lifelong learning are better equipped to contribute to research and innovation in the field. This can involve participating in clinical trials, developing new treatment protocols, or contributing to professional guidelines.

4.2.1.2 Enhancing Professional Competence

Continuous Improvement of Knowledge and Skills:

Continuing education is essential for the continuous improvement of pharmacists' knowledge and skills, ensuring they remain competent and effective in their roles. Key aspects include:

1. **Clinical Competence:** Continuous education helps pharmacists stay current with pharmacological developments, clinical guidelines, and therapeutic strategies. This ensures they can provide informed clinical advice and make sound decisions regarding patient care.

2. **Professional Development:** Engaging in lifelong learning supports professional growth and career advancement. Pharmacists can pursue specialized certifications, advanced degrees, and leadership roles within their institutions or professional organizations.

3. **Skill Enhancement:** Continuing education programs offer opportunities to develop new skills and refine existing ones. This includes advanced compounding techniques, medication therapy management, patient counseling, and the use of new pharmacy technologies.

4. **Interprofessional Collaboration:** Lifelong learning fosters better collaboration with other healthcare professionals. By understanding the latest advancements in various medical fields, pharmacists can communicate more effectively with physicians, nurses, and other healthcare providers, contributing to integrated and holistic patient care.

5. **Patient Education and Advocacy:** Updated knowledge allows pharmacists to educate patients more effectively about their medications, potential side effects, and the importance of adherence to therapy. This empowers patients to take an active role in their health management and improves overall health outcomes.

6. **Ethical and Legal Awareness:** Continuing education ensures that pharmacists are aware of the latest ethical guidelines and legal requirements related to pharmacy practice. This knowledge helps them navigate complex ethical dilemmas and maintain professional integrity.

Methods for Lifelong Learning:

1. **Professional Development Programs:** Enrolling in structured professional development programs, such as those offered by pharmacy associations, universities, and healthcare organizations, provides comprehensive and up-to-date education.

2. **Conferences and Seminars:** Attending conferences and seminars allows pharmacists to learn about the latest research, network with peers, and gain insights from experts in the field.

3. **Online Courses and Webinars:** Online platforms offer flexible learning options, enabling pharmacists to access courses and webinars on various

topics at their convenience.

4. **Peer-Reviewed Journals:** Regularly reading peer-reviewed journals keeps pharmacists informed about the latest research findings, clinical trials, and advancements in pharmacy practice.

5. **Workshops and Hands-On Training:** Participating in workshops and hands-on training sessions enhances practical skills and provides opportunities for experiential learning.

6. **Mentorship and Peer Learning:** Engaging in mentorship programs and peer learning groups fosters knowledge sharing and collaborative learning among pharmacists.

By prioritizing lifelong learning, pharmacists can maintain their professional competence, stay current with advancements in their field, and continue to provide safe, effective, and high-quality care to their patients.

4.2.2 Certification Programs

4.2.2.1 Types of Certification Programs

Board Certifications, Specialty Certifications:

Certification programs are essential for pharmacists seeking to demonstrate their expertise and advance their careers. These programs offer a structured pathway to gaining specialized knowledge and skills in various areas of pharmacy practice. The two main types of certification programs are board certifications and specialty certifications.

1. **Board Certifications:**

   - **Board of Pharmacy Specialties (BPS) Certifications:** The BPS offers several board certifications for pharmacists who wish to specialize in specific areas of pharmacy practice. These certifications include:

     - **Board Certified Pharmacotherapy Specialist (BCPS):** Focuses on optimizing medication therapy outcomes across various disease states.

     - **Board Certified Oncology Pharmacist (BCOP):** Specializes in the management and treatment of cancer patients, including chemotherapy and supportive care.

     - **Board Certified Ambulatory Care Pharmacist (BCACP):** Concentrates on providing care to ambulatory patients, focusing on chronic disease management and medication therapy management.

- **Board Certified Critical Care Pharmacist (BCCCP):** Specializes in the care of critically ill patients, managing complex medication regimens in intensive care settings.
- **Board Certified Pediatric Pharmacy Specialist (BCPPS):** Focuses on the unique medication needs of pediatric patients.
- **Board Certified Geriatric Pharmacist (BCGP):** Specializes in the care of older adults, addressing polypharmacy and age-related pharmacokinetic changes.

2. **Specialty Certifications:**

- **Certified Diabetes Educator (CDE):** Specializes in diabetes management, providing education and support to patients with diabetes.
- **Certified Anticoagulation Care Provider (CACP):** Focuses on the management of anticoagulant therapy, including monitoring and adjusting dosages.
- **Certified Pain Educator (CPE):** Specializes in pain management, helping patients manage chronic pain conditions.
- **Certified Specialty Pharmacist (CSP):** Focuses on specialty pharmacy practice, including the management of high-cost, high-complexity medications.

4.2.2.2 Benefits of Certification
Recognition of Expertise and Career Advancement:

1. **Recognition of Expertise:**

- **Professional Credibility:** Certification demonstrates a pharmacist's commitment to excellence and expertise in their chosen field. It provides formal recognition of their advanced knowledge and skills, enhancing their professional credibility among peers, employers, and patients.
- **Increased Trust:** Certified pharmacists are often perceived as more knowledgeable and reliable, leading to increased trust from patients, healthcare providers, and other stakeholders. This trust can improve patient outcomes and collaborative efforts within the healthcare

team.

2. **Career Advancement:**

- **Expanded Career Opportunities:** Certification can open doors to advanced clinical roles, leadership positions, and specialized practice areas. Pharmacists with certifications may be eligible for positions that require advanced expertise, such as clinical pharmacy specialists, pharmacy managers, or educators.
- **Higher Earning Potential:** Certified pharmacists often have higher earning potential due to their specialized skills and qualifications. Employers may offer higher salaries, bonuses, or other financial incentives to attract and retain certified professionals.
- **Professional Development:** Certification programs require ongoing education and recertification, encouraging pharmacists to stay current with the latest advancements in their field. This continuous learning fosters professional growth and ensures that pharmacists remain at the forefront of their practice.
- **Networking Opportunities:** Participation in certification programs and related professional organizations provides opportunities for networking with other experts in the field. These connections can lead to collaborative projects, mentorship, and further career advancement.
- **Enhanced Job Satisfaction:** Achieving certification can lead to increased job satisfaction by providing a sense of accomplishment and recognition. Certified pharmacists often report higher levels of professional fulfillment and confidence in their practice.

4.2.2.3 Obtaining and Maintaining Certification
Requirements and Processes for Certification Renewal:
Obtaining Certification:

1. **Eligibility Criteria:**

- **Education:** Candidates typically need to hold a Doctor of Pharmacy (Pharm.D.) degree from an accredited pharmacy school.
- **Licensure:** Candidates must be licensed pharmacists in good standing with their respective state board of pharmacy.

- **Experience:** Many certification programs require a certain amount of professional experience in the relevant area of practice. For example, board certifications may require several years of practice experience or completion of a residency program in the specialty area.

2. Application Process:

- **Application Submission:** Candidates must complete and submit an application form, which usually includes details about their educational background, professional experience, and any prior certifications.
- **Documentation:** Candidates often need to provide documentation such as transcripts, proof of licensure, and letters of recommendation from colleagues or supervisors.
- **Fees:** There are usually application fees associated with the certification process. These fees cover the cost of processing the application and administering the examination.

3. Examination:

- **Study and Preparation:** Candidates should prepare for the certification exam by studying relevant materials, attending review courses, and using practice exams. Many certification bodies provide study guides and resources to help candidates prepare.
- **Examination:** The certification exam typically consists of multiple-choice questions that assess the candidate's knowledge and skills in the specialty area. The exam may cover clinical guidelines, pharmacotherapy, patient care, and other relevant topics.
- **Passing Score:** Candidates must achieve a passing score on the exam to earn the certification.

Maintaining Certification:

1. Continuing Education:

- **Continuing Education Units (CEUs):** Certified pharmacists are required to earn a specified number of CEUs within a certain period (e.g., every 3 to 7 years) to maintain their certification. CEUs can be earned through various activities, including attending conferences, completing online courses, and participating in workshops.

- **Relevant Topics:** Continuing education activities should be relevant to the pharmacist's specialty area and cover topics such as new drug therapies, clinical guidelines, and advances in pharmacy practice.

2. **Practice Experience:**

- **Ongoing Practice:** Many certification programs require pharmacists to continue practicing in their specialty area to maintain certification. This ensures that they remain actively engaged in patient care and stay current with clinical practices.
- **Documentation:** Pharmacists may need to provide documentation of their ongoing practice experience, such as letters from employers or detailed logs of their professional activities.

3. **Recertification Examination:**

- **Periodic Testing:** Some certification programs require pharmacists to pass a recertification exam periodically to demonstrate that they have maintained their knowledge and skills. The recertification exam may be similar in format to the initial certification exam but focuses on recent advancements and current best practices.
- **Preparation:** Pharmacists should prepare for the recertification exam by reviewing recent literature, guidelines, and clinical updates in their specialty area.

4. **Professional Involvement:**

- **Professional Activities:** Participation in professional activities, such as serving on committees, publishing research, or presenting at conferences, can also contribute to maintaining certification. These activities demonstrate a commitment to advancing the profession and staying engaged with the pharmacy community.

5. **Renewal Application:**

- **Submission:** Pharmacists must submit a renewal application to the certifying body, providing evidence of their continuing education, practice experience, and any other requirements.
- **Fees:** There may be renewal fees associated with maintaining certification, which cover the cost of processing the renewal application and administering any required exams.

4.3 Training for Medical and Nursing Staff
4.3.1 Collaborative Training Programs
4.3.1.1 Interdisciplinary Training Sessions
Joint Training Programs with Medical and Nursing Staff:

Interdisciplinary training sessions are designed to foster collaboration and improve communication among pharmacists, medical staff, and nursing staff. These joint training programs are essential for creating a cohesive healthcare team that works together effectively to provide high-quality patient care. Interdisciplinary training enhances understanding of each other's roles, encourages mutual respect, and improves overall coordination in patient care.

Benefits of Interdisciplinary Training:

1. **Improved Patient Outcomes:** Collaborative training helps ensure that all healthcare providers are on the same page regarding patient care protocols, leading to more consistent and effective treatment plans.
2. **Enhanced Communication:** By training together, medical, nursing, and pharmacy staff can develop better communication skills, reducing misunderstandings and improving the clarity of patient care instructions.
3. **Increased Efficiency:** Understanding each other's roles and workflows allows for more efficient coordination of tasks, reducing delays and improving the overall efficiency of patient care.
4. **Professional Development:** Interdisciplinary training provides opportunities for professional growth, as participants learn from each other's expertise and perspectives.

Components of Interdisciplinary Training Sessions:

1. **Role Understanding and Clarification:**

- **Overview of Roles:** Sessions begin with an overview of the roles and responsibilities of each discipline, highlighting how they contribute to patient care.
- **Case Studies:** Use real-world case studies to illustrate how collaboration among pharmacists, doctors, and nurses can enhance patient outcomes.

2. **Communication Skills:**

- **Effective Communication:** Training on effective communication strategies, including active listening, clear and concise verbal communication, and proper documentation practices.
- **SBAR Technique:** Teach the SBAR (Situation-Background-Assessment-Recommendation) technique to standardize communication about patient conditions and care plans.

3. **Clinical Guidelines and Protocols:**

- **Joint Review of Guidelines:** Conduct joint reviews of clinical guidelines and protocols to ensure all team members are familiar with best practices and standard procedures.
- **Simulations:** Implement simulation-based training to practice adherence to clinical guidelines in a controlled environment, allowing participants to refine their skills and responses.

4. **Team-Based Care:**

- **Interdisciplinary Rounds:** Organize interdisciplinary rounds where the healthcare team discusses patient cases collectively, ensuring comprehensive care planning.
- **Collaboration Exercises:** Engage in exercises that require team members to work together to solve clinical problems, fostering a sense of teamwork and shared responsibility.

5. **Medication Management:**

- **Joint Medication Review:** Conduct joint medication review sessions where pharmacists, doctors, and nurses assess patient medication regimens, addressing potential issues such as drug interactions and adherence.

- **Safe Medication Practices:** Train all team members on safe medication practices, including proper prescribing, administration, and monitoring of medications.

6. **Patient Education and Counseling:**

- **Unified Approach:** Develop a unified approach to patient education and counseling, ensuring that all team members provide consistent and accurate information to patients and their families.
- **Role-Playing:** Use role-playing scenarios to practice patient counseling techniques and improve confidence in delivering patient education.

Implementation Strategies:

1. **Scheduling Flexibility:** Schedule training sessions at times that accommodate the busy schedules of all healthcare providers, possibly through multiple sessions or online modules.
2. **Leadership Support:** Ensure support from hospital leadership to prioritize interdisciplinary training and provide necessary resources.
3. **Feedback Mechanisms:** Implement feedback mechanisms to gather input from participants on the effectiveness of the training sessions and areas for improvement.
4. **Continuous Improvement:** Regularly update the training programs based on feedback, new clinical guidelines, and emerging best practices to ensure they remain relevant and effective.

By incorporating interdisciplinary training sessions into the professional development programs of medical, nursing, and pharmacy staff, hospitals can enhance collaboration, improve patient outcomes, and create a more cohesive and efficient healthcare team.

4.3.1.2 Focus Areas for Collaborative Training

Medication Management, Patient Safety, and Interprofessional Communication:

Collaborative training programs for medical, nursing, and pharmacy staff should focus on key areas that directly impact patient care and safety. By targeting these focus areas, interdisciplinary training sessions can enhance the knowledge and skills of healthcare providers, promote effective teamwork, and improve overall patient outcomes.

Medication Management:

1. **Comprehensive Understanding of Medications:**

   - **Pharmacology and Therapeutics:** Ensure that all team members have a solid understanding of the pharmacology, therapeutic uses, side effects, and interactions of commonly used medications.
   - **Medication Reconciliation:** Train staff on the importance and process of medication reconciliation at all transitions of care to prevent discrepancies and ensure continuity of therapy.

2. **Prescribing and Administration:**

   - **Safe Prescribing Practices:** Educate medical staff on evidence-based prescribing guidelines, appropriate dosing, and adjustments for special populations (e.g., pediatrics, geriatrics, renal impairment).
   - **Proper Administration Techniques:** Train nursing staff on correct medication administration techniques, including the use of infusion pumps, injection protocols, and oral medication delivery.

3. **Monitoring and Adherence:**

   - **Adverse Drug Reactions (ADRs):** Equip healthcare providers with the knowledge to monitor, recognize, and manage ADRs effectively.
   - **Patient Adherence:** Develop strategies to improve patient adherence to medication regimens, including patient education, motivational interviewing, and the use of adherence aids (e.g., pill organizers, reminder systems).

Patient Safety:

1. **Error Prevention and Reporting:**

   - **Medication Errors:** Educate staff on the types and causes of medication errors, and implement protocols to prevent them.

Encourage a non-punitive culture of error reporting and continuous improvement.

- **Safety Checklists:** Utilize checklists and standardized procedures to ensure consistency and reduce the risk of errors during medication preparation, administration, and documentation.

2. **Infection Control:**

- **Aseptic Techniques:** Reinforce the importance of aseptic techniques in medication preparation and administration to prevent infections.
- **Hand Hygiene:** Train staff on proper hand hygiene practices and the use of personal protective equipment (PPE) to minimize the risk of healthcare-associated infections (HAIs).

3. **Patient Identification:**

- **Verification Processes:** Implement and train staff on robust patient identification processes, such as using at least two identifiers (e.g., name and date of birth) before administering medications or performing procedures.

Interprofessional Communication:

1. **Effective Communication Techniques:**

- **SBAR Technique:** Train staff on the Situation-Background-Assessment-Recommendation (SBAR) technique to standardize communication about patient conditions and care plans.
- **Active Listening:** Encourage active listening skills to ensure that all team members understand and consider each other's perspectives and contributions.

2. **Team Huddles and Rounds:**

- **Interdisciplinary Rounds:** Conduct regular interdisciplinary rounds where the healthcare team discusses patient cases collectively, ensuring comprehensive care planning and decision-making.

- **Team Huddles:** Use brief, focused team huddles to review daily goals, address concerns, and coordinate care activities.

3. Conflict Resolution:

- **Conflict Management:** Provide training on conflict resolution strategies to handle disagreements or misunderstandings within the healthcare team constructively.
- **Collaborative Decision-Making:** Foster a culture of collaborative decision-making where all team members' input is valued and considered in patient care decisions.

Implementation Strategies:

1. **Integrated Curriculum:** Develop an integrated training curriculum that incorporates these focus areas and ensures that all healthcare providers receive consistent and comprehensive training.
2. **Simulation-Based Learning:** Use simulation-based training to practice real-life scenarios and reinforce learning in a safe, controlled environment.
3. **Continuous Feedback:** Establish mechanisms for continuous feedback and evaluation of the training program to identify areas for improvement and ensure its effectiveness.

By focusing on medication management, patient safety, and interprofessional communication, collaborative training programs can enhance the competency and coordination of medical, nursing, and pharmacy staff, leading to improved patient care and safety.

4.3.2 Continuing Education for Medical and Nursing Staff

4.3.2.1 Workshops and Seminars

Topics on Pharmacotherapy, New Medications, and Best Practices:

Continuing education for medical and nursing staff is essential for maintaining high standards of patient care and keeping abreast of the latest developments in pharmacotherapy and healthcare practices. Workshops and seminars play a crucial role in this ongoing professional development, providing opportunities for staff to learn about new medications, therapeutic approaches, and best practices in patient care.

Workshops:

1. **Pharmacotherapy Updates:**

   - **Advanced Pharmacotherapy:** Workshops focusing on advanced pharmacotherapy cover the latest treatment protocols for managing chronic diseases such as diabetes, hypertension, and heart failure. These sessions include case studies and practical applications to enhance clinical decision-making skills.
   - **Personalized Medicine:** Training on the principles of personalized medicine and how genetic, environmental, and lifestyle factors influence drug therapy. This includes understanding pharmacogenomics and its application in tailoring treatments to individual patients.

2. **New Medications:**

   - **Drug Mechanisms and Applications:** Workshops that provide detailed information on the mechanisms of action, clinical applications, and potential side effects of newly approved medications. This helps healthcare providers stay informed about the latest therapeutic options available for their patients.
   - **Clinical Trials and Research:** Sessions that review recent clinical trials and research studies, discussing their implications for clinical practice and how new evidence can be integrated into patient care.

3. **Best Practices in Medication Management:**

   - **Medication Reconciliation:** Training on best practices for medication reconciliation to ensure accuracy and continuity of care during patient transitions between different healthcare settings.
   - **Polypharmacy Management:** Strategies for managing polypharmacy, particularly in elderly patients, to minimize the risk of adverse drug interactions and improve patient outcomes.

Seminars:

1. **Pharmacotherapy Topics:**

- **Emerging Therapies:** Seminars on emerging therapies and their potential impact on patient care. This includes innovative treatments such as biologics, gene therapy, and novel drug delivery systems.
- **Antimicrobial Stewardship:** Education on antimicrobial stewardship programs, focusing on the responsible use of antibiotics to combat antibiotic resistance and ensure effective treatment of infections.

2. **New Medications:**

- **Therapeutic Advances:** Seminars that explore therapeutic advances in specific fields, such as oncology, cardiology, and neurology. These sessions highlight the latest drug developments and their clinical implications.
- **Safety and Efficacy:** Discussions on the safety and efficacy of new medications, including post-marketing surveillance data and real-world evidence to provide a comprehensive understanding of their use in clinical practice.

3. **Best Practices:**

- **Interdisciplinary Collaboration:** Seminars that emphasize the importance of interdisciplinary collaboration in patient care. Topics include effective communication, teamwork, and the integration of pharmacy services into the broader healthcare team.
- **Patient-Centered Care:** Training on patient-centered care approaches, focusing on improving patient engagement, adherence to therapy, and shared decision-making.

Implementation Strategies:

1. **Regular Scheduling:** Schedule workshops and seminars regularly to ensure that all medical and nursing staff have opportunities to participate and stay updated with the latest knowledge and skills.
2. **Expert Instructors:** Engage expert instructors and guest speakers from various fields of medicine and pharmacy to provide high-quality, evidence-based education.
3. **Interactive Learning:** Incorporate interactive learning methods, such as case discussions, role-playing, and hands-on activities, to enhance

engagement and retention of information.

4. **Accreditation and Credits:** Ensure that workshops and seminars are accredited and provide continuing education credits, encouraging staff participation and meeting professional licensure requirements.

5. **Feedback and Evaluation:** Collect feedback from participants to evaluate the effectiveness of the sessions and identify areas for improvement. Use this feedback to continuously refine and enhance the continuing education program.

By offering comprehensive workshops and seminars on pharmacotherapy, new medications, and best practices, hospitals can ensure that their medical and nursing staff remain knowledgeable, skilled, and capable of providing the highest quality of care to their patients.

4.3.2 Continuing Education for Medical and Nursing Staff

4.3.2.2 Simulation-Based Training

Use of Simulations to Enhance Practical Skills and Emergency Preparedness:

Simulation-based training is an effective educational tool that enhances practical skills and prepares medical and nursing staff for emergency situations. This method uses realistic scenarios to mimic clinical environments, allowing healthcare providers to practice and refine their skills in a controlled, risk-free setting.

1. **Enhancing Practical Skills:**

   - **Clinical Procedures:** Simulations provide hands-on practice for various clinical procedures, such as IV insertion, catheterization, wound care, and medication administration. By rehearsing these skills in a simulated environment, staff can build confidence and competence.

   - **Complex Cases:** Simulation-based training allows healthcare providers to manage complex cases that they may not encounter frequently in real practice. This includes rare medical conditions, multi-system trauma, and intricate surgical procedures.

2. **Emergency Preparedness:**

- **Code Blue Scenarios:** Simulations of cardiac arrest situations (Code Blue) help staff practice rapid response, effective communication, and the use of emergency equipment like defibrillators. Regular practice in these high-stress scenarios enhances readiness and performance during actual emergencies.
- **Disaster Drills:** Simulating large-scale emergencies, such as natural disasters or mass casualty incidents, prepares healthcare providers for coordinated responses. These drills involve triage, resource allocation, and interdepartmental collaboration.

3. **Interprofessional Collaboration:**

- **Team-Based Scenarios:** Simulation exercises often involve multidisciplinary teams, fostering collaboration and improving communication among physicians, nurses, pharmacists, and other healthcare professionals. These team-based scenarios enhance teamwork and ensure cohesive patient care.
- **Communication Skills:** Practicing handoffs, patient consultations, and crisis communication in simulations helps improve verbal and non-verbal communication skills, reducing the risk of miscommunication in real clinical settings.

Implementation of Simulation-Based Training:

- **High-Fidelity Simulators:** Use high-fidelity mannequins and advanced simulation technology to create realistic and immersive training scenarios.
- **Scenario Development:** Develop detailed scenarios that reflect common clinical situations and potential emergencies, ensuring a wide range of experiences for trainees.
- **Debriefing Sessions:** Conduct thorough debriefing sessions after each simulation exercise to discuss performance, identify strengths, and address areas for improvement. This reflective practice is crucial for learning and skill development.

4.3.2.3 Evaluation and Feedback

Assessing the Effectiveness of Training Programs and Providing Feedback:

Regular evaluation and feedback are critical components of effective continuing education programs. They ensure that training sessions meet their objectives and contribute to the ongoing development of medical and nursing staff.

1. **Assessing Effectiveness:**

   - **Pre- and Post-Training Assessments:** Implement assessments before and after training sessions to measure knowledge gain and skill improvement. These assessments can include written tests, practical exams, and self-evaluations.
   - **Simulation Performance Metrics:** Use specific metrics to evaluate performance during simulation-based training, such as time to intervention, accuracy of procedures, and adherence to protocols.
   - **Participant Feedback:** Collect feedback from participants through surveys, focus groups, and informal discussions. This feedback provides insights into the perceived value of the training, areas of strength, and suggestions for improvement.

2. **Providing Feedback:**

   - **Immediate Feedback:** Provide immediate feedback during hands-on training and simulations. Real-time feedback helps participants correct mistakes and reinforce correct practices.
   - **Constructive Criticism:** Offer constructive criticism that highlights specific areas for improvement while acknowledging strengths. Use a balanced approach to maintain motivation and encourage professional growth.
   - **Peer Feedback:** Encourage peer feedback during team-based training sessions. Peer evaluations can provide additional perspectives and promote a collaborative learning environment.

3. **Continuous Improvement:**

   - **Program Review:** Regularly review and update training programs based on evaluation results, participant feedback, and advancements in medical knowledge and technology.

- **Outcome Tracking:** Track the long-term outcomes of training programs, such as improvements in clinical performance, patient outcomes, and staff competency. Use this data to refine and enhance training initiatives.

Implementation of Evaluation and Feedback:

- **Structured Evaluation Tools:** Develop structured evaluation tools and forms to systematically assess training effectiveness and collect consistent feedback.
- **Debriefing Protocols:** Establish protocols for debriefing sessions that include structured discussions, feedback from instructors, and opportunities for self-reflection.
- **Ongoing Education:** Integrate evaluation and feedback into a continuous learning cycle, ensuring that training programs evolve and adapt to meet the changing needs of healthcare providers and patients.

By incorporating simulation-based training and robust evaluation and feedback mechanisms, hospitals can enhance the practical skills, emergency preparedness, and overall competency of their medical and nursing staff, ultimately improving patient care and safety.

4.4 Educational Programs for Pharmacy Students

4.4.1 Internship Programs

4.4.1.1 Structure and Objectives of Internship Programs

Duration, Goals, and Learning Outcomes:

Internship programs are essential components of pharmacy education, providing students with hands-on experience in real-world clinical settings. These programs are structured to bridge the gap between academic learning and professional practice, ensuring that students develop the practical skills and competencies required for successful careers in pharmacy.

Duration:

- **Typical Length:** Internship programs usually span several months to a year, depending on the requirements of the pharmacy school and the specific program. Common durations include 6-month, 9-month, or 12-month internships.
- **Flexible Schedules:** Programs may offer flexible schedules to accommodate students' academic commitments, allowing for part-time

or full-time participation.

Goals:

- **Professional Development:** To enhance students' professional development by providing practical experience in various pharmacy practice settings.
- **Skill Acquisition:** To develop essential skills in medication dispensing, patient counseling, clinical decision-making, and interprofessional collaboration.
- **Clinical Exposure:** To expose students to diverse clinical scenarios, enabling them to apply theoretical knowledge in real-world contexts.
- **Ethical Practice:** To instill a strong sense of professional ethics and responsibility in pharmacy practice.

Learning Outcomes:

- **Competency in Dispensing:** Students will demonstrate proficiency in accurately dispensing medications, including verifying prescriptions, preparing medications, and labeling.
- **Effective Patient Counseling:** Students will develop effective communication skills for counseling patients on medication use, potential side effects, and adherence strategies.
- **Clinical Decision-Making:** Students will enhance their ability to make informed clinical decisions based on patient history, clinical guidelines, and evidence-based practices.
- **Interprofessional Collaboration:** Students will learn to collaborate effectively with other healthcare professionals, contributing to a multidisciplinary approach to patient care.
- **Understanding of Pharmacy Operations:** Students will gain a comprehensive understanding of the operational aspects of pharmacy practice, including inventory management, regulatory compliance, and quality assurance.

4.4.1.2 Roles and Responsibilities of Interns
Practical Experience in Dispensing, Patient Counseling, and Clinical Rotations:

Internship programs provide pharmacy students with a wide range of responsibilities, ensuring they gain practical experience across various aspects of pharmacy practice.

Dispensing:

- **Prescription Verification:** Interns assist in verifying prescriptions for accuracy, appropriateness, and potential drug interactions.
- **Medication Preparation:** Interns are involved in preparing medications, including compounding, packaging, and labeling.
- **Inventory Management:** Interns help manage inventory levels, track medication usage, and ensure proper storage conditions to maintain drug efficacy.

Patient Counseling:

- **Medication Education:** Interns counsel patients on the correct use of their medications, including dosage instructions, administration methods, and potential side effects.
- **Adherence Strategies:** Interns provide strategies to improve medication adherence, such as using reminder tools and addressing barriers to compliance.
- **Health Promotion:** Interns educate patients on lifestyle modifications, preventive care, and the importance of following their treatment plans.

Clinical Rotations:

- **Hospital Pharmacy:** Interns rotate through hospital pharmacy settings, gaining experience in inpatient care, IV admixture preparation, and clinical pharmacy services.
- **Community Pharmacy:** Interns work in community pharmacies, focusing on outpatient care, OTC medication recommendations, and chronic disease management.
- **Specialty Clinics:** Interns may rotate through specialty clinics, such as oncology, cardiology, or infectious disease, to gain experience in managing complex medication regimens and specialized patient populations.

Supervision and Mentorship:

- **Preceptor Guidance:** Interns work under the supervision of experienced pharmacists (preceptors) who provide guidance, mentorship, and feedback on their performance.
- **Performance Evaluation:** Interns receive regular evaluations to assess their progress, identify strengths, and address areas for improvement.

Professional Development:

- **Ethics and Compliance:** Interns are educated on the ethical and legal aspects of pharmacy practice, ensuring adherence to professional standards and regulatory requirements.
- **Continuous Learning:** Interns are encouraged to engage in continuous learning through participation in workshops, seminars, and professional development activities.

4.4.1.3 Supervision and Mentorship
Role of Preceptors in Guiding and Evaluating Interns:
Preceptors play a crucial role in the professional development of pharmacy interns by providing supervision, mentorship, and evaluation throughout their internship programs. Their guidance helps interns transition from academic learning to practical application, ensuring they acquire the skills and confidence needed for successful careers in pharmacy.
Supervision:

1. **Direct Oversight:**

   - **Daily Supervision:** Preceptors provide day-to-day oversight of interns' activities, ensuring they perform tasks accurately and safely. This includes monitoring medication dispensing, compounding, and patient interactions.
   - **Task Delegation:** Preceptors assign specific tasks and responsibilities to interns, gradually increasing their level of autonomy as they demonstrate competence and confidence in their skills.

2. **Ensuring Compliance:**

   - **Adherence to Protocols:** Preceptors ensure that interns adhere to established pharmacy protocols, guidelines, and safety standards.

This includes proper hand hygiene, aseptic techniques, and compliance with regulatory requirements.

- **Patient Safety:** Preceptors prioritize patient safety by closely supervising interns during high-risk tasks, such as IV admixture preparation and medication reconciliation.

Mentorship:

1. **Guidance and Support:**

- **Knowledge Sharing:** Preceptors share their expertise and knowledge with interns, providing insights into best practices, clinical decision-making, and effective patient communication.
- **Professional Development:** Preceptors support interns' professional growth by offering advice on career planning, specialization opportunities, and continuing education.

2. **Role Modeling:**

- **Demonstrating Professionalism:** Preceptors serve as role models, exemplifying professionalism, ethical behavior, and a patient-centered approach to care. Interns learn by observing their preceptors' interactions with patients, colleagues, and other healthcare professionals.
- **Encouraging Reflection:** Preceptors encourage interns to reflect on their experiences, successes, and challenges. This reflective practice helps interns develop critical thinking skills and a deeper understanding of their roles.

Evaluation:

1. **Performance Assessment:**

- **Regular Evaluations:** Preceptors conduct regular evaluations of interns' performance, using structured assessment tools and criteria. These evaluations cover various aspects of pharmacy practice, including technical skills, clinical knowledge, communication, and professionalism.

- **Feedback Sessions:** Preceptors provide constructive feedback during scheduled feedback sessions, highlighting strengths and identifying areas for improvement. This feedback helps interns understand their progress and set goals for further development.

2. Competency Development:

- **Skills Checklist:** Preceptors use skills checklists to track interns' progress in mastering essential competencies. This ensures that interns receive comprehensive training and meet the required standards for practice.
- **Addressing Deficiencies:** When performance deficiencies are identified, preceptors work with interns to develop action plans for improvement. This may involve additional training, practice, or targeted learning activities.

Supportive Learning Environment:

1. Encouraging Questions:

- **Open Communication:** Preceptors foster an environment where interns feel comfortable asking questions and seeking clarification. This open communication promotes a culture of continuous learning and improvement.
- **Problem-Solving:** Preceptors guide interns through problem-solving processes, encouraging them to think critically and develop effective solutions to clinical challenges.

2. Emotional Support:

- **Building Confidence:** Preceptors provide positive reinforcement and encouragement, helping interns build confidence in their abilities. This support is especially important during challenging or stressful situations.
- **Mentoring Relationships:** Preceptors develop mentoring relationships with interns, offering ongoing support and guidance beyond the duration of the internship program.

4.4.2 Residency Programs
4.4.2.1 Overview of Pharmacy Residency Programs
Types (PGY1, PGY2) and Specialization Options:

Pharmacy residency programs provide advanced training and experience beyond the Doctor of Pharmacy (Pharm.D.) degree. These programs are designed to enhance clinical skills, prepare pharmacists for specialized practice, and provide opportunities for professional development.

1. **PGY1 (Postgraduate Year One):**

   - **General Focus:** PGY1 residency programs offer a broad-based training experience that covers various aspects of pharmacy practice, including clinical, administrative, and distributive functions. The goal is to develop well-rounded pharmacists capable of providing comprehensive patient care.
   - **Core Areas:** Training typically includes rotations in internal medicine, critical care, ambulatory care, infectious disease, and pharmacy administration. Residents gain exposure to different patient populations and healthcare settings.

2. **PGY2 (Postgraduate Year Two):**

   - **Specialized Focus:** PGY2 residency programs provide advanced training in a specific area of pharmacy practice. These programs are designed for pharmacists who have completed a PGY1 residency and wish to specialize further.
   - **Specialization Options:** PGY2 specializations include areas such as oncology, cardiology, infectious diseases, critical care, ambulatory care, psychiatry, and pediatric pharmacy. Each program focuses on developing expertise in the chosen specialty.

4.4.2.2 Curriculum and Training Components
Clinical Practice, Research, and Teaching Responsibilities:

Pharmacy residency programs have a comprehensive curriculum that includes clinical practice, research, and teaching components. These elements are designed to provide a well-rounded training experience that prepares residents for advanced practice and leadership roles.

1. **Clinical Practice:**

- **Patient Care Rotations:** Residents participate in various clinical rotations, working alongside experienced pharmacists and healthcare providers. These rotations provide hands-on experience in managing patient care, conducting medication reviews, and optimizing therapeutic regimens.
- **Interdisciplinary Collaboration:** Residents collaborate with physicians, nurses, and other healthcare professionals to develop and implement patient care plans. This interdisciplinary approach enhances communication skills and promotes a team-based approach to healthcare.
- **Direct Patient Interaction:** Residents engage in direct patient care activities, such as conducting patient interviews, providing medication counseling, and monitoring therapy outcomes. This experience helps residents build clinical competence and improve patient outcomes.

2. **Research:**

- **Research Projects:** Residents are required to complete a research project during their residency. This involves identifying a research question, designing a study, collecting and analyzing data, and presenting the findings. The project aims to develop research skills and contribute to the advancement of pharmacy practice.
- **Publication and Presentation:** Residents are encouraged to publish their research findings in peer-reviewed journals and present their work at professional conferences. This helps disseminate knowledge and promotes professional development.

3. **Teaching Responsibilities:**

- **Didactic Teaching:** Residents may have opportunities to teach pharmacy students through lectures, workshops, and seminars. This teaching experience enhances residents' communication and instructional skills.
- **Precepting:** Residents often serve as preceptors for pharmacy students during clinical rotations. This involves mentoring students,

providing guidance, and evaluating their performance. Precepting helps residents develop leadership and supervisory skills.

- **Continuing Education:** Residents may also be involved in providing continuing education sessions for pharmacy staff and other healthcare professionals. This contributes to the ongoing education and professional development of the healthcare team.

4.4.2.3 Benefits of Residency Training
Career Opportunities and Professional Development:

1. **Enhanced Career Opportunities:**

- **Specialized Roles:** Completing a residency program opens up opportunities for specialized roles in various healthcare settings, including hospitals, clinics, academia, and research institutions. Residents can pursue careers as clinical specialists, clinical coordinators, or faculty members.
- **Leadership Positions:** Residency training equips pharmacists with the skills and experience needed for leadership positions, such as pharmacy directors, managers, and administrators. These roles involve overseeing pharmacy operations, implementing policies, and managing staff.

2. **Professional Development:**

- **Advanced Clinical Skills:** Residency programs provide extensive clinical training, allowing pharmacists to develop advanced skills in patient care, disease management, and therapeutic decision-making. This enhances their ability to provide high-quality care and improve patient outcomes.
- **Networking:** Residents have the opportunity to build professional networks by working with experienced practitioners, participating in professional organizations, and attending conferences. Networking can lead to collaborative opportunities, mentorship, and career advancement.
- **Certifications:** Residency training prepares pharmacists for board certification in various specialties, such as Board Certified Pharmacotherapy Specialist (BCPS) or Board Certified Critical Care

Pharmacist (BCCCP). These certifications demonstrate expertise and enhance professional credibility.

By participating in residency programs, pharmacists gain valuable experience, advanced clinical skills, and professional development opportunities that prepare them for successful careers in specialized areas of pharmacy practice.

4.5 Drug and Therapeutics Newsletters

4.5.1 Creating Informative Newsletters

4.5.1.1 Identifying Relevant Topics

Selecting Topics Based on Current Trends and Clinical Needs:

Creating an informative and engaging drug and therapeutics newsletter begins with selecting relevant topics that resonate with the target audience, typically healthcare professionals such as pharmacists, physicians, and nurses. The process involves:

1. **Current Trends:** Monitoring the latest developments in pharmacy practice, including new drug approvals, updates to clinical guidelines, and emerging therapeutic areas. This ensures that the newsletter covers timely and important issues that impact patient care.

2. **Clinical Needs:** Identifying common clinical challenges and gaps in knowledge that healthcare providers face. Topics might include drug interactions, adverse drug reactions, management of chronic diseases, and new treatment modalities.

3. **Feedback from Readers:** Gathering input from readers about their interests and informational needs through surveys, feedback forms, and direct conversations. This helps tailor the content to meet the specific needs of the audience.

4. **Professional Recommendations:** Consulting with clinical experts, pharmacy leaders, and medical professionals to identify high-priority topics. These experts can provide insights into critical issues that require attention and education.

4.5.1.2 Content Development

Writing Articles, Drug Monographs, and Clinical Updates:

Once topics are selected, the next step is content development, which involves writing comprehensive and informative articles, drug monographs, and clinical updates. Key components include:

1. **Articles:**

   - **In-Depth Analysis:** Writing detailed articles that explore topics thoroughly, providing evidence-based information and practical insights. These articles should address clinical implications, best practices, and case studies.
   - **Clear and Concise Writing:** Ensuring that the content is written clearly and concisely, avoiding jargon and overly complex language. The goal is to make the information accessible and understandable to a broad audience.

2. **Drug Monographs:**

   - **Comprehensive Information:** Developing drug monographs that provide detailed information about specific medications, including pharmacology, indications, dosing, administration, side effects, and contraindications.
   - **Clinical Pearls:** Including practical tips and clinical pearls that help healthcare providers use the medication effectively and safely in their practice.

3. **Clinical Updates:**

   - **Recent Developments:** Providing updates on recent developments in drug therapy, such as new clinical trials, changes in treatment guidelines, and safety alerts from regulatory agencies.
   - **Implications for Practice:** Discussing the implications of these updates for clinical practice, helping healthcare providers stay current with the latest advancements and incorporate them into patient care.

4.5.1.3 Design and Layout

Effective Use of Graphics, Tables, and Formatting for Readability:

An engaging and well-designed newsletter not only conveys information effectively but also enhances readability and retention. Key aspects of design and layout include:

1. **Graphics:**

- **Visual Aids:** Using graphics such as charts, graphs, and infographics to visually represent data and complex information. Visual aids can make the content more engaging and easier to understand.
- **Images and Illustrations:** Incorporating relevant images and illustrations that complement the text and enhance visual appeal.

2. Tables:

- **Organized Information:** Using tables to organize and present information in a structured format. Tables are particularly useful for comparing drug properties, summarizing clinical guidelines, and presenting dosage charts.
- **Clarity and Precision:** Ensuring that tables are clearly labeled and easy to interpret, with concise headings and precise data.

3. Formatting:

- **Consistent Style:** Maintaining a consistent style throughout the newsletter, including font choices, headings, and color schemes. Consistency enhances readability and creates a professional appearance.
- **Readable Layout:** Designing the layout to be reader-friendly, with adequate white space, bullet points, and short paragraphs. This helps prevent information overload and keeps readers engaged.
- **Highlighted Sections:** Using headings, subheadings, and highlighted sections to break up the text and guide readers through the content. Key points and important information should be easily identifiable.

By carefully selecting relevant topics, developing high-quality content, and utilizing effective design and layout techniques, drug and therapeutics newsletters can become valuable resources for healthcare professionals. These newsletters help keep readers informed about the latest developments, best practices, and clinical updates, ultimately enhancing patient care and professional knowledge.

4.5.2 Distributing Newsletters

4.5.2.1 Distribution Channels

Print and Electronic Formats, Email Subscriptions, and Hospital Intranet:

To effectively distribute drug and therapeutics newsletters and ensure they reach the intended audience, it is important to use a variety of distribution channels:

1. **Print Formats:**

    - **Hard Copies:** Distribute printed copies of the newsletter within the hospital, placing them in common areas such as staff lounges, break rooms, and nursing stations. Printed newsletters can also be mailed to healthcare professionals who prefer physical copies.
    - **Bulletin Boards:** Post key articles and updates on bulletin boards in high-traffic areas, ensuring that important information is visible to all staff members.

2. **Electronic Formats:**

    - **PDF Versions:** Create PDF versions of the newsletter that can be easily downloaded and viewed on computers, tablets, and smartphones. PDFs can be emailed directly to staff or made available for download from the hospital intranet.
    - **Interactive Digital Editions:** Develop interactive digital editions of the newsletter with embedded links, videos, and other multimedia elements to enhance engagement.

3. **Email Subscriptions:**

    - **Email Distribution List:** Maintain an up-to-date email distribution list of healthcare professionals within the hospital. Send newsletters directly to their email inboxes, ensuring timely and convenient access to the latest information.
    - **Subscription Service:** Offer an email subscription service where staff can sign up to receive newsletters regularly. Provide an easy opt-in process and clear instructions on how to manage subscription preferences.

4. **Hospital Intranet:**

- **Intranet Posting:** Post the newsletter on the hospital's intranet site, making it accessible to all staff members. Use the intranet's notification system to alert staff when a new edition is available.
- **Intranet Announcements:** Highlight key articles and updates on the intranet homepage or through announcements to encourage staff to read the full newsletter.

4.5.2.2 Ensuring Wide Reach

Strategies to Increase Readership Among Healthcare Professionals:

To maximize the readership of the newsletter among healthcare professionals, implement strategies that enhance visibility and encourage engagement:

1. **Promotion and Awareness:**

- **Launch Campaigns:** Run promotional campaigns when new issues are released, using posters, emails, and intranet announcements to generate excitement and awareness.
- **Staff Meetings:** Announce new editions during staff meetings and departmental huddles, highlighting key articles and encouraging staff to read and share the newsletter.

2. **Engagement Incentives:**

- **Interactive Content:** Include interactive content, such as quizzes, polls, and case studies, to engage readers and encourage them to spend more time with the newsletter.
- **Recognition and Rewards:** Recognize and reward staff members who contribute articles or participate in newsletter activities. Offer incentives such as certificates, gift cards, or professional development opportunities.

3. **Feedback Mechanisms:**

- **Surveys and Feedback Forms:** Include surveys and feedback forms within the newsletter to gather input from readers about the content and format. Use this feedback to make improvements and address readers' preferences.

- **Reader Contributions:** Encourage readers to submit questions, case studies, and suggestions for future topics. This involvement creates a sense of ownership and investment in the newsletter.

4. Collaboration with Departments:

- **Departmental Champions:** Identify champions within each department who can promote the newsletter and encourage their colleagues to read it. These champions can also provide valuable feedback on content relevance and engagement.
- **Cross-Departmental Collaboration:** Collaborate with different departments to include content that is relevant to various specialties. This broadens the appeal of the newsletter and ensures it meets the diverse needs of the healthcare team.

4.5.2.3 Feedback and Evaluation

Collecting Feedback from Readers and Measuring the Impact:

To ensure the newsletter remains relevant and effective, it is important to regularly collect feedback from readers and evaluate its impact:

1. Feedback Collection:

- **Reader Surveys:** Conduct regular reader surveys to gather feedback on the content, format, and overall quality of the newsletter. Ask specific questions about what readers find useful and what improvements they would like to see.
- **Comment Sections:** Include comment sections or feedback forms in both print and electronic versions of the newsletter, allowing readers to share their thoughts and suggestions easily.

2. Measuring Engagement:

- **Analytics Tools:** Use analytics tools to track engagement with the electronic version of the newsletter. Monitor metrics such as open rates, click-through rates, and time spent on different sections to understand reader behavior.
- **Participation Metrics:** Track participation in interactive content, such as quizzes and polls, to gauge reader interest and engagement

levels.

3. Impact Assessment:

- **Knowledge Improvement:** Assess the impact of the newsletter on readers' knowledge and practice by conducting pre- and post-newsletter quizzes or surveys on key topics covered.
- **Behavioral Changes:** Evaluate whether the newsletter has led to any changes in clinical practice or decision-making by gathering anecdotal evidence and case studies from readers.

4. Continuous Improvement:

- **Regular Updates:** Use the feedback and evaluation data to make regular updates and improvements to the newsletter. Ensure that content remains current, relevant, and aligned with the needs and interests of the readership.
- **Editorial Board:** Establish an editorial board comprising representatives from different departments to oversee the content development process, review feedback, and ensure the newsletter maintains high standards.

By effectively distributing the newsletter through multiple channels, employing strategies to increase readership, and continuously collecting feedback and evaluating its impact, the drug and therapeutics newsletter can become an invaluable resource for healthcare professionals, enhancing their knowledge and improving patient care.

CHAPTER FIVE

Community Pharmacy Practice

5.1 Definition, Roles, and Responsibilities of Community Pharmacists

5.1.1 Definition of Community Pharmacy

5.1.1.1 Overview of Community Pharmacy

Community pharmacy, often referred to as retail pharmacy, is a vital component of the healthcare system, serving as the frontline interface between patients and healthcare providers. It encompasses establishments where licensed pharmacists dispense prescription medications, provide over-the-counter medications, offer health-related products, and deliver pharmaceutical care services to the general public. Community pharmacies are typically located within neighborhoods or retail settings, easily accessible to the population they serve. The primary objective of community pharmacies is to ensure safe and effective medication use, promote health and wellness, and enhance patient outcomes through comprehensive pharmaceutical services.

Explanation of Community Pharmacy and its Role in the Healthcare System

Community pharmacies play a multifaceted role in the healthcare system, contributing significantly to public health and patient care. One of the fundamental responsibilities of community pharmacists is to accurately dispense medications prescribed by healthcare professionals while ensuring adherence to regulatory standards and guidelines. Beyond dispensing, pharmacists serve as medication experts, providing counseling and education to patients on proper medication usage, potential side effects, drug interactions, and lifestyle modifications to optimize therapeutic outcomes.

Moreover, community pharmacists actively engage in medication therapy management (MTM) services, collaborating with other healthcare providers to optimize medication regimens, identify and resolve medication-related problems, and promote medication adherence. These services are particularly crucial for patients with chronic conditions requiring complex medication regimens, such as diabetes, hypertension, or asthma.

In addition to medication-related services, community pharmacies offer various healthcare screenings and immunization services to promote preventive care and early detection of health issues. Pharmacists conduct screenings for conditions like blood pressure, cholesterol levels, and diabetes, providing valuable insights into patients' health status and facilitating appropriate interventions or referrals to primary care providers.

Furthermore, community pharmacies serve as accessible resources for health information and support, addressing patients' inquiries regarding medications, health conditions, and general wellness concerns. Pharmacists leverage their expertise to provide evidence-based recommendations, guidance on self-care practices, and referrals to appropriate healthcare providers when necessary.

Community pharmacies play a pivotal role in enhancing patient access to essential healthcare services, promoting medication safety and efficacy, and fostering collaborative relationships among healthcare providers to deliver comprehensive patient-centered care. Through their diverse range of services and expertise, community pharmacists contribute significantly to improving public health outcomes and advancing the quality of healthcare delivery in communities.

5.1.1.2 Importance of Community Pharmacy

Community pharmacies hold significant importance in the realm of public health and primary care, serving as accessible hubs for healthcare services and resources within local communities. Their contributions span various dimensions, encompassing public health promotion, disease prevention, and the provision of primary care services.

Contribution to Public Health:

Community pharmacies actively contribute to public health initiatives by providing convenient access to essential healthcare services, including medication dispensing, health screenings, and immunizations. Their strategic placement within neighborhoods facilitates widespread accessibility, especially for individuals with limited mobility or those residing in underserved areas. By offering preventive care services such as blood pressure monitoring, cholesterol screenings, and diabetes management, community pharmacists play a crucial role in early detection and intervention for various health conditions.

Moreover, community pharmacies serve as valuable platforms for health education and promotion, empowering patients to make informed decisions about their health and well-being. Pharmacists utilize their expertise to deliver personalized counseling on medication adherence, lifestyle modifications, and disease management strategies, thereby fostering patient empowerment and self-care practices. Through educational initiatives, community pharmacies contribute to raising awareness about prevalent health issues, promoting healthy behaviors, and reducing the burden of chronic diseases within communities.

Contribution to Primary Care:

In addition to promoting public health, community pharmacies serve as frontline providers of primary care services, bridging the gap between patients and healthcare professionals. Pharmacists are equipped to address a wide range of acute and chronic health concerns, offering timely interventions, medication therapy management, and referral services as needed. Patients often seek the guidance of pharmacists for minor ailments, medication-related inquiries, and self-care advice, highlighting the integral role of community pharmacies in delivering patient-centered primary care.

Furthermore, community pharmacists collaborate closely with other healthcare providers, including physicians, nurse practitioners, and allied health professionals, to ensure coordinated and comprehensive care for patients. Through interdisciplinary communication and collaboration, pharmacists contribute to optimizing medication regimens, preventing medication errors, and promoting medication safety within the primary care continuum.

Community pharmacies play a pivotal role in advancing public health and primary care objectives by providing accessible healthcare services, promoting health education, and facilitating collaborative patient care efforts. Their significance extends beyond medication dispensing to encompass a holistic approach to health promotion, disease prevention, and patient-centered care delivery within local communities.

5.1.2 Scope of Practice

Community pharmacists operate within a defined scope of practice that encompasses various roles and responsibilities aimed at optimizing patient care and promoting public health. Within this scope, one of the central aspects is patient counseling and education, where pharmacists provide invaluable medication advice and health information to enhance patient understanding and engagement in their healthcare journey.

5.1.2.1 Patient Counseling and Education

Pharmacists serve as trusted healthcare advisors, offering personalized counseling and education to patients on various aspects of medication therapy, health management, and wellness promotion. This facet of their practice involves delivering clear, concise, and evidence-based information tailored to individual patient needs and preferences.

Providing Medication Advice:

Community pharmacists play a pivotal role in providing medication advice to patients, ensuring safe and effective medication use. This includes explaining medication instructions, dosing schedules, potential side effects, and precautions to be observed. Pharmacists address patient concerns, clarifying misconceptions, and providing reassurance to foster medication adherence and treatment success.

Moreover, pharmacists offer guidance on medication storage, administration techniques, and proper disposal of unused medications, promoting medication safety and minimizing the risk of adverse events. Through proactive medication counseling, pharmacists empower patients to take ownership of their health and make informed decisions regarding their treatment plans.

Health Information Provision:

In addition to medication-specific counseling, pharmacists serve as valuable sources of health information, addressing a wide range of health-related inquiries and concerns. Patients rely on pharmacists for guidance on managing common ailments, navigating self-care options, and adopting healthy lifestyle practices. Pharmacists leverage their expertise to provide evidence-based recommendations, dietary advice, and preventive health strategies tailored to individual patient needs.

Furthermore, pharmacists offer information on healthcare resources, community support services, and referral options, facilitating access to additional care and support as needed. By serving as accessible healthcare providers and educators, pharmacists contribute to health literacy enhancement and empowerment, enabling patients to make informed decisions about their health and well-being.

Patient counseling and education represent integral components of the community pharmacist's scope of practice, encompassing medication advice, health information provision, and patient empowerment initiatives. Through effective communication and education strategies, pharmacists empower patients to optimize medication outcomes, improve health outcomes, and achieve greater engagement in their healthcare journey.

5.1.2.2 Prescription Management

Community pharmacists play a critical role in prescription management, ensuring the safe and accurate dispensing of medications while actively monitoring for potential drug interactions and medication errors.

Dispensing Medications:

One of the primary responsibilities of community pharmacists is to accurately dispense medications prescribed by healthcare providers. Pharmacists meticulously review prescription orders to verify their accuracy, ensuring that the medication, dosage, and instructions align with the patient's needs and therapy plan. They utilize their pharmacological knowledge and expertise to interpret prescription instructions, identify any discrepancies or concerns, and communicate with prescribers when necessary to resolve issues or clarify instructions.

Checking for Drug Interactions:

In addition to dispensing medications, pharmacists conduct comprehensive medication reviews to assess for potential drug interactions, contraindications, or adverse effects. They utilize electronic drug databases and clinical decision support systems to screen prescriptions for interactions between medications, allergies, and patient-specific factors. Pharmacists identify and mitigate potential risks by providing counseling to patients on the importance of medication adherence, monitoring for signs of adverse effects, and reporting any unexpected symptoms to their healthcare providers promptly.

Ensuring Accuracy:

Pharmacists uphold stringent quality assurance standards to ensure the accuracy and integrity of the medication dispensing process. They meticulously label medications with clear instructions and safety information, verifying the correct medication and dosage before dispensing to patients. Pharmacists utilize barcode scanning technology and double-check procedures to minimize the risk of medication errors and enhance patient safety. Additionally, they provide patient counseling on proper medication administration techniques, storage requirements, and potential side effects to promote medication adherence and therapeutic efficacy.

5.1.2.3 Health Screening and Monitoring

Community pharmacists extend their role beyond medication management to include health screening and monitoring services, facilitating early detection and prevention of common health conditions.

Conducting Health Checks:

Pharmacists offer a range of health screening services to assess patients' health status and identify potential risk factors for chronic diseases. This may include conducting screenings for conditions such as high blood pressure, elevated cholesterol levels, and diabetes. Pharmacists utilize validated screening tools and equipment to measure vital signs, perform point-of-care testing, and interpret results accurately. They engage patients in meaningful discussions about their health risks, providing personalized recommendations for lifestyle modifications, preventive interventions, and follow-up care as needed.

Collaborative Care:

Furthermore, pharmacists collaborate with other healthcare providers to facilitate comprehensive health screening and monitoring initiatives. They communicate screening results and relevant clinical findings to patients' primary care providers, enabling coordinated care and informed decision-making regarding further diagnostic evaluation or treatment interventions. Pharmacists may also provide referrals to specialized healthcare services or community resources to address identified health needs and promote continuity of care.

Prescription management and health screening are integral components of the community pharmacist's scope of practice, emphasizing their commitment to patient safety, medication efficacy, and preventive healthcare. Through meticulous medication dispensing, proactive drug interaction screening, and comprehensive health assessments, pharmacists contribute to enhancing patient outcomes, promoting public health, and fostering collaborative relationships within the healthcare system.

5.1.2.4 Administration of Vaccinations

Pharmacists play a pivotal role in immunization programs by administering vaccines, promoting vaccination awareness, and expanding access to preventive healthcare services within the community.

Role of Pharmacists in Immunization Programs:

Community pharmacists have emerged as key providers of immunization services, offering convenient access to vaccines and vaccination clinics in retail pharmacy settings. Pharmacists undergo specialized training and certification in vaccine administration techniques, ensuring adherence to best practices and safety protocols established by public health authorities. Pharmacists administer a wide range of vaccines, including routine childhood immunizations, adult vaccinations for influenza, pneumonia, and travel-related diseases, as well as emerging vaccines for infectious diseases and pandemics. By leveraging their accessibility and expertise, pharmacists play a crucial role in increasing vaccination rates, reducing vaccine-preventable diseases, and promoting herd immunity within the community.

Vaccination Advocacy and Education:

In addition to administering vaccines, pharmacists serve as advocates for vaccination awareness and education, addressing vaccine hesitancy and misinformation among patients and caregivers. Pharmacists provide evidence-based information on the safety, efficacy, and importance of vaccines, addressing common concerns and misconceptions to promote informed decision-making. They engage in community outreach initiatives, educational campaigns, and collaborative efforts with healthcare providers to emphasize the value of immunization in preventing infectious diseases and protecting public health. By fostering a culture of vaccination acceptance, pharmacists contribute to achieving immunization goals and safeguarding community health.

5.1.2.5 Chronic Disease Management

Community pharmacists play an integral role in assisting patients in managing long-term conditions such as diabetes, hypertension, and other chronic diseases through comprehensive medication management, lifestyle counseling, and patient support services.

Assisting Patients in Managing Long-Term Conditions:

Pharmacists collaborate with patients and healthcare providers to develop personalized care plans tailored to the unique needs and goals of individuals with chronic diseases. They conduct medication reviews, assess treatment adherence, and optimize medication regimens to achieve therapeutic goals and prevent disease progression. Pharmacists provide ongoing monitoring and support to patients, addressing medication-related issues, monitoring disease parameters, and facilitating timely interventions to minimize complications and improve health outcomes. Through patient education and counseling, pharmacists empower individuals with chronic diseases to adopt healthy lifestyle behaviors, self-management strategies, and adherence to treatment recommendations, promoting disease control and enhancing quality of life.

Interdisciplinary Collaboration:

Furthermore, pharmacists engage in interdisciplinary collaboration with healthcare teams, including physicians, nurses, dietitians, and other allied health professionals, to ensure coordinated and holistic care for patients with chronic diseases. They participate in care coordination meetings, medication reconciliation processes, and shared decision-making discussions to optimize patient outcomes and promote continuity of care. Pharmacists serve as valuable resources for healthcare providers, offering clinical expertise, medication management strategies, and patient-centered interventions to address complex healthcare needs and improve patient outcomes. Through collaborative practice models and team-based care approaches, pharmacists contribute to enhancing the quality, efficiency, and effectiveness of chronic disease management within the healthcare system.

5.1.3 Professional Duties

Community pharmacists uphold a range of professional duties encompassing ethical conduct, adherence to legal regulations, and meticulous record-keeping practices to ensure patient safety and maintain the integrity of pharmaceutical services.

5.1.3.1 Ethical and Legal Responsibilities

Community pharmacists are entrusted with ethical and legal responsibilities to uphold professional standards, safeguard patient welfare, and maintain the public's trust in the pharmacy profession.

Adhering to Regulations and Professional Standards:

Pharmacists adhere to a comprehensive framework of regulations and professional standards established by regulatory bodies, such as state pharmacy boards, professional organizations, and governmental agencies. They comply with laws governing pharmacy practice, including the dispensing and distribution of medications, controlled substances management, prescription drug monitoring programs, and patient privacy protections under the Health Insurance Portability and Accountability Act (HIPAA). Pharmacists conduct their practice with integrity, honesty, and transparency, ensuring the ethical delivery of pharmaceutical care services and fostering trustful relationships with patients, healthcare providers, and regulatory authorities.

Moreover, pharmacists engage in continuing education and professional development activities to stay abreast of evolving legal requirements, emerging healthcare trends, and advancements in pharmaceutical practice. They participate in regulatory compliance initiatives, quality assurance programs, and adherence to professional codes of conduct to uphold the highest standards of ethical conduct and professional integrity in their practice.

5.1.3.2 Record Keeping and Documentation

Community pharmacists maintain meticulous record-keeping and documentation practices to ensure accurate documentation of patient care activities, prescription dispensing, and medication-related interventions.

Maintaining Accurate Patient Records and Prescription Logs:

Pharmacists are responsible for maintaining comprehensive and up-to-date patient records, including medication profiles, medical histories, allergies, and relevant clinical information. They document medication dispensing transactions, prescription orders, medication counseling sessions, and any medication-related interventions or consultations conducted with patients or healthcare providers. Pharmacists utilize electronic health record systems, pharmacy information management systems, and prescription monitoring databases to facilitate efficient documentation and information retrieval processes.

Furthermore, pharmacists maintain accurate prescription logs and dispensing records in compliance with regulatory requirements and record-keeping standards. They ensure the integrity, confidentiality, and security of patient information, adhering to HIPAA regulations and data protection protocols to safeguard patient privacy and confidentiality. Pharmacists implement appropriate measures for data storage, backup, and security to prevent unauthorized access, data breaches, or information loss, thereby maintaining the trust and confidence of patients and stakeholders in the confidentiality and integrity of pharmacy records.

Professional duties of community pharmacists encompass ethical conduct, compliance with legal regulations, and meticulous record-keeping practices to ensure patient safety, regulatory compliance, and the highest standards of pharmaceutical care delivery. By upholding ethical principles, adhering to legal requirements, and maintaining accurate documentation, pharmacists fulfill their professional obligations and contribute to promoting public health, patient welfare, and the integrity of pharmacy practice.

5.1.3.3 Continuing Professional Development

Community pharmacists recognize the importance of continuous learning and professional growth to maintain competence, stay abreast of advancements in pharmaceutical practice, and provide high-quality patient care.

Engaging in Ongoing Education and Training:

Pharmacists actively participate in continuing professional development (CPD) activities, including educational programs, workshops, seminars, and certification courses, to enhance their knowledge, skills, and competencies. They pursue opportunities for lifelong learning in various areas of pharmacy practice, such as pharmacotherapy updates, medication management technologies, patient counseling techniques, and emerging healthcare trends. Pharmacists also engage in self-directed learning, literature review, and peer collaboration to stay informed about evidence-based practices, clinical guidelines, and regulatory changes impacting pharmacy practice. By investing in continuous education and training, pharmacists maintain their professional relevance, adaptability, and effectiveness in meeting the evolving needs of patients and the healthcare system.

5.1.3.4 Patient Safety and Quality Assurance

Community pharmacists prioritize patient safety and quality assurance through proactive measures to prevent medication errors, optimize medication use, and enhance the quality of pharmaceutical care services.

Implementing Measures to Prevent Medication Errors:

Pharmacists implement a range of strategies to minimize the risk of medication errors and adverse drug events, ensuring the safe and effective use of medications by patients. They employ systematic approaches to medication dispensing, including medication reconciliation, double-check procedures, and verification processes, to reduce errors in prescription interpretation, dosage calculation, and medication selection. Pharmacists leverage technology-enabled solutions, such as electronic prescribing systems, barcode scanning, and automated dispensing machines, to enhance medication safety, accuracy, and efficiency in pharmacy operations.

Furthermore, pharmacists engage in medication error reporting, root cause analysis, and quality improvement initiatives to identify system weaknesses, workflow inefficiencies, and opportunities for error reduction and prevention. They collaborate with healthcare teams, including prescribers, nurses, and pharmacists, to implement evidence-based strategies, best practices, and error-reduction protocols to mitigate risks and enhance patient safety across the medication use continuum.

Through their commitment to continuous learning, professional development, and quality improvement efforts, community pharmacists demonstrate their dedication to patient safety, quality assurance, and the highest standards of pharmaceutical care delivery. By proactively addressing medication errors, implementing safety measures, and promoting a culture of quality and accountability, pharmacists contribute to improving patient outcomes, reducing healthcare costs, and fostering public trust in pharmacy services.

5.2 Relationship with Other Healthcare Providers

In the complex landscape of healthcare delivery, community pharmacists recognize the significance of fostering collaborative relationships with other healthcare providers to enhance patient care, improve outcomes, and optimize healthcare resources.

5.2.1 Importance of Interprofessional Collaboration

Interprofessional collaboration is integral to delivering comprehensive, patient-centered care that addresses the diverse healthcare needs of individuals and communities. Community pharmacists engage in collaborative practice models with other healthcare providers to leverage their unique expertise, perspectives, and resources for the benefit of patients.

5.2.1.1 Enhancing Patient Care

Collaborative practice among healthcare providers, including pharmacists, physicians, nurses, and allied health professionals, enhances the quality and effectiveness of patient care. By working together as a cohesive team, healthcare providers can leverage their respective knowledge and skills to develop holistic care plans, tailor treatment approaches, and address complex health conditions comprehensively. Pharmacists contribute their medication expertise, medication management strategies, and patient counseling skills to optimize medication regimens, prevent drug interactions, and improve medication adherence. This collaborative approach ensures that patients receive personalized, evidence-based care that aligns with their individual needs, preferences, and treatment goals, ultimately leading to improved health outcomes and patient satisfaction.

Benefits of Collaborative Practice in Improving Patient Outcomes

Interprofessional collaboration has been shown to yield numerous benefits in improving patient outcomes across various healthcare settings and patient populations. By fostering open communication, shared decision-making, and coordinated care delivery, collaborative practice models facilitate early detection and intervention for health issues, reduce hospital readmissions, and enhance medication safety and efficacy. Pharmacists collaborate with physicians and other providers to identify and address medication-related problems, optimize therapy outcomes, and promote patient self-management skills. This team-based approach enables healthcare providers to deliver timely, comprehensive care that addresses the root causes of health problems, prevents disease complications, and promotes long-term wellness and quality of life for patients.

5.2.1.2 Reducing Healthcare Costs

In addition to improving patient outcomes, interprofessional collaboration offers significant potential for reducing healthcare costs and optimizing resource utilization. By leveraging the expertise of multiple healthcare disciplines, collaborative practice models can identify cost-effective strategies for managing chronic diseases, preventing hospital admissions, and reducing unnecessary healthcare expenditures. Pharmacists play a key role in cost containment efforts through medication therapy management, medication optimization initiatives, and medication adherence interventions that help minimize medication-related complications and healthcare utilization. Furthermore, collaborative care models enable healthcare providers to implement preventive measures, health promotion activities, and early intervention strategies that mitigate the progression of diseases, reduce healthcare utilization, and lower overall healthcare costs over time.

Interprofessional collaboration is essential for maximizing the effectiveness, efficiency, and value of healthcare delivery. By working collaboratively with other healthcare providers, community pharmacists contribute to enhancing patient care, improving outcomes, and reducing healthcare costs through coordinated, patient-centered approaches that prioritize evidence-based practice, communication, and teamwork.

5.2.2 Communication with Healthcare Providers

Effective communication with other healthcare providers is essential for facilitating collaborative care, ensuring patient safety, and optimizing treatment outcomes. Community pharmacists employ various techniques and technologies to enhance communication and coordination within the healthcare team.

5.2.2.1 Effective Communication Techniques

Clear and efficient communication among healthcare providers is vital for exchanging critical patient information, coordinating care plans, and addressing patient needs effectively. Community pharmacists utilize several techniques to ensure effective communication with other providers:

Methods for Clear and Efficient Communication:

1. **Interprofessional Meetings and Consultations:** Pharmacists participate in interprofessional meetings, case conferences, and team huddles to discuss patient cases, share insights, and collaborate on care plans. These face-to-face interactions facilitate open dialogue, foster mutual understanding, and promote collaborative decision-making among healthcare team members.

2. **Structured Communication Tools:** Pharmacists utilize structured communication tools, such as SBAR (Situation, Background, Assessment, Recommendation), to convey important patient information, clinical updates, and medication-related concerns to other providers in a concise and standardized format. These tools help streamline communication, reduce misunderstandings, and ensure key information is effectively communicated and acted upon.

3. **Electronic Communication Platforms:** Pharmacists leverage electronic communication platforms, such as secure messaging systems or shared electronic health record (EHR) platforms, to communicate with other providers asynchronously. These platforms enable pharmacists to transmit medication-related inquiries, clinical recommendations, and care coordination updates in real-time, promoting timely collaboration and continuity of care.

4. **Follow-Up and Feedback:** Pharmacists prioritize follow-up communication with other providers to ensure care plans are implemented, medication adjustments are made as needed, and patient progress is monitored effectively. They seek feedback from other providers regarding the outcomes of medication interventions, adherence to treatment recommendations, and opportunities for improvement in care coordination processes.

By employing these effective communication techniques, community pharmacists facilitate seamless collaboration, enhance interdisciplinary communication, and promote patient-centered care delivery within the healthcare team.

5.2.2.2 Use of Technology

Technology plays a crucial role in enhancing communication and collaboration among healthcare providers, enabling efficient information exchange, remote consultations, and access to patient data. Community pharmacists leverage various technological tools to streamline communication and enhance patient care:

Electronic Health Records (EHR): Pharmacists utilize EHR systems to access comprehensive patient records, medication histories, and clinical information in real-time. EHR platforms facilitate seamless information sharing among healthcare providers, enabling pharmacists to review medication orders, document interventions, and communicate with other providers electronically. By having access to up-to-date patient information, pharmacists can make informed decisions, identify potential medication-related issues, and collaborate effectively with other providers to optimize patient care.

Telepharmacy Services: Telepharmacy technology enables pharmacists to provide remote pharmacy services, including medication counseling, medication therapy management, and prescription verification, to patients located in underserved or remote areas. Pharmacists utilize telepharmacy platforms to conduct virtual consultations, answer medication-related inquiries, and deliver patient education sessions via video conferencing or telecommunication channels. Telepharmacy services enhance access to pharmacy care, particularly in rural or isolated communities, and facilitate communication between pharmacists and other healthcare providers involved in the patient's care.

By leveraging technology-enabled communication tools such as EHR systems and telepharmacy services, community pharmacists overcome geographical barriers, enhance communication efficiency, and promote collaborative care delivery across diverse healthcare settings. These technological advancements enable pharmacists to play an active role in the healthcare team, contribute to patient-centered care initiatives, and optimize treatment outcomes through seamless communication and information exchange with other providers.

5.2.3 Collaborative Practice Models

Community pharmacists engage in various collaborative practice models to optimize patient care, improve treatment outcomes, and enhance healthcare delivery. These models involve partnering with other healthcare professionals to leverage complementary expertise and resources in delivering comprehensive, patient-centered care.

5.2.3.1 Integrated Care Teams

Integrated care teams represent a collaborative practice model in which pharmacists work closely with physicians, nurses, and other healthcare professionals to provide coordinated, holistic care for patients across the continuum of healthcare settings.

Working with Physicians, Nurses, and Other Healthcare Professionals:

In integrated care teams, pharmacists collaborate with physicians, nurse practitioners, physician assistants, and other healthcare providers to deliver patient-centered care that addresses the full spectrum of patients' healthcare needs. Pharmacists contribute their medication expertise, clinical knowledge, and medication management skills to assist in diagnosing, treating, and monitoring patients with acute and chronic health conditions. They collaborate with physicians and other prescribers to optimize medication regimens, prevent drug interactions, and ensure medication safety and efficacy. Pharmacists also work closely with nurses to coordinate patient care activities, provide medication counseling, and monitor patients' responses to therapy.

Furthermore, pharmacists actively engage in interdisciplinary care planning, case conferences, and team-based rounds to develop comprehensive care plans, set treatment goals, and evaluate patient progress collaboratively. By working collaboratively with other healthcare professionals, pharmacists contribute to improving care coordination, enhancing communication, and promoting seamless transitions of care for patients across different healthcare settings.

5.2.3.2 Pharmacist-Led Clinics

Pharmacist-led clinics represent a specialized practice model in which pharmacists take on expanded roles and responsibilities in providing direct patient care services, such as chronic disease management and medication therapy management (MTM).

Establishing Clinics for Chronic Disease Management and MTM:

In pharmacist-led clinics, pharmacists assume leadership roles in managing chronic diseases, conducting medication reviews, and delivering medication therapy management services to patients. These clinics may focus on specific chronic conditions, such as diabetes, hypertension, asthma, or anticoagulation therapy, where pharmacists provide comprehensive medication management, monitoring, and education to optimize treatment outcomes and improve patients' quality of life.

Pharmacist-led clinics offer a range of services, including medication reconciliation, medication therapy reviews, adherence counseling, laboratory monitoring, and patient education. Pharmacists collaborate with patients' primary care providers and specialists to develop individualized care plans, adjust medication regimens, and address medication-related issues effectively. By offering dedicated time and attention to patient care, pharmacist-led clinics enhance medication safety, promote treatment adherence, and empower patients to actively participate in managing their health.

Furthermore, pharmacist-led clinics play a crucial role in promoting preventive care, early intervention, and health promotion initiatives within the community. Pharmacists conduct health screenings, immunizations, and wellness assessments to identify risk factors, prevent disease complications, and promote healthy lifestyle behaviors among patients.

Collaborative practice models such as integrated care teams and pharmacist-led clinics enable community pharmacists to expand their roles, enhance patient care, and contribute to improving health outcomes through interdisciplinary collaboration, patient-centered care delivery, and specialized medication management services. These models represent innovative approaches to healthcare delivery that leverage pharmacists' expertise and capabilities to address the evolving healthcare needs of patients and communities effectively.

5.2.4 Overcoming Barriers to Collaboration

Effective collaboration among healthcare providers is essential for delivering high-quality patient care and optimizing treatment outcomes. However, various barriers can impede collaboration efforts. Community pharmacists employ strategies to overcome these barriers and promote seamless interdisciplinary collaboration within the healthcare team.

5.2.4.1 Identifying Common Barriers

Several common barriers can hinder effective collaboration among healthcare providers, including community pharmacists:

Communication Gaps: Communication breakdowns or inconsistencies between healthcare providers can hinder information sharing, care coordination, and decision-making processes. Communication gaps may arise from differences in communication styles, lack of standardized communication protocols, or limited access to shared patient information.

Professional Silos: Professional silos or organizational boundaries can restrict collaboration and hinder interdisciplinary teamwork. Healthcare providers may operate within their respective professional domains, leading to fragmented care delivery, duplication of efforts, and missed opportunities for collaboration.

Resource Constraints: Limited resources, such as time, staffing, and financial support, can pose significant challenges to collaborative practice initiatives. Healthcare organizations may face resource constraints that impede the implementation of collaborative care models or hinder pharmacists' ability to expand their roles and responsibilities within the healthcare team.

5.2.4.2 Strategies to Enhance Collaboration

Community pharmacists employ various strategies to overcome barriers to collaboration and promote effective interdisciplinary teamwork:

Building Trust: Establishing trust and mutual respect among healthcare providers is essential for fostering collaboration and communication. Pharmacists cultivate trust by demonstrating their expertise, reliability, and commitment to patient care. Building trusting relationships with other providers encourages open communication, promotes collaboration, and facilitates shared decision-making.

Creating Joint Protocols: Developing standardized protocols, guidelines, and workflows for collaborative practice can enhance communication, streamline care processes, and promote consistency in patient care delivery. Pharmacists collaborate with other healthcare providers to develop joint protocols for medication management, care coordination, and patient follow-up, ensuring alignment with best practices and evidence-based guidelines.

Engaging in Regular Interdisciplinary Meetings: Regular interdisciplinary meetings, case conferences, and team huddles provide opportunities for healthcare providers to collaborate, discuss patient cases, and share insights. Pharmacists actively participate in these meetings to contribute their expertise, provide medication-related recommendations, and coordinate care plans with other providers. Interdisciplinary meetings promote shared decision-making, enhance communication, and foster a collaborative culture within the healthcare team.

Utilizing Technology: Leveraging technology-enabled communication tools, such as secure messaging systems, electronic health records (EHR), and telehealth platforms, can facilitate information exchange, collaboration, and coordination among healthcare providers. Pharmacists utilize technology to communicate with other providers, access patient information remotely, and participate in virtual consultations or care planning sessions, overcoming geographical barriers and enhancing interdisciplinary collaboration.

By implementing these strategies, community pharmacists can overcome barriers to collaboration, enhance communication, and promote effective interdisciplinary teamwork to optimize patient care delivery and improve treatment outcomes.

CHAPTER SIX

Management of Community Pharmacy

6.1 Legal Requirements for Starting a Community Pharmacy

6.1.1 Licensing and Regulatory Compliance

6.1.1.1 Overview of Licensing Requirements

To operate a community pharmacy in India, obtaining necessary licenses and permits is crucial. This includes a Drug License from the State Drug Control Organization under the provisions of the Drugs and Cosmetics Act, 1940. A pharmacist must also be registered with the State Pharmacy Council.

6.1.1.2 Regulatory Bodies and Guidelines

The key regulatory authorities include the Central Drugs Standard Control Organization (CDSCO) and respective State Drug Control Organizations. These bodies ensure compliance with the Drugs and Cosmetics Act, 1940, the Pharmacy Act, 1948, and other relevant regulations.

6.1.1.3 Compliance with Laws and Regulations

Community pharmacies must adhere to all relevant laws, including those related to the sale of controlled substances, prescription handling, and health codes. Compliance ensures the legal and ethical operation of the pharmacy, maintaining public safety and trust.

6.2 Site Selection, Layout, and Design

6.2.1 Strategic Location

6.2.1.1 Factors Influencing Site Selection

Selecting a site for a community pharmacy involves considering population demographics, local competition, and accessibility. High footfall areas near clinics, hospitals, or residential zones are ideal to attract more customers.

6.2.1.2 Impact of Location on Business Success

The success of a pharmacy significantly depends on its location. A visible and convenient site increases customer footfall, enhancing business prospects.

6.2.2 Efficient Layout Planning

6.2.2.1 Designing the Pharmacy Interior

The interior layout should facilitate optimal workflow, ensuring easy navigation for customers and staff. This includes organized shelving, clear signage, and dedicated areas for dispensing and counseling.

6.2.2.2 Compliance with Building Codes and Standards

Adhering to safety, accessibility, and health regulations is essential. This includes ensuring proper ventilation, lighting, and space for secure medication storage.

6.2.2.3 Ergonomic Design Principles

Implementing ergonomic design principles creates a comfortable and efficient work environment, reducing staff fatigue and enhancing productivity.

6.3 Drug Display and Super Drug Store Model

6.3.1 Effective Merchandising Techniques

6.3.1.1 Principles of Drug Display

Strategically placing medications and health products improves accessibility and promotes sales. Key items should be placed at eye level, and high-demand products should be easily reachable.

6.3.1.2 Promoting Over-the-Counter (OTC) Products

Effective promotion techniques, such as special displays and promotions, can maximize visibility and sales of OTC products.

6.3.2 Super Drug Store Model

6.3.2.1 Concept and Benefits

The super drug store model integrates pharmacy services with a wider range of health and wellness products, enhancing customer experience and increasing revenue streams.

6.3.2.2 Implementation Strategies

Adopting the super drug store model involves expanding the product range, training staff, and optimizing store layout to accommodate additional products and services.

6.4 Accounts and Audits

6.4.1 Financial Management

6.4.1.1 Basics of Pharmacy Accounting

Maintaining accurate financial records involves understanding key financial statements such as profit and loss accounts, balance sheets, and cash flow statements.

6.4.1.2 Budgeting and Financial Planning

Creating and managing budgets is crucial for ensuring the pharmacy's profitability. This includes forecasting expenses, setting financial goals, and monitoring performance.

6.4.2 Compliance and Audits

6.4.2.1 Importance of Regular Audits

Regular audits ensure financial accuracy, regulatory compliance, and help identify areas for improvement.

6.4.2.2 Types of Audits

Understanding the differences between internal and external audits helps in preparing and maintaining the required financial documentation.

6.4.2.3 Preparing for Audits

Best practices include maintaining organized records, regularly updating financial information, and ensuring compliance with legal standards.

6.5 Good Dispensing Practices

6.5.1 Ensuring Safe and Accurate Dispensing

6.5.1.1 Principles of Good Dispensing

Following guidelines for accurate and safe medication dispensing ensures patient safety and trust.

6.5.1.2 Preventing Dispensing Errors

Identifying common causes of errors and implementing strategies to mitigate them, such as double-checking prescriptions and using technology for verification.

6.5.1.3 Patient Counseling

Providing patients with clear information and advice on medication use, potential side effects, and adherence improves health outcomes.

6.6 Software and Databases in Community Pharmacies

6.6.1 Technology for Efficient Management

6.6.1.1 Types of Pharmacy Management Software

Common software solutions include inventory management, billing systems, and electronic health records (EHR).

6.6.1.2 Benefits of Using Technology

Implementing technology enhances efficiency, accuracy, and customer service, reducing manual errors and saving time.

6.6.2 Implementing and Utilizing Databases

6.6.2.1 Inventory Management Systems

Tracking and managing stock levels ensures the availability of essential medications and reduces wastage.

6.6.2.2 Patient Record Systems

Maintaining comprehensive and secure patient records supports better patient care and compliance with legal requirements.

6.6.2.3 Integration with Healthcare Systems

Ensuring interoperability with other healthcare providers and systems facilitates seamless patient care and information sharing.

6.7 Entrepreneurship in Community Pharmacy

6.7.1 Business Skills and Opportunities

6.7.1.1 Fundamentals of Pharmacy Entrepreneurship

Successful pharmacy business owners need key skills such as financial management, marketing, and strategic planning.

6.7.1.2 Identifying Business Opportunities

Conducting market analysis and identifying gaps in services helps in seizing new business opportunities.

6.7.2 Developing a Business Plan

6.7.2.1 Creating a Comprehensive Business Plan

A robust business plan includes market research, financial projections, and a marketing strategy.

6.7.2.2 Securing Funding and Investment

Exploring various sources of funding and developing strategies to attract investors is crucial for starting and expanding the business.

6.7.2.3 Launching and Growing the Business

Effective steps for launching the pharmacy and strategies for sustainable growth and expansion ensure long-term success.

6.1 Legal Requirements for Starting a Community Pharmacy 6.1.1 Licensing and Regulatory Compliance 6.1.1.1 Overview of Licensing Requirements To operate a community pharmacy in India, obtaining necessary licenses and permits is crucial. This includes a Drug License from the State Drug Control Organization under the provisions of the Drugs and Cosmetics Act, 1940. A pharmacist must also be registered with the State Pharmacy Council.:please expand this in the form of long Paragraphs with values, minute details etc if any in academic tone but not using very complex sentences with clarity: sub Section headings are bold font. Give answer only no need to give Conclusion SumMrARy etc at the end . it is not required. Please remember all prompts for future reference)

6.1.1.1 Overview of Licensing Requirements

To operate a community pharmacy in India, obtaining necessary licenses and permits is crucial. This process ensures that the pharmacy complies with all legal and regulatory standards set forth by governing authorities, thus safeguarding public health and maintaining professional integrity within the pharmacy sector. The cornerstone of these licensing requirements is obtaining a Drug License from the State Drug Control Organization. This license is issued under the provisions of the Drugs and Cosmetics Act, 1940, a pivotal piece of legislation that regulates the import, manufacture, distribution, and sale of drugs and cosmetics in India. The Drug License is categorized into two types: the Retail Drug License (RDL) and the Wholesale Drug License (WDL), depending on the nature of the business. For a community pharmacy, the Retail Drug License is essential, permitting the sale of medications directly to consumers.

In addition to the Drug License, the pharmacy must have a registered pharmacist who is responsible for overseeing the dispensing of medications and ensuring compliance with pharmaceutical regulations. This pharmacist must be registered with the State Pharmacy Council, an authoritative body established under the Pharmacy Act, 1948. Registration with the State Pharmacy Council requires the pharmacist to hold a valid degree or diploma in pharmacy from an institution recognized by the Pharmacy Council of India (PCI). The registration process involves submitting various documents, including proof of qualifications, identity verification, and professional conduct certificates.

Furthermore, pharmacies must also obtain a business registration from the local municipal authorities or the Ministry of Micro, Small & Medium Enterprises (MSME), depending on the business structure, whether it is a sole proprietorship, partnership, or private limited company. This registration is necessary to legally operate a business within the jurisdiction and to comply with local business laws and tax regulations.

Another critical requirement is the Goods and Services Tax (GST) registration, which is mandatory for all businesses with an annual turnover exceeding a specified threshold. GST registration enables the pharmacy to conduct business transactions legally, collect GST from customers, and claim input tax credits on purchases.

Moreover, the premises of the pharmacy must meet specific infrastructural standards as outlined by the regulatory authorities. This includes adequate space for the storage of medications, proper ventilation, refrigeration for temperature-sensitive drugs, and a clean and hygienic environment to ensure the safety and efficacy of pharmaceutical products. Regular inspections by the Drug Control Authority ensure that these standards are maintained consistently.

6.1.1.3 Compliance with Laws and Regulations

Community pharmacies in India are mandated to comply with a comprehensive framework of laws and regulations to ensure the legal, ethical, and safe operation of their services. This compliance is crucial for maintaining public safety, upholding professional standards, and fostering trust within the community. The cornerstone of these regulatory requirements is the Drugs and Cosmetics Act, 1940, which provides guidelines on the sale, storage, and distribution of pharmaceutical products. This act mandates that pharmacies must only dispense medications that are prescribed by a licensed medical practitioner and must maintain accurate records of all transactions.

A critical aspect of compliance involves the handling and sale of controlled substances, which are regulated under the Narcotic Drugs and Psychotropic Substances (NDPS) Act, 1985. Pharmacies must ensure that these substances are dispensed strictly according to the prescriptions, and comprehensive records must be maintained to track their inventory and usage. Any deviation or non-compliance with these regulations can result in severe legal consequences, including fines and revocation of licenses.

In addition to controlled substances, pharmacies must adhere to stringent prescription handling protocols. This includes verifying the authenticity of prescriptions, ensuring that medications are dispensed in the correct dosages, and providing appropriate patient counseling to ensure the safe and effective use of medications. Pharmacists must also be vigilant in checking for potential drug interactions and contraindications, thereby safeguarding patient health and wellbeing.

Health codes and standards set by various regulatory authorities, such as the Central Drugs Standard Control Organization (CDSCO) and State Drug Control Organizations, must also be strictly followed. These codes cover a wide range of operational aspects, including the storage conditions for medications, which must meet specific temperature and humidity requirements to ensure their efficacy. Regular inspections by regulatory authorities ensure that pharmacies adhere to these standards, and any lapses can result in penalties or suspension of operations.

Furthermore, pharmacies must comply with the Pharmacy Act, 1948, which governs the qualifications and practice of pharmacists in India. This act requires that all dispensing activities are supervised by a registered pharmacist, who is responsible for ensuring that all regulatory and ethical standards are met. The pharmacist must also stay abreast of the latest developments in pharmaceutical practice through continuous professional development.

Compliance with the Goods and Services Tax (GST) regulations is another critical requirement. Pharmacies must ensure accurate calculation, collection, and remittance of GST on all taxable supplies. Proper financial record-keeping and regular filing of GST returns are essential to avoid legal issues and maintain smooth business operations.

6.2 Site Selection, Layout, and Design

6.2.1 Strategic Location

6.2.1.1 Factors Influencing Site Selection

Selecting an appropriate site for a community pharmacy is a critical decision that can significantly impact its success. Several key factors must be considered to ensure optimal location. One of the primary considerations is **population demographics**. Understanding the age, income levels, health conditions, and buying behaviors of the local population can help tailor the services and products offered by the pharmacy to meet community needs effectively. For instance, an area with a high proportion of elderly residents may benefit from a pharmacy offering specialized services for chronic conditions and convenient access to medications.

Local competition is another vital factor. It is essential to analyze the number and types of existing pharmacies in the area, their service offerings, and their customer base. Opening a pharmacy in a location with limited or no competition can provide a significant business advantage. However, even in areas with existing competition, a pharmacy can differentiate itself by offering superior customer service, a broader range of products, or unique services such as home delivery.

Accessibility is crucial for attracting and retaining customers. Pharmacies should ideally be located in high footfall areas, such as near clinics, hospitals, residential zones, or shopping centers. These locations ensure that the pharmacy is easily accessible to a large number of potential customers. Proximity to healthcare facilities can create a synergistic relationship, where patients visiting doctors or hospitals can conveniently fill their prescriptions nearby. Additionally, the pharmacy should be easily accessible by public transportation and have adequate parking facilities for customers who drive.

6.2.1.2 Impact of Location on Business Success

The success of a community pharmacy is profoundly influenced by its location. A pharmacy situated in a **visible and convenient site** is more likely to attract high customer footfall, which directly translates to higher sales and profitability. Visibility ensures that the pharmacy is easily noticed by passersby, increasing the likelihood of attracting walk-in customers. Convenient locations reduce the effort and time required for customers to reach the pharmacy, enhancing customer satisfaction and loyalty.

For example, a pharmacy located in a busy commercial area or a bustling residential neighborhood is likely to experience a steady flow of customers throughout the day. Such locations benefit from the natural traffic of people in the area, who may visit the pharmacy as part of their routine activities. On the other hand, a pharmacy in a remote or hard-to-reach location may struggle to attract customers, regardless of the quality of its services and products.

Moreover, the location can influence the type of products and services offered by the pharmacy. Pharmacies in affluent areas may focus on high-end health and wellness products, while those in areas with a higher prevalence of specific health conditions may stock a wide range of medications for those conditions. Strategic site selection also enables pharmacies to establish partnerships with nearby healthcare providers, fostering a collaborative environment that benefits both the pharmacy and its customers.

6.2.2 Efficient Layout Planning

6.2.2.1 Designing the Pharmacy Interior

Designing the interior of a community pharmacy involves creating a space that promotes optimal workflow and enhances the customer experience. The layout should ensure that both customers and staff can navigate the space easily and efficiently. **Organized shelving** is crucial for this purpose. Medications and products should be arranged systematically, making it easy for staff to locate items quickly and for customers to find what they need without confusion. Shelves should be labeled clearly, with categories such as prescription medications, over-the-counter drugs, health supplements, and personal care items.

Clear signage is another important element. Signs should direct customers to various sections of the pharmacy, such as the prescription counter, consultation area, and product aisles. This not only improves the flow of traffic within the pharmacy but also enhances the overall customer experience by reducing confusion and wait times. The layout should include **dedicated areas** for specific functions. For example, a separate dispensing area ensures that prescription medications are handled with care and privacy. A designated **counseling area** provides a quiet and confidential space for pharmacists to discuss medication regimens, potential side effects, and health concerns with customers. This separation of spaces helps maintain organization and improves service delivery.

6.2.2.2 Compliance with Building Codes and Standards

Adhering to building codes and standards is essential for the safe and legal operation of a community pharmacy. Compliance with **safety regulations** includes ensuring that the pharmacy is equipped with proper fire safety measures, such as fire extinguishers, smoke detectors, and emergency exits. These measures are critical for protecting both customers and staff in case of an emergency. **Accessibility regulations** must also be followed to ensure that the pharmacy is accessible to all individuals, including those with disabilities. This includes installing ramps, providing wide aisles for wheelchair access, and ensuring that counters are at an appropriate height for all customers.

Health regulations are equally important. Proper **ventilation** is necessary to maintain a healthy indoor environment, preventing the buildup of dust, chemicals, and other pollutants. Adequate **lighting** is essential for both safety and functionality, ensuring that staff can read labels and prescriptions accurately and that customers can navigate the space comfortably. There should also be sufficient space for the **secure storage** of medications. This includes both temperature-controlled storage for drugs that require specific conditions and locked cabinets for controlled substances, ensuring compliance with regulations and preventing theft or misuse.

6.2.2.3 Ergonomic Design Principles

Implementing **ergonomic design principles** in the pharmacy layout is vital for creating a comfortable and efficient work environment. Ergonomics focuses on designing workspaces that reduce strain and fatigue, thereby enhancing productivity and employee well-being. For example, **workstations** should be designed to minimize repetitive movements and awkward postures. Adjustable chairs and desks, along with properly positioned computer monitors and keyboards, can help reduce the risk of musculoskeletal disorders among staff.

Shelving and storage should be placed at heights that reduce the need for excessive bending, reaching, or lifting. Frequently used items should be stored within easy reach, while heavier items should be stored at waist height to prevent injury. The layout should also include **break areas** where staff can rest and recharge. Comfortable seating, adequate lighting, and a quiet environment can help reduce stress and improve overall job satisfaction.

Incorporating these ergonomic principles not only enhances the physical comfort of staff but also contributes to a more efficient workflow. When staff are comfortable and not experiencing fatigue or pain, they are more likely to be productive and provide better service to customers. In summary, thoughtful interior design, compliance with building codes, and the application of ergonomic principles are all essential components of efficient layout planning in a community pharmacy.

6.3 Drug Display and Super Drug Store Model

6.3.1 Effective Merchandising Techniques

6.3.1.1 Principles of Drug Display

Strategically placing medications and health products within a community pharmacy is vital for enhancing accessibility and boosting sales. The layout of product displays should be designed to guide customers naturally through the store, making it easy for them to find what they need while also encouraging impulse purchases. **Key items should be placed at eye level**, as this is the most visible and convenient location for customers. Products that are frequently purchased, such as common over-the-counter (OTC) medications, personal care items, and health supplements, should be positioned in these prime spots to maximize visibility and sales.

High-demand products should be easily reachable to ensure customer convenience. Placing popular items within easy reach can enhance the customer experience, making it more likely that they will complete their purchase and return in the future. Additionally, it is beneficial to group related products together. For example, placing cough and cold remedies alongside tissues, throat lozenges, and nasal sprays can create a cohesive section that meets all of a customer's needs in one place. This not only improves the shopping experience but also increases the likelihood of additional purchases.

Clear signage and labeling play a critical role in effective drug display. Signs should be used to direct customers to various sections of the pharmacy, such as prescription medications, OTC drugs, and wellness products. Labels should provide clear information about the product, including its use, benefits, and any promotional offers. This helps customers make informed decisions and enhances their overall shopping experience.

6.3.1.2 Promoting Over-the-Counter (OTC) Products

Promoting OTC products effectively can significantly boost sales and enhance customer satisfaction. One of the most effective techniques for promoting OTC products is through **special displays**. End-cap displays, for example, are highly visible locations at the end of aisles that can showcase promotional items or new products. These displays are particularly effective because they catch the customer's eye as they navigate the store.

Promotional offers, such as discounts, buy-one-get-one-free deals, or bundling related products together, can also drive sales of OTC products. These promotions should be clearly advertised using eye-catching signs and labels. For example, a promotion on allergy medications during allergy season can attract customers who are looking for relief and encourage them to purchase additional related products.

Seasonal displays are another effective strategy. Creating displays that align with the time of year—such as flu season, allergy season, or summer travel—can highlight relevant OTC products and remind customers of their needs. These seasonal displays can be positioned prominently to draw attention and encourage purchases.

In-store marketing materials such as brochures, flyers, and posters can provide additional information about OTC products, including their benefits, usage instructions, and any current promotions. These materials can be placed near the products or in waiting areas where customers are likely to see them.

Staff recommendations can also play a significant role in promoting OTC products. Pharmacists and pharmacy staff can suggest products based on customer inquiries and needs, providing personalized recommendations that enhance customer trust and satisfaction. Training staff to be knowledgeable about OTC products and promotions can further support these efforts.

6.3.2 Super Drug Store Model

6.3.2.1 Concept and Benefits

The **super drug store model** represents a comprehensive approach to community pharmacy, integrating traditional pharmacy services with an extensive range of health and wellness products. This model aims to create a one-stop destination for customers, providing them with access to medications, health supplements, beauty products, personal care items, and even basic groceries and lifestyle products. By diversifying the product offerings, pharmacies can cater to a broader audience, addressing various health and wellness needs in one convenient location.

Enhancing customer experience is a primary benefit of the super drug store model. Customers appreciate the convenience of finding a wide array of products under one roof, reducing the need to visit multiple stores. This approach fosters customer loyalty, as people are more likely to return to a store that meets a broad spectrum of their needs. Additionally, providing a wider range of products can attract different customer segments, such as fitness enthusiasts, beauty-conscious individuals, and those seeking natural or organic products.

Increasing revenue streams is another significant advantage of this model. By offering a variety of products beyond prescription medications, pharmacies can tap into additional market segments and generate higher sales. The inclusion of high-margin items like cosmetics and health supplements can significantly boost profitability. Furthermore, the super drug store model can lead to increased foot traffic, as customers drawn by the extensive product range are likely to make additional impulse purchases.

Building a stronger community presence is also a benefit of adopting this model. Pharmacies that offer comprehensive services and products can become central hubs for health and wellness in their communities. This enhanced role can lead to stronger relationships with customers and an improved reputation, further driving business success.

6.3.2.2 Implementation Strategies

Successfully adopting the **super drug store model** requires careful planning and execution. Key strategies for implementation include expanding the product range, training staff, and optimizing the store layout to accommodate additional offerings.

Expanding the product range involves conducting market research to identify popular and high-demand items that complement the pharmacy's existing offerings. This may include health and wellness products like vitamins, dietary supplements, fitness equipment, organic foods, and personal care items. It's crucial to maintain a balanced inventory that meets diverse customer needs without overwhelming the store's space and management capacity.

Training staff is essential to ensure they are knowledgeable about the expanded range of products and capable of providing excellent customer service. Staff should be able to answer questions, offer recommendations, and guide customers in their purchasing decisions. Investing in regular training sessions can help employees stay updated on new products and industry trends, enhancing their ability to serve customers effectively.

Optimizing store layout is critical to accommodate the additional product categories and ensure a seamless shopping experience. The layout should be designed to facilitate easy navigation and efficient workflows. Key considerations include:

- **Zoning**: Grouping related products together, such as creating sections for health supplements, beauty products, and personal care items, can make it easier for customers to find what they need.
- **Accessibility**: Ensuring that high-demand and frequently purchased items are easily accessible and prominently displayed can drive sales and improve customer satisfaction.
- **Aesthetics and ambiance**: Creating a visually appealing environment with appropriate lighting, clear signage, and attractive displays can enhance the shopping experience and encourage longer store visits.

Leveraging technology can further support the implementation of the super drug store model. Utilizing point-of-sale (POS) systems that integrate inventory management, customer relationship management (CRM), and sales analytics can streamline operations and provide valuable insights into customer preferences and purchasing patterns. Additionally, offering online shopping options and home delivery services can expand the store's reach and convenience for customers.

In conclusion, the super drug store model offers numerous benefits, including enhanced customer experience, increased revenue streams, and a stronger community presence. By strategically expanding the product range, training staff, and optimizing store layout, community pharmacies can successfully transition to this model and achieve long-term business growth and success.

6.4 Accounts and Audits

6.4.1 Financial Management

6.4.1.1 Basics of Pharmacy Accounting

Maintaining accurate financial records is fundamental for the successful operation of a community pharmacy. Key financial statements that must be meticulously managed include the **profit and loss (P&L) account**, the **balance sheet**, and the **cash flow statement**. The **P&L account** provides a detailed summary of the pharmacy's revenues, costs, and expenses over a specific period, offering insights into profitability. It includes various line items such as sales revenue, cost of goods sold (COGS), gross profit, operating expenses, and net profit. The **balance sheet** is a snapshot of the pharmacy's financial position at a given point in time, detailing assets, liabilities, and shareholders' equity. It helps in understanding the financial stability and liquidity of the business. The **cash flow statement** tracks the flow of cash in and out of the business, highlighting operational, investing, and financing activities. This statement is crucial for ensuring that the pharmacy maintains sufficient liquidity to meet its obligations and invest in growth opportunities.

Accurate bookkeeping practices involve recording every financial transaction in a systematic manner. This includes sales, purchases, payroll, and other operational expenses. Utilizing accounting software can streamline these processes, reduce errors, and provide real-time financial insights. Regularly reconciling accounts, reviewing financial statements, and conducting variance analysis are essential practices that help in identifying discrepancies, managing cash flow effectively, and making informed business decisions. Proper financial management not only ensures compliance with legal and regulatory requirements but also enhances the overall financial health and sustainability of the pharmacy.

6.4.1.2 Budgeting and Financial Planning

Creating and managing budgets is crucial for ensuring the pharmacy's profitability and financial stability. Budgeting involves forecasting revenues and expenses, setting financial goals, and allocating resources effectively. The process begins with **revenue forecasting**, which estimates the pharmacy's expected income based on historical data, market trends, and seasonal variations. This is followed by **expense forecasting**, where anticipated costs for inventory, payroll, rent, utilities, marketing, and other operational expenses are projected.

Setting financial goals is an integral part of budgeting. These goals could include targets for sales growth, cost reduction, profit margins, and return on investment. Once the budget is established, **monitoring performance** against the budget is essential. This involves regularly reviewing actual financial results, comparing them with budgeted figures, and analyzing variances. Significant variances should be investigated to understand their causes and take corrective actions if necessary.

Financial planning also encompasses long-term strategies for growth and sustainability. This includes planning for capital investments, such as opening new branches, upgrading technology, or expanding product lines. It may also involve financial risk management strategies to mitigate potential financial uncertainties and challenges. By maintaining a well-structured budgeting and financial planning process, the pharmacy can ensure optimal resource utilization, enhance profitability, and achieve its long-term financial objectives.

6.4.2 Compliance and Audits

6.4.2.1 Importance of Regular Audits

Regular audits are critical for ensuring financial accuracy, regulatory compliance, and overall operational efficiency. Audits help in verifying the accuracy of financial records, identifying discrepancies, and ensuring that financial statements reflect the true financial position of the pharmacy. They also assess compliance with legal and regulatory requirements, such as tax laws, accounting standards, and industry-specific regulations. Conducting regular audits helps in identifying areas for improvement, enhancing internal controls, and mitigating risks. Furthermore, audits build credibility and trust with stakeholders, including investors, lenders, and regulatory authorities.

6.4.2.2 Types of Audits

Understanding the differences between internal and external audits is essential for effective audit preparation and management. **Internal audits** are conducted by the pharmacy's own staff or an internal audit team. They focus on evaluating the effectiveness of internal controls, risk management processes, and compliance with internal policies and procedures. Internal audits provide management with insights into operational efficiencies and areas that require improvement.

External audits, on the other hand, are conducted by independent auditors from outside the organization. They provide an objective assessment of the pharmacy's financial statements and compliance with regulatory requirements. External audits offer assurance to stakeholders that the financial information presented is accurate and reliable. Both types of audits play a crucial role in maintaining the integrity and transparency of the pharmacy's financial and operational practices.

6.4.2.3 Preparing for Audits

Best practices for preparing for audits include maintaining organized and up-to-date financial records, ensuring compliance with legal standards, and being proactive in addressing potential audit issues. This involves regularly reviewing and reconciling accounts, updating financial information, and ensuring that all transactions are accurately recorded. Documentation should be readily available and well-organized, including invoices, receipts, bank statements, and other supporting documents.

Creating a comprehensive audit preparation checklist can be beneficial. This checklist should include tasks such as reviewing internal controls, conducting preliminary self-audits, and ensuring that all necessary documentation is in place. Additionally, staff should be trained and informed about the audit process to facilitate smooth cooperation with auditors. By adhering to these best practices, the pharmacy can ensure a successful audit outcome, demonstrating financial transparency, regulatory compliance, and operational efficiency.

6.5 Good Dispensing Practices

6.5.1 Ensuring Safe and Accurate Dispensing

6.5.1.1 Principles of Good Dispensing

Following established guidelines for accurate and safe medication dispensing is crucial for maintaining patient safety and trust. Good dispensing practices involve several key principles aimed at ensuring that patients receive the correct medication in the correct dosage and form. Pharmacists must accurately interpret prescriptions, verify the legitimacy of the prescriber, and ensure that the medication is appropriate for the patient's condition. This includes checking for potential drug interactions, contraindications, and allergies.

Pharmacists should also ensure that medications are stored under proper conditions to maintain their efficacy and safety. Labeling must be clear and accurate, providing patients with essential information such as dosage instructions, usage directions, and warnings. Additionally, maintaining confidentiality and privacy of patient information is a critical aspect of good dispensing practices. Adhering to these principles not only helps in preventing medication errors but also enhances the overall quality of care provided to patients.

6.5.1.2 Preventing Dispensing Errors

Preventing dispensing errors is a fundamental aspect of ensuring patient safety. Common causes of dispensing errors include misinterpretation of prescriptions, look-alike/sound-alike (LASA) medications, and manual transcription errors. To mitigate these risks, pharmacists should adopt several strategies. Double-checking prescriptions before dispensing is an effective method to catch potential errors. This involves verifying the medication, dosage, patient information, and instructions against the original prescription.

Using technology, such as electronic prescribing systems and barcode verification, can significantly reduce the likelihood of errors. These systems help in ensuring accuracy by providing real-time alerts for potential drug interactions, dosage errors, and duplications. Implementing a standardized workflow and adhering to protocols for dispensing can also minimize the risk of errors. Training and continuous education for pharmacy staff on best practices and new technologies are essential in maintaining high standards of dispensing accuracy.

6.5.1.3 Patient Counseling

Providing patients with clear information and advice on medication use is a crucial component of good dispensing practices. Effective patient counseling ensures that patients understand how to take their medications correctly, what to expect from their treatment, and how to manage potential side effects. This process begins with verifying the patient's understanding of the medication's purpose, dosage regimen, and duration of therapy.

Pharmacists should educate patients on the importance of adherence to their prescribed treatment plan, highlighting the potential consequences of non-compliance. Discussing possible side effects and how to handle them can empower patients to manage their health more effectively. Additionally, pharmacists should provide advice on lifestyle modifications and other non-pharmacological measures that can complement the medication therapy. Encouraging patients to ask questions and express concerns fosters a collaborative relationship, enhancing patient satisfaction and health outcomes. By prioritizing patient counseling, pharmacists play a vital role in promoting safe and effective medication use.

6.6 Software and Databases in Community Pharmacies

6.6.1 Technology for Efficient Management

6.6.1.1 Types of Pharmacy Management Software

Community pharmacies can significantly benefit from implementing various types of pharmacy management software. **Inventory management**

systems are essential for tracking and managing stock levels, ensuring that essential medications are always available while minimizing overstock and wastage. These systems can automate reordering processes, alerting pharmacists when stock levels are low and helping to maintain optimal inventory levels.

Billing systems streamline the financial transactions within the pharmacy, including processing sales, managing insurance claims, and handling payments. These systems can integrate with inventory management software to automatically update stock levels and financial records, reducing the likelihood of manual errors.

Electronic health records (EHR) systems enable pharmacies to maintain detailed and secure patient records. EHRs can store patient information, prescription histories, allergy information, and other relevant health data. This comprehensive record-keeping supports better patient care by providing pharmacists with a complete overview of each patient's medication history and health status.

6.6.1.2 Benefits of Using Technology

Implementing technology in community pharmacies offers numerous benefits, enhancing efficiency, accuracy, and customer service. Automation of routine tasks, such as inventory management and billing, **reduces manual errors** and frees up staff time for more critical tasks, such as patient counseling and clinical services. This increased efficiency leads to **faster service**, improving customer satisfaction and loyalty.

Technology also enhances **accuracy** in dispensing medications, billing, and record-keeping. Barcode scanning and electronic prescriptions reduce the risk of dispensing errors, while automated billing systems ensure correct pricing and insurance claims processing.

Moreover, technology improves **customer service** by providing staff with quick access to patient records and medication information, enabling them to answer queries promptly and accurately. EHRs facilitate better communication and coordination with other healthcare providers, ensuring that patients receive cohesive and well-informed care.

6.6.2 Implementing and Utilizing Databases

6.6.2.1 Inventory Management Systems

Implementing inventory management systems in community pharmacies is crucial for maintaining efficient operations. These systems enable pharmacists to **track and manage stock levels** in real-time, ensuring that essential medications are always available and reducing the likelihood of stockouts. Automated reordering features can predict inventory needs based on historical data and current trends, helping pharmacies maintain optimal stock levels without overstocking.

Inventory management systems also help in **reducing wastage** by monitoring expiration dates and rotating stock accordingly. By providing detailed insights into inventory turnover rates and usage patterns, these systems support better inventory planning and cost management, ultimately improving the pharmacy's profitability.

6.6.2.2 Patient Record Systems

Maintaining comprehensive and secure patient records is essential for providing high-quality care and complying with legal requirements. Patient record systems, such as EHRs, allow pharmacies to **store and access detailed patient information**, including medical histories, current medications, allergies, and treatment plans. This comprehensive data helps pharmacists make informed decisions about medication dispensing and patient counseling.

Secure patient record systems also ensure **compliance with legal and regulatory requirements** related to patient privacy and data protection. By implementing robust security measures, such as encryption and access controls, pharmacies can protect sensitive patient information from unauthorized access and breaches.

6.6.2.3 Integration with Healthcare Systems

Ensuring interoperability with other healthcare providers and systems is crucial for seamless patient care and information sharing. Integrated systems enable pharmacies to **exchange information** with hospitals, clinics, and other healthcare providers, facilitating coordinated care and reducing the risk of medication errors. For instance, electronic prescriptions can be sent directly from a prescriber to the pharmacy, reducing the potential for transcription errors and ensuring that patients receive their medications promptly.

Interoperability also supports **comprehensive care** by allowing pharmacists to access relevant patient health information, such as lab results and treatment plans, from other healthcare providers. This integrated approach enables pharmacists to provide more informed and personalized care, improving patient outcomes.

6.7 Entrepreneurship in Community Pharmacy

6.7.1 Business Skills and Opportunities

6.7.1.1 Fundamentals of Pharmacy Entrepreneurship

Successful pharmacy business owners require a blend of key skills to navigate the complexities of running a community pharmacy. **Financial management** is crucial, involving budgeting, forecasting, and maintaining accurate financial records. Owners must understand profit margins, manage cash flow, and control expenses to ensure profitability. **Marketing skills** are essential to attract and retain customers. This includes knowledge of digital marketing, customer relationship management, and community engagement strategies. Effective marketing helps to build the pharmacy's brand and establish a loyal customer base.

Strategic planning involves setting long-term goals, identifying growth opportunities, and adapting to market changes. Entrepreneurs must stay informed about industry trends, regulatory changes, and technological advancements. They need to be innovative, continuously seeking ways to improve services and expand their product offerings. Additionally, strong **leadership and management skills** are vital for motivating staff, fostering a positive work environment, and ensuring efficient operations. By developing these fundamental skills, pharmacy entrepreneurs can build and sustain a successful business.

6.7.1.2 Identifying Business Opportunities

Identifying new business opportunities is a critical aspect of entrepreneurship in community pharmacy. Conducting **market analysis** helps entrepreneurs understand the local healthcare landscape, including the needs and preferences of the community. This involves analyzing demographic data, health trends, and competitor offerings. Identifying **gaps in services** presents opportunities for pharmacies to differentiate themselves and meet unmet needs. For example, offering specialized services such as compounding, chronic disease management, or wellness programs can attract new customers and increase revenue.

Entrepreneurs should also stay informed about emerging **healthcare technologies and innovations**. Adopting new technologies, such as telepharmacy services or automated dispensing systems, can improve efficiency and enhance patient care. Networking with other healthcare providers and participating in industry events can provide insights into potential collaboration opportunities and emerging market trends. By proactively seeking and capitalizing on business opportunities, pharmacy entrepreneurs can achieve sustainable growth and competitive advantage.

6.7.2 Developing a Business Plan

6.7.2.1 Creating a Comprehensive Business Plan

A comprehensive business plan is the foundation of a successful community pharmacy. It serves as a roadmap, outlining the business's objectives, strategies, and financial projections. **Market research** is a critical component, providing insights into the target market, customer needs, and competitive landscape. This information helps entrepreneurs identify unique selling points and develop effective marketing strategies. **Financial projections** include detailed estimates of startup costs, operating expenses, revenue streams, and profitability. Accurate financial forecasting helps entrepreneurs secure funding and manage resources effectively.

A robust business plan also includes a **marketing strategy**, detailing how the pharmacy will attract and retain customers. This involves defining the brand, identifying marketing channels, and setting promotional activities. Additionally, the plan should outline the organizational structure, staffing requirements, and operational processes. By creating a comprehensive business plan, entrepreneurs can clearly articulate their vision, align their team, and guide the business toward achieving its goals.

6.7.2.2 Securing Funding and Investment

Securing adequate funding is crucial for starting and expanding a community pharmacy. Entrepreneurs need to explore various **sources of funding**, including personal savings, bank loans, venture capital, and government grants. Each funding source has its advantages and considerations. For instance, bank loans require a solid credit history and collateral, while venture capital may involve giving up equity in the business. **Developing strategies to attract investors** is essential. This includes preparing a compelling business plan, showcasing the pharmacy's potential for growth, and demonstrating a strong return on investment.

Effective **networking and relationship-building** can also help entrepreneurs connect with potential investors and financial advisors. Entrepreneurs should be prepared to pitch their business idea confidently, highlighting the unique aspects of their pharmacy and the benefits it offers to the community. By securing adequate funding, entrepreneurs can cover startup costs, invest in necessary technology and infrastructure, and support the pharmacy's growth and expansion.

6.7.2.3 Launching and Growing the Business

Launching a community pharmacy involves several key steps to ensure a successful start. This includes **finalizing the business location**, obtaining necessary licenses and permits, and setting up the pharmacy's interior layout and technology systems. Effective **marketing and promotional**

activities are crucial during the launch phase to attract initial customers and create awareness about the new pharmacy. This can include grand opening events, special promotions, and targeted advertising.

Once the pharmacy is operational, **strategies for sustainable growth and expansion** become important. This involves continuously evaluating and improving services, expanding the product range, and exploring new market opportunities. Building strong relationships with customers, healthcare providers, and the community can enhance the pharmacy's reputation and drive business growth. Regularly reviewing financial performance and adjusting strategies as needed ensures the pharmacy remains competitive and profitable. By implementing effective launch and growth strategies, entrepreneurs can achieve long-term success and establish a thriving community pharmacy.

Prescription Handling and Minor Ailments

7.1 Legal Requirements and Interpretation of Prescriptions

7.1.1 Ensuring Compliance with Regulations

7.1.1.1 Overview of Prescription Regulations

In India, handling prescriptions requires adherence to a comprehensive set of legal requirements to ensure safe and effective patient care. The primary regulations governing prescription handling include the **Drugs and Cosmetics Act, 1940**, and the **Pharmacy Act, 1948**. These laws mandate that only qualified pharmacists can dispense medications, and prescriptions must be issued by registered medical practitioners. Each prescription should include specific information: the patient's name and address, the prescriber's details, the date of issue, and a clear description of the prescribed medications, including dosage and administration instructions. Adherence to these regulations helps prevent medication errors, ensures proper patient treatment, and maintains public health and safety.

7.1.1.2 Verification of Prescription Validity

Verifying the validity of prescriptions is a critical responsibility of pharmacists. This process involves checking the **completeness and authenticity** of the prescription to prevent fraud and ensure accurate medication dispensing. Pharmacists must confirm that all required information is present, including the patient's name, prescriber's details, date, and specific medication instructions. Additionally, they must verify the prescriber's registration and license to practice. In cases where the prescription appears unclear or questionable, pharmacists should contact the prescriber for clarification. Implementing robust verification procedures minimizes the risk of dispensing errors, enhances patient safety, and maintains the integrity of the pharmacy practice.

7.1.1.3 Confidentiality and Data Protection

Ensuring patient **confidentiality and secure handling of prescription information** is paramount in pharmacy practice. The **Information Technology Act, 2000**, and the **Personal Data Protection Bill, 2019** (pending enactment) provide the legal framework for data protection in India. Pharmacists must implement measures to safeguard patient information, such as secure storage of physical and electronic prescription records, restricting access to authorized personnel only, and using encrypted systems for digital data. Maintaining confidentiality not only complies with legal requirements but also fosters trust between patients and healthcare providers. Pharmacists must be vigilant about data breaches and have protocols in place to address any security incidents promptly. By upholding stringent confidentiality standards, pharmacies contribute to the overall integrity and reliability of the healthcare system.

7.1.2 Interpretation of Prescriptions

7.1.2.1 Reading and Understanding Prescription Components

Interpreting prescriptions accurately is a fundamental skill for pharmacists. This involves **decoding medical abbreviations**, understanding dosage instructions, and interpreting the prescriber's notes. Medical abbreviations and shorthand are commonly used in prescriptions, and pharmacists must be proficient in interpreting these terms to ensure correct medication dispensing. For example, abbreviations such as "b.i.d." (twice a day), "t.i.d." (three times a day), and "q.h.s." (every night at bedtime) must be understood accurately. Dosage instructions must be clearly interpreted to ensure the correct amount of medication is dispensed and administered. Pharmacists must also be adept at reading prescribers' handwriting, which can often be challenging. Ensuring clarity in these areas is critical for patient safety and effective treatment outcomes.

7.1.2.2 Identifying Potential Drug Interactions

Recognizing and managing potential drug interactions is a crucial aspect of prescription interpretation. Pharmacists must have a thorough understanding of pharmacology to identify interactions that could lead to adverse effects or reduced efficacy of medications. This involves checking the patient's medication history and cross-referencing new prescriptions with existing medications. Drug interactions can occur between prescription medications, over-the-counter drugs, herbal supplements, and even certain foods. Utilizing drug interaction databases and clinical decision support systems can aid pharmacists in identifying potential interactions. When a potential interaction is detected, the pharmacist must assess the clinical significance and take appropriate action, such as adjusting the medication regimen or consulting with the prescriber. By effectively managing drug interactions, pharmacists play a vital role in optimizing patient safety and therapeutic outcomes.

7.1.2.3 Communicating with Prescribers

Effective communication with healthcare providers is essential for clarifying prescription details and ensuring accurate dispensing. When a prescription is unclear or raises concerns, pharmacists must **communicate with prescribers** to seek clarification. This can involve discussing unclear handwriting, ambiguous dosage instructions, or potential drug interactions. Establishing a professional and collaborative relationship with prescribers facilitates open communication and timely resolution of issues. Pharmacists should use clear and concise language, provide relevant patient information, and document all communications for future reference. Additionally, understanding the workflow and constraints of prescribers can help pharmacists communicate more effectively and enhance interprofessional collaboration. By maintaining open lines of communication, pharmacists ensure that patients receive the correct medications and dosages, ultimately improving patient care and safety.

7.2 Prescription-Related Problems

7.2.1 Identifying Issues in Prescriptions

7.2.1.1 Common Prescription Errors

One of the critical roles of a pharmacist is to identify and rectify common prescription errors to ensure patient safety and effective treatment. **Incorrect dosages** are a frequent issue, which can lead to underdosing or overdosing, potentially resulting in therapeutic failure or adverse effects. Pharmacists must verify the prescribed dosage against standard dosing guidelines and consider patient-specific factors such as age, weight, and renal function. **Missing information** is another common problem, including the absence of the patient's name, dosage instructions, or the prescriber's signature. Such omissions can cause confusion and increase the risk of medication errors. **Illegible handwriting** can also pose significant challenges, as it may lead to misinterpretation of the prescribed medication or dosage. Pharmacists should not hesitate to contact the prescriber for clarification in such cases. Identifying and addressing these errors is essential to ensure the accurate dispensing of medications and to maintain patient safety.

7.2.1.2 Drug Interactions and Contraindications

Recognizing harmful drug interactions and contraindications is a fundamental aspect of prescription review. Pharmacists must thoroughly evaluate each prescription in the context of the patient's overall medication regimen to identify potential **drug interactions** that could lead to adverse effects or diminished therapeutic efficacy. This includes interactions between prescription medications, over-the-counter drugs, herbal supplements, and dietary components. Pharmacists should use drug interaction databases and clinical decision support tools to aid in this assessment. **Contraindications** are specific conditions or factors that render a particular treatment unsafe or inappropriate for a patient. Pharmacists must be aware of contraindications related to each medication and assess whether any prescribed drug poses a risk to the patient based on their medical history. By identifying and managing drug interactions and contraindications, pharmacists play a crucial role in preventing adverse drug events and optimizing patient outcomes.

7.2.1.3 Allergies and Adverse Reactions

Checking for patient **allergies and potential adverse drug reactions** is a critical safety measure in prescription handling. Pharmacists must review the patient's allergy history before dispensing any medication to ensure that it does not contain any known allergens. This includes common allergens such as penicillin, sulfa drugs, and specific excipients or preservatives found in medications. Additionally, pharmacists should be vigilant about potential **adverse drug reactions (ADRs)**, which can range from mild side effects to severe, life-threatening conditions. Reviewing the patient's medication history and consulting available pharmacovigilance data can help identify any previous adverse reactions to medications. Pharmacists should educate patients on possible side effects and instruct them on what to do if they experience any adverse reactions. By proactively managing allergies and ADRs, pharmacists enhance patient safety and contribute to more effective and personalized healthcare.

7.2.2 Resolving Prescription Issues

7.2.2.1 Corrective Measures

When prescription errors are identified, pharmacists must take immediate and appropriate steps to correct these issues to ensure patient safety and effective treatment. The first step is to **verify the error** by cross-referencing the prescription with standard dosing guidelines, the patient's medical history, and any available clinical data. Once the error is confirmed, the pharmacist should make the necessary corrections. This may involve adjusting the dosage, completing missing information, or clarifying ambiguous instructions. For example, if a dosage is found to be incorrect, the pharmacist should calculate the correct dosage based on the patient's age, weight, and clinical condition. Any changes or corrections should be clearly documented, and a note should be made in the patient's record to maintain a comprehensive and accurate medication history.

7.2.2.2 Consultation with Healthcare Providers

Collaborating with prescribers is essential for resolving prescription-related problems effectively. When an issue is identified, the pharmacist should promptly **consult with the healthcare provider** who issued the prescription. This consultation can occur via phone, electronic communication, or face-to-face meetings, depending on the urgency and complexity of the issue. During the consultation, the pharmacist should clearly communicate the identified problem, provide relevant patient information, and suggest possible solutions or alternative treatments. Effective communication and collaboration with prescribers help ensure that any necessary changes are made accurately and promptly, thereby minimizing the risk of adverse events and improving patient outcomes. Establishing a good rapport and regular communication channels with healthcare providers can enhance the overall coordination of patient care.

7.2.2.3 Patient Communication and Education

Informing patients about identified issues and recommended actions is a crucial component of resolving prescription problems. Pharmacists should **communicate with patients** in a clear and empathetic manner, explaining the nature of the issue, the corrective measures taken, and any changes to their medication regimen. It is important to ensure that patients understand why the changes were made and how they should take their medications moving forward. Providing written instructions or educational materials can help reinforce this information. Additionally, pharmacists should encourage patients to ask questions and express any concerns they may have. By involving patients in the resolution process and ensuring they are well-informed, pharmacists can enhance patient adherence, improve therapeutic outcomes, and foster trust and confidence in the pharmacy services.

7.3 Responding to Symptoms of Minor Ailments

7.3.1 Headache

7.3.1.1 Common Causes and Symptoms

Headaches are a prevalent minor ailment that can significantly affect daily life. Understanding the common causes and symptoms of different types of headaches is essential for effective management. The three main types of headaches are **tension headaches, migraines,** and **cluster headaches.**

Tension headaches are the most common type, often caused by stress, poor posture, or muscle strain. Symptoms include a dull, aching pain on both sides of the head, a sensation of tightness or pressure around the forehead or the back of the head and neck, and tenderness in the scalp, neck, and shoulder muscles.

Migraines are more severe and can be debilitating. They are characterized by intense, throbbing pain usually on one side of the head. Migraines may be accompanied by nausea, vomiting, and sensitivity to light and sound. Some individuals experience an aura, which can include visual disturbances, tingling, or speech difficulties, before the onset of a migraine.

Cluster headaches are the least common but are extremely painful. They occur in cyclical patterns or clusters, often waking individuals from sleep. Symptoms include severe burning or piercing pain around or behind one eye, which can radiate to other areas of the face, head, and neck. These headaches can also cause redness, swelling, and tearing in the affected eye, as well as nasal congestion or runny nose on the same side as the headache.

7.3.1.2 Over-the-Counter Treatments

Over-the-counter (OTC) treatments for headaches include various medications and non-pharmacological remedies. Common OTC medications include:

- **Acetaminophen** (paracetamol): Effective for mild to moderate pain relief and is generally well-tolerated with few side effects.
- **Nonsteroidal anti-inflammatory drugs (NSAIDs)** such as ibuprofen and aspirin: These are useful for reducing inflammation and relieving pain. They can be particularly effective for tension headaches and migraines but should be used with caution in individuals with gastrointestinal issues or other contraindications.
- **Combination medications**: Products that combine acetaminophen, aspirin, and caffeine can be more effective for some types of headaches, particularly migraines.

Non-pharmacological remedies include:

- **Applying a cold or warm compress**: A cold compress can help reduce migraine pain, while a warm compress can alleviate tension headache symptoms.
- **Hydration**: Ensuring adequate fluid intake can prevent dehydration-related headaches.
- **Rest and relaxation techniques**: Stress reduction methods such as deep breathing, meditation, and gentle exercise can help manage and prevent headaches.
- **Maintaining a regular sleep schedule**: Consistent sleep patterns can prevent headaches caused by irregular sleep.

7.3.1.3 Patient Counseling

Effective patient counseling involves advising patients on the appropriate use of OTC treatments and non-pharmacological remedies, as well as recognizing when to seek medical attention. Pharmacists should educate patients on the proper dosage and potential side effects of OTC medications, emphasizing the importance of not exceeding recommended doses. For example, patients should be aware of the risks associated with excessive use of NSAIDs, such as gastrointestinal bleeding and kidney damage.

Pharmacists should also discuss lifestyle modifications that can help prevent headaches, such as maintaining good hydration, practicing stress management techniques, and ensuring regular sleep patterns. Additionally, advising patients to keep a headache diary can help identify triggers and patterns, enabling more effective management strategies.

It is crucial to inform patients about the signs and symptoms that warrant medical attention. For instance, if headaches are frequent, severe, or accompanied by neurological symptoms such as vision changes, confusion, or weakness, patients should seek prompt medical evaluation. Similarly, if headaches do not respond to OTC treatments or worsen over time, a healthcare provider should be consulted.

By providing comprehensive counseling, pharmacists can empower patients to manage their headaches effectively, improve their quality of life, and ensure timely medical intervention when necessary.

7.3.2 Pyrexia (Fever)

7.3.2.1 Causes and Symptoms

Fever, or pyrexia, is a common medical sign characterized by an elevated body temperature. It is typically a response to an underlying condition, often an infection. Common causes of fever include **viral infections** (such as the common cold, influenza, and COVID-19), **bacterial infections** (such as strep throat, urinary tract infections, and pneumonia), **fungal infections**, and **parasitic infections** (such as malaria). Non-infectious causes can include **inflammatory conditions** (such as rheumatoid arthritis), **heat exhaustion**, and **certain medications**.

The symptoms of fever can vary but generally include an elevated body temperature (typically above 38°C or 100.4°F), chills, sweating, headache, muscle aches, loss of appetite, dehydration, and general weakness. In children, fever can sometimes cause febrile seizures, which, while often alarming, are typically benign and self-limiting.

7.3.2.2 Treatment Options

The primary goal in treating fever is to alleviate discomfort and address the underlying cause. **Antipyretic medications** are commonly used to reduce fever and provide symptomatic relief. These include:

- **Acetaminophen (paracetamol)**: Effective in reducing fever and relieving pain. It is generally safe when used as directed but should be used cautiously to avoid overdose, which can cause liver damage.
- **Nonsteroidal anti-inflammatory drugs (NSAIDs)** such as ibuprofen: These medications help reduce fever, pain, and inflammation. They should be used with caution in individuals with gastrointestinal issues, kidney problems, or those at risk of cardiovascular events.

In addition to antipyretics, **supportive measures** can help manage fever and improve comfort:

- **Hydration**: Encouraging adequate fluid intake is essential to prevent dehydration, which can be exacerbated by fever.
- **Rest**: Ensuring ample rest helps the body recover from the underlying illness causing the fever.
- **Cooling techniques**: Applying cool compresses to the forehead, taking lukewarm baths, and dressing in light clothing can help lower body temperature and provide relief.

7.3.2.3 Monitoring and Follow-Up

Effective management of fever involves **monitoring the condition** and providing clear guidance on when to seek further medical care. Patients should be advised to regularly check their temperature using a reliable thermometer and to keep track of any additional symptoms.

Pharmacists should inform patients about signs that warrant medical attention, such as:

- **Persistent high fever**: A fever lasting more than three days without improvement should be evaluated by a healthcare provider.
- **Severe symptoms**: Symptoms such as severe headache, neck stiffness, shortness of breath, chest pain, persistent vomiting, or confusion require prompt medical evaluation.
- **Fever in vulnerable populations**: Infants, elderly individuals, or those with compromised immune systems may need medical attention sooner due to their increased risk of complications.

Pharmacists should also educate patients on the importance of not overusing antipyretics and following the recommended dosage guidelines. Overuse can lead to adverse effects and potentially serious health issues.

By providing comprehensive advice on treatment options, monitoring, and follow-up, pharmacists can play a crucial role in managing fever effectively, ensuring patient safety, and improving health outcomes.

7.3.3 Menstrual Pain

7.3.3.1 Causes and Symptoms

Menstrual pain, also known as dysmenorrhea, is a common condition that affects many women during their menstrual cycles. **Primary dysmenorrhea** refers to common menstrual cramps caused by uterine contractions during menstruation and is not associated with any underlying condition. **Secondary dysmenorrhea** is menstrual pain resulting from an underlying reproductive health issue, such as endometriosis, fibroids, or pelvic inflammatory disease.

Symptoms of dysmenorrhea include **cramping pain in the lower abdomen** that can radiate to the lower back and thighs, **nausea, vomiting, diarrhea, fatigue,** and **headaches**. These symptoms typically begin one to two days before menstruation starts and can last from 12 to 72 hours. The intensity of the pain can vary from mild to severe, significantly affecting daily activities and quality of life.

7.3.3.2 Pharmacological and Non-Pharmacological Treatments

Managing menstrual pain involves a combination of **pharmacological and non-pharmacological treatments**.

Pharmacological treatments include:

- **Nonsteroidal anti-inflammatory drugs (NSAIDs)**: Medications such as ibuprofen and naproxen are commonly used to reduce menstrual pain and inflammation. They work by inhibiting the production of prostaglandins, which are chemicals that trigger uterine contractions and pain.
- **Oral contraceptives**: Birth control pills can help regulate menstrual cycles and reduce the severity of menstrual cramps by thinning the uterine lining and decreasing prostaglandin production.
- **Other prescription medications**: In cases where NSAIDs and oral contraceptives are ineffective, healthcare providers may prescribe stronger pain relievers or hormonal treatments.

Non-pharmacological treatments include:

- **Lifestyle changes**: Regular physical exercise can help alleviate menstrual pain by improving blood flow and reducing stress. Dietary changes, such as reducing caffeine and salt intake, can also help.
- **Heat therapy**: Applying heat to the lower abdomen using a heating pad, hot water bottle, or warm bath can help relax the muscles and reduce cramping.
- **Alternative therapies**: Acupuncture, acupressure, and herbal remedies like ginger and turmeric have been found to provide relief for some women. It's important to consult with a healthcare provider before starting any alternative therapies.

7.3.3.3 Patient Counseling

Effective patient counseling for menstrual pain involves providing advice on **pain management strategies** and recognizing when to seek medical attention. Pharmacists should educate patients on the proper use of medications, including dosing instructions and potential side effects. For example, NSAIDs should be taken with food to reduce the risk of gastrointestinal upset, and patients should be aware of the maximum recommended daily dose.

Pharmacists should also discuss **non-pharmacological approaches**, such as the benefits of regular exercise, dietary modifications, and the use of heat therapy. Encouraging patients to maintain a menstrual diary can help track the severity and pattern of symptoms, aiding in the identification of effective management strategies and potential triggers.

It's crucial to inform patients about the signs that warrant a consultation with a healthcare provider. These include severe or worsening pain, pain that does not respond to over-the-counter treatments, symptoms of secondary dysmenorrhea (such as heavy menstrual bleeding, irregular periods, or pain during intercourse), and any other unusual or concerning symptoms.

By providing comprehensive counseling, pharmacists can empower patients to manage their menstrual pain effectively, improve their quality of life, and ensure timely medical intervention when necessary.

7.3.4 Food and Drug Allergies

7.3.4.1 Recognizing Allergic Reactions

Recognizing allergic reactions promptly is critical for effective management and patient safety. Allergic reactions to food and drugs can range from mild to severe and can present with a variety of symptoms. **Common symptoms of food allergies** include hives, itching, swelling of the lips, face, tongue, and throat, abdominal pain, diarrhea, vomiting, and anaphylaxis, which is a severe, life-threatening reaction that requires immediate medical attention. **Drug allergies** can manifest similarly, with symptoms such as rashes, itching, fever, swelling, and anaphylaxis. Additional symptoms can include respiratory problems like wheezing and shortness of breath, as well as cardiovascular symptoms such as low blood pressure and rapid pulse. Early recognition of these symptoms is essential for initiating appropriate treatment and preventing complications.

7.3.4.2 Emergency Management

Emergency management of allergic reactions involves immediate intervention to mitigate symptoms and prevent severe outcomes. In cases of mild allergic reactions, **antihistamines** like diphenhydramine or loratadine can help alleviate symptoms such as itching, hives, and mild swelling. For more severe reactions, such as anaphylaxis, **epinephrine** is the first-line treatment. Patients at risk of severe allergic reactions should carry an **epinephrine auto-injector** (e.g., EpiPen) and be trained on its proper use.

During an anaphylactic reaction, it is crucial to administer epinephrine immediately and seek emergency medical help. If the patient is conscious, they should be placed in a comfortable position, often lying down with their legs elevated to maintain blood flow to vital organs. Additional measures include keeping the airway open and administering oxygen if available. Continuous monitoring of the patient's vital signs until emergency services arrive is essential. Quick and decisive action during an allergic reaction can save lives and minimize complications.

7.3.4.3 Preventive Measures

Preventive measures play a crucial role in managing food and drug allergies and preventing future reactions. **Educating patients** about their allergies and how to avoid allergens is the first step. Patients should be informed about how to read food labels and recognize potential allergens in ingredients. For drug allergies, they should be aware of the names and classes of drugs they are allergic to and inform healthcare providers and pharmacists about their allergies.

Management of mild reactions involves having over-the-counter antihistamines readily available and knowing how to use them. Patients should also be educated on recognizing early symptoms of an allergic reaction and taking prompt action. Keeping a detailed record of past allergic reactions, including the suspected allergen, symptoms, and treatments used, can help healthcare providers manage the patient's allergies more effectively.

Patients should also be advised to wear **medical alert identification** that lists their allergies. This can be crucial in emergencies where the patient might be unable to communicate their condition. Regular follow-ups with an allergist or healthcare provider can help manage allergies and update the patient's action plan based on their latest health status.

By providing comprehensive education and preventive strategies, pharmacists can empower patients to effectively manage their allergies, avoid triggers, and respond appropriately in case of an allergic reaction. This proactive approach enhances patient safety and quality of life.

7.4.2 Patient Education

7.4.2.1 Counseling on Safe Use of OTC Medications

Providing guidance on the safe and effective use of over-the-counter (OTC) medications is a crucial aspect of patient education. Pharmacists should explain the proper use of these medications, including dosage instructions, frequency, and duration of use. Patients should be made aware of the importance of reading the medication label and following the recommended dosage to avoid potential overdose or misuse. It is also essential to discuss the potential side effects and interactions with other medications, supplements, or underlying health conditions. For example, NSAIDs like ibuprofen should be used with caution in patients with gastrointestinal issues, kidney problems, or those taking anticoagulants. By providing detailed counseling, pharmacists can help patients use OTC medications safely and effectively, enhancing treatment outcomes and minimizing risks.

7.4.2.2 Addressing Patient Concerns and Questions

Pharmacists play a vital role in addressing patient concerns and answering questions about OTC medications. Common concerns may include the effectiveness of the medication, potential side effects, interactions with other drugs, and the suitability of the medication for specific conditions. Pharmacists should provide clear and accurate information, using language that is easy to understand. Encouraging patients to ask questions and express any concerns helps build trust and ensures that they feel confident in their medication choices. For instance, if a patient is worried about taking an OTC cold medication while on prescription blood pressure medication, the pharmacist should explain potential interactions and suggest safer alternatives if necessary. By being approachable and knowledgeable, pharmacists can alleviate patient anxieties and promote better health outcomes.

7.4.2.3 Monitoring and Follow-Up

Advising patients on what to watch for and when to seek further medical advice is a critical component of patient education. Pharmacists should inform patients about the signs and symptoms that indicate their condition is not improving or is worsening, which may necessitate professional medical evaluation. For example, if a patient is taking an OTC pain reliever for a headache and the pain persists for several days or is accompanied by other symptoms such as fever or visual disturbances, they should be advised to seek medical attention.

Pharmacists should also emphasize the importance of monitoring for potential side effects and adverse reactions. Patients should be instructed to report any unexpected symptoms or changes in their condition promptly. Follow-up is essential for ensuring that the medication is effective and that the patient is not experiencing any adverse effects. Scheduling a follow-up consultation or phone call can help assess the patient's progress and make any necessary adjustments to their treatment plan. By providing ongoing support and monitoring, pharmacists can ensure that patients achieve the best possible outcomes from their OTC medications.

Medication Counseling and Adherence

8.1 Medication Counseling Techniques

8.1.1 Effective Communication with Patients

8.1.1.1 Building Rapport with Patients

Establishing trust and a comfortable environment is the foundation of effective medication counseling. Building rapport with patients involves showing genuine interest and concern for their well-being. Pharmacists should greet patients warmly, introduce themselves, and use the patient's name during the conversation to create a personal connection. Demonstrating empathy and understanding, and respecting the patient's privacy and confidentiality, further strengthens the relationship. When patients feel comfortable and trust their pharmacist, they are more likely to share important information about their health and adhere to their medication regimen.

8.1.1.2 Active Listening Skills

Active listening is crucial for understanding patients' concerns and needs. Techniques for active listening include making eye contact, nodding, and providing verbal acknowledgments like "I see" or "Go on." Pharmacists should avoid interrupting the patient and allow them to express their thoughts fully. Reflective listening, where the pharmacist paraphrases what the patient has said to confirm understanding, can also be beneficial. For example, if a patient expresses concern about side effects, the pharmacist might say, "It sounds like you're worried about how this medication might affect you. Let's discuss these concerns in more detail."

8.1.1.3 Clear and Simple Language

Using clear and simple language is essential to ensure patients understand their medication instructions. Pharmacists should avoid medical jargon and use terms that are easy to comprehend. For example, instead of saying "antihypertensive," a pharmacist might say "medicine to lower your blood pressure." Providing information in a straightforward manner helps patients feel more confident about their treatment and reduces the risk of misunderstandings. Additionally, pharmacists can use visual aids, such as diagrams or pill organizers, to reinforce verbal instructions and improve patient comprehension.

8.1.1.4 Non-Verbal Communication

Non-verbal communication, including body language, eye contact, and gestures, plays a significant role in effective counseling. Positive body language, such as leaning slightly forward and maintaining an open posture, shows that the pharmacist is engaged and interested in the conversation. Maintaining eye contact conveys attentiveness and sincerity, while appropriate gestures can emphasize key points and make the information more relatable. For instance, demonstrating how to use an inhaler with hand movements can be more effective than verbal instructions alone. Being mindful of non-verbal cues helps create a supportive environment where patients feel heard and valued.

By incorporating these communication techniques, pharmacists can enhance their medication counseling efforts, leading to better patient understanding, adherence, and overall health outcomes.

8.2 Use of Patient Information Leafletsa

8.2.1 Enhancing Understanding and Compliance

8.2.1.1 Designing Effective Leaflets

Designing effective patient information leaflets is crucial for enhancing patient understanding and medication compliance. A well-designed leaflet should include key elements such as clear headings, simple language, and visually appealing graphics. The leaflet should be structured logically, beginning with an introduction to the medication, followed by sections on dosage instructions, potential side effects, storage information, and contact details for further inquiries. Using bullet points and short paragraphs can make the content more digestible. Additionally, including visuals such as diagrams or pictograms can help illustrate important points and make the information more accessible to patients with varying literacy levels.

8.2.1.2 Distributing Leaflets Effectively

Effective distribution of patient information leaflets ensures that patients receive and read the necessary information about their medications. Pharmacists should provide the leaflet at the point of dispensing and verbally highlight its importance. Ensuring that leaflets are available in multiple languages can accommodate non-native speakers. For patients with visual impairments, offering large-print versions or digital formats can be beneficial. Pharmacists should also consider placing leaflets in visible areas of the pharmacy, such as near the counter or in waiting areas, to encourage patients to pick them up. Additionally, integrating digital leaflets accessible via QR codes or pharmacy websites can cater to tech-savvy patients.

8.2.1.3 Explaining Leaflet Content

Helping patients understand the information provided in the leaflet is essential for ensuring compliance and safe medication use. Pharmacists should take the time to review the key points of the leaflet with the patient, answering any questions they may have. This includes explaining the purpose of the medication, how and when to take it, potential side effects, and what to do in case of missed doses or adverse reactions. Using the leaflet as a reference during the counseling session can reinforce the information and provide patients with a tangible resource to consult later. Encouraging patients to read the leaflet thoroughly and highlighting the importance of following the instructions can further enhance their understanding and adherence to their medication regimen.

By incorporating these strategies for designing, distributing, and explaining patient information leaflets, pharmacists can significantly improve patient understanding, compliance, and overall health outcomes.

8.3 Medication Adherence

8.3.1 Definition and Importance

8.3.1.1 Understanding Medication Adherence

Medication adherence refers to the extent to which patients take their medications as prescribed by their healthcare providers. This includes following the correct dosage, timing, and frequency, as well as completing the full course of treatment. Adherence is crucial for achieving the desired therapeutic outcomes and managing chronic conditions effectively. Good medication adherence can lead to improved health outcomes, better quality of life, and reduced healthcare costs. For instance, patients with chronic conditions like hypertension, diabetes, or asthma who adhere to their medication regimens are more likely to maintain control over their conditions, preventing complications and hospitalizations.

8.3.1.2 Consequences of Non-Adherence

Non-adherence to medication regimens can have serious health risks and adverse impacts on patient outcomes. It can lead to the progression of disease, treatment failure, and the development of drug resistance, particularly in conditions like tuberculosis and HIV/AIDS. Non-adherence can also result in increased morbidity and mortality. For example, patients with heart disease who do not take their medications as prescribed are at higher risk of heart attacks and strokes. Additionally, non-adherence can lead to higher healthcare costs due to increased hospital admissions, additional treatments, and longer recovery times. Understanding the reasons behind non-adherence, which can include forgetfulness, side effects, cost, and lack of understanding, is essential for healthcare providers to address these issues and improve patient adherence.

By emphasizing the definition and importance of medication adherence, pharmacists can educate patients on the critical role adherence plays in their overall health and the potential consequences of not following prescribed regimens. This understanding can motivate patients to take their medications consistently and correctly, leading to better health outcomes.

8.3.2 Factors Influencing Adherence

8.3.2.1 Patient-Related Factors

Several patient-related factors can influence medication adherence. **Age** plays a significant role, as elderly patients may face challenges such as multiple comorbidities, polypharmacy, and age-related cognitive decline, making it harder to adhere to complex medication regimens. Conversely, younger patients may not prioritize medication adherence due to a lack of perceived immediate benefit or a tendency to forget doses. **Literacy** and **health literacy** are also critical, as patients with limited reading skills or understanding of medical information may struggle to follow instructions accurately. **Cognitive ability** affects a patient's capacity to understand and remember medication schedules. **Motivation** is a crucial factor; patients who understand the importance of their medications and are motivated to manage their health are more likely to adhere to their regimens. Education and counseling by healthcare providers can significantly enhance patient motivation and adherence.

8.3.2.2 Medication-Related Factors

The characteristics of the medication itself can also impact adherence. The **complexity of the regimen**, such as the number of pills, frequency of doses, and specific timing requirements, can be daunting for patients. Simplifying regimens, such as using combination pills or extended-release formulations, can improve adherence. **Side effects** are a common deterrent; if a medication causes unpleasant or severe side effects, patients may be less inclined to take it regularly. Effective management of side effects through dose adjustments or switching to alternative medications can help maintain adherence. **Cost** is another significant factor; high out-of-pocket costs for medications can be a barrier, particularly for uninsured or underinsured patients. Providing information about generic alternatives, patient assistance programs, or other financial resources can help alleviate this burden.

8.3.2.3 Healthcare System Factors

The healthcare system itself can influence medication adherence through various mechanisms. **Accessibility** to healthcare services, including proximity to pharmacies and availability of medications, is essential. Patients who have difficulty accessing their medications due to geographic or logistical barriers are less likely to adhere to their treatment plans. The **provider-patient relationship** is crucial; patients who trust their healthcare providers and feel supported are more likely to follow their recommendations. Effective communication and a collaborative approach to care can strengthen this relationship. **Follow-up** is also important; regular check-ins, whether in-person, by phone, or through digital means, can help ensure patients remain adherent and address any issues that arise. Implementing reminder systems and follow-up appointments can provide the necessary support to maintain adherence.

By understanding and addressing these factors, healthcare providers can develop targeted strategies to improve medication adherence, ultimately enhancing patient outcomes and quality of life.

8.3.3 Strategies to Improve Adherence

8.3.3.1 Patient Education and Counseling

Patient education and counseling are fundamental strategies for improving medication adherence. Providing **clear instructions** about how and when to take medications, the importance of adherence, and the potential consequences of non-adherence can significantly enhance understanding and compliance. Pharmacists should also address **patient concerns** about their medications, including side effects, efficacy, and interactions with other drugs or foods. Using simple, non-technical language and confirming patient understanding through techniques like the teach-back method can be very effective. Personalized counseling sessions that take into account the patient's specific health conditions, lifestyle, and preferences can also help build trust and encourage adherence.

8.3.3.2 Simplifying Medication Regimens

Simplifying medication regimens can make it easier for patients to adhere to their treatment plans. This may involve reducing the number of daily doses by using **extended-release formulations** or **combination pills** that contain multiple medications in a single tablet. For patients on multiple medications, consolidating doses to align with daily routines (e.g., taking all morning medications together) can also help. Whenever possible, prescribers should aim to prescribe the simplest regimen that achieves the therapeutic goals, as this reduces the likelihood of missed doses and improves overall adherence.

8.3.3.3 Use of Reminders and Support Systems

Implementing reminders and support systems can significantly improve medication adherence. **Pill organizers** are a simple and effective tool for helping patients keep track of their medications. They are especially useful for those with complex regimens or memory challenges. **Alarms and digital reminders**, such as phone alerts or mobile apps, can prompt patients to take their medications at the correct times. Follow-up calls from pharmacists or automated reminder systems can provide additional support. These tools can be particularly beneficial for patients with busy schedules or those who are prone to forgetfulness.

8.3.3.4 Collaborative Care Approach

A collaborative care approach involves engaging **family members and caregivers** in the treatment process. This strategy can provide additional layers of support and accountability, especially for elderly patients or those with cognitive impairments. Educating family members and caregivers about the patient's medication regimen, potential side effects, and the importance of adherence can help them assist in managing the treatment plan. Regular communication and coordination among healthcare providers, patients, and their support networks can ensure that everyone is informed and involved in promoting adherence. This holistic approach recognizes that medication adherence is not solely the responsibility of the patient but a shared goal among all stakeholders in the patient's health.

By implementing these strategies, healthcare providers can effectively improve medication adherence, leading to better health outcomes, reduced healthcare costs, and enhanced patient quality of life.

8.4 Patient Referrals to Doctors

8.4.1 Identifying Referral Needs

8.4.1.1 Recognizing Symptoms Requiring Medical Attention

Pharmacists play a crucial role in identifying symptoms that may require medical attention. Recognizing these symptoms is essential for ensuring that patients receive timely and appropriate care. Symptoms that warrant a doctor's consultation include persistent or severe pain, unexplained weight loss, prolonged fever, shortness of breath, chest pain, and significant changes in bodily functions such as urination or bowel movements. Additionally, symptoms that do not improve with over-the-counter treatments or that worsen over time should prompt a referral. For example, a patient presenting with severe headache unresponsive to OTC medications, or experiencing neurological symptoms such as vision changes or numbness, should be advised to seek medical evaluation.

8.4.1.2 Criteria for Referral

Determining when a referral is necessary involves following specific guidelines and criteria. These include evaluating the severity, duration, and nature of the symptoms, as well as considering the patient's medical history and current medication regimen. Pharmacists should refer patients to a doctor if they suspect serious underlying conditions such as cardiovascular disease, diabetes complications, infections, or mental health issues. Other criteria for referral include adverse drug reactions, potential drug interactions, and non-adherence to prescribed medications that could compromise the patient's health. Using clinical judgment and established protocols helps ensure that referrals are made appropriately and effectively.

8.4.2 Acting on Referral Needs

8.4.2.1 Effective Communication with Physicians

Clear and concise communication with healthcare providers is essential for effective referrals. Pharmacists should provide a detailed account of the patient's symptoms, relevant medical history, current medications, and any interventions attempted. This information can be communicated through written referral notes, electronic health records, or direct communication via phone or email. When communicating with physicians, it is important to use clear, professional language and to focus on the key points that need addressing. Establishing a good rapport with local healthcare providers can facilitate smoother and more efficient referrals, ensuring that patients receive the necessary follow-up care promptly.

8.4.2.2 Informing and Assisting Patients

Guiding patients through the referral process involves ensuring they understand the need for a referral and the next steps to take. Pharmacists should explain the reason for the referral clearly, addressing any concerns or questions the patient may have. Providing written instructions or referral forms can help clarify the process. Pharmacists should also assist patients in scheduling appointments with their healthcare providers and offer to follow up to ensure the referral was completed. For patients who may face barriers such as transportation issues or financial constraints, pharmacists can provide information on available resources and support services. By being proactive and supportive, pharmacists can help patients navigate the referral process smoothly and effectively.

By identifying referral needs accurately and facilitating the referral process through effective communication and patient support, pharmacists play a vital role in ensuring patients receive comprehensive and timely medical care.

8.5 Adverse Drug Reaction (ADR) Monitoring

8.5.1 Ensuring Patient Safety in Community Pharmacies

8.5.1.1 Identifying Adverse Drug Reactions

Identifying adverse drug reactions (ADRs) is crucial for ensuring patient safety in community pharmacies. ADRs are unintended and harmful reactions that occur at normal doses used for prophylaxis, diagnosis, or treatment. Common types of ADRs include **allergic reactions**, such as rashes, itching, or anaphylaxis; **gastrointestinal issues**, like nausea, vomiting, or diarrhea; and **central nervous system effects**, including dizziness, sedation, or confusion. More serious ADRs can include organ-specific toxicity, such as hepatotoxicity or nephrotoxicity. Pharmacists should be vigilant in recognizing these reactions, paying close attention to patient reports of new or worsening symptoms after starting a medication. Using tools like patient interviews, medication history reviews, and electronic health records can help in identifying potential ADRs early.

8.5.1.2 Reporting ADRs

Reporting adverse drug reactions is an essential component of pharmacovigilance. Pharmacists should follow established procedures for documenting and reporting ADRs to the relevant authorities, such as the Pharmacovigilance Programme of India (PvPI). This involves completing an ADR reporting form, which includes details about the patient, the suspected drug, the reaction, and any other relevant information. Accurate and timely reporting helps in identifying potential safety issues with medications, leading to better regulatory decisions and improved patient safety. Pharmacists should also report ADRs to the prescribing physician and ensure that the information is recorded in the patient's medical record for future reference.

8.5.1.3 Educating Patients on ADRs

Educating patients about potential side effects and what to do if they experience an ADR is critical for patient safety. Pharmacists should provide clear and concise information about the common side effects of prescribed medications and instruct patients on how to recognize and respond to them. This includes advising patients on which side effects are minor and manageable, and which require immediate medical attention. For example, while mild gastrointestinal discomfort might be tolerable, symptoms like severe rash, difficulty breathing, or swelling should prompt immediate medical consultation. Providing written information, such as patient information leaflets, can reinforce verbal counseling and serve as a reference for patients.

8.5.1.4 Follow-Up and Monitoring

Continuous monitoring of patients for ADRs and providing necessary interventions are essential for ensuring ongoing patient safety. Pharmacists should schedule follow-up consultations, either in person or by phone, to check on the patient's response to the medication and identify any emerging ADRs. This follow-up should include a review of the patient's symptoms, adherence to the medication regimen, and any challenges they might be facing. If an ADR is identified, the pharmacist should assess the severity and take appropriate action, such as advising discontinuation of the medication, switching to an alternative therapy, or adjusting the dose. Collaboration with the prescribing physician is crucial to ensure that the patient receives comprehensive care and that any necessary changes to the treatment plan are implemented promptly.

By effectively identifying, reporting, educating, and monitoring ADRs, pharmacists play a vital role in safeguarding patient health and enhancing the overall quality of care in community pharmacies.

Health Promotion in Community Pharmacy

9.1 Definition and Health Promotion Activities

9.1.1 Role of Pharmacists in Health Education

9.1.1.1 Defining Health Promotion

Health promotion involves enabling people to increase control over and improve their health. It is a holistic approach that encompasses a wide range of social and environmental interventions designed to benefit and protect individual people's health and quality of life by addressing and preventing the root causes of ill health, not just focusing on treatment and cure. The **objectives of health promotion** include enhancing awareness about health issues, encouraging healthy behaviors, reducing risk factors, and fostering environments that support good health practices.

In community pharmacies, health promotion is an integral part of the pharmacist's role. Pharmacists are uniquely positioned to influence public health due to their accessibility and frequent interactions with the public. They can provide education on a variety of topics, including the importance of vaccinations, healthy eating, physical activity, smoking cessation, and the management of chronic conditions such as diabetes and hypertension. By promoting health and wellness, pharmacists help to prevent illness, improve health outcomes, and reduce healthcare costs.

Health promotion activities in community pharmacies can include one-on-one counseling, organizing health camps, providing informational leaflets, conducting health screenings, and participating in public health campaigns. These activities aim to empower individuals with the knowledge and resources they need to make healthier choices and take proactive steps towards maintaining their health.

9.1.1.2 Educating the Community

Pharmacists play a crucial role in educating the community about health and wellness. Their accessibility and frequent interactions with the public place them in an ideal position to influence health behaviors and promote healthy lifestyles. Effective health education by pharmacists involves various methods and strategies designed to reach and engage the community. These methods include personalized counseling, group education sessions, and leveraging digital platforms.

Personalized Counseling

One-on-one counseling allows pharmacists to provide tailored health information and advice based on individual patient needs. During these interactions, pharmacists can educate patients about their medications, potential side effects, lifestyle modifications, and preventive health measures. For example, a pharmacist can counsel a patient with diabetes on the importance of blood sugar monitoring, diet, and exercise. Personalized counseling also allows for the identification of barriers to adherence and the development of individualized strategies to overcome these challenges.

Group Education Sessions

Group education sessions are an effective way to disseminate health information to a larger audience. Pharmacists can organize workshops, seminars, or health talks on various topics such as smoking cessation, weight management, and disease prevention. These sessions can be held in the pharmacy, community centers, schools, or workplaces. Group education fosters peer support and encourages community members to share their experiences and knowledge. Interactive activities, such as demonstrations, Q&A sessions, and role-playing, can enhance engagement and retention of information.

Health Screenings and Campaigns

Pharmacists can conduct health screenings and participate in public health campaigns to promote awareness and early detection of health issues. Screenings for blood pressure, cholesterol, blood glucose, and body mass index (BMI) can identify individuals at risk of chronic diseases and provide an opportunity for early intervention. Public health campaigns, such as those promoting vaccination or heart health, can be supported by distributing educational materials, hosting events, and collaborating with other healthcare providers and community organizations.

Informational Leaflets and Posters

Providing educational materials such as leaflets, brochures, and posters in the pharmacy can help raise awareness about various health topics. These materials should be clear, concise, and visually appealing, with easy-to-understand language and graphics. Topics can range from managing specific health conditions to general wellness tips. Pharmacists can use these materials to reinforce verbal counseling and provide patients with a resource to refer to at home.

Digital Platforms and Social Media

Leveraging digital platforms and social media can extend the reach of health education efforts. Pharmacists can use the pharmacy's website, social media channels, and email newsletters to share health tips, informational videos, and updates on health events. Online platforms can also facilitate virtual consultations and interactive webinars, allowing pharmacists to engage with the community remotely. Digital tools, such as mobile apps, can support medication adherence, track health metrics, and provide reminders for health appointments.

Collaboration with Healthcare Providers

Collaborating with other healthcare providers and community organizations can enhance the effectiveness of health education initiatives. Pharmacists can work with doctors, nurses, dietitians, and public health officials to deliver comprehensive health education programs. Joint efforts can help address broader health issues and ensure that patients receive consistent and coordinated care.

Evaluating Health Education Efforts

Regularly evaluating the impact of health education activities is essential for continuous improvement. Pharmacists should gather feedback from participants, assess changes in knowledge and behavior, and track health outcomes. This information can guide future educational efforts and ensure that they meet the needs of the community effectively.

By employing these methods and strategies, pharmacists can play a pivotal role in educating the community, promoting health, and preventing disease. Their efforts can lead to improved health literacy, healthier behaviors, and better health outcomes for the population they serve.

9.1.1.3 Community Engagement

Community engagement is a vital component of health promotion in community pharmacies. Engaging with the community helps build trust, increase awareness, and encourage participation in health initiatives. Pharmacists can employ various techniques to effectively engage with the community and promote health awareness.

Hosting Health Events

Organizing health fairs, workshops, and seminars can draw community members to the pharmacy for educational and interactive activities. These events can focus on various health topics such as nutrition, exercise, disease prevention, and medication management. Health fairs can include screenings for blood pressure, cholesterol, and glucose levels, as well as demonstrations on proper medication use and healthy lifestyle practices. Workshops can provide hands-on experiences, such as cooking classes for healthy eating or exercise sessions for physical fitness.

Collaborating with Local Organizations

Partnering with local schools, community centers, non-profits, and healthcare providers can enhance the reach and impact of health promotion efforts. These collaborations can help organize joint events, share resources, and promote health initiatives through established community networks. For example, working with schools to provide health education to students and parents or collaborating with local fitness centers to offer exercise programs can foster a more comprehensive approach to community health.

Utilizing Social Media and Digital Platforms

Engaging with the community through social media and digital platforms allows for broader and more consistent communication. Pharmacists can use social media channels to share health tips, updates on health events, and educational videos. Creating a pharmacy blog or YouTube channel can provide a platform for in-depth discussions on various health topics. Hosting live Q&A sessions or webinars can offer real-time interaction with community members, allowing them to ask questions and receive immediate feedback.

Creating Educational Campaigns

Developing targeted educational campaigns can raise awareness about specific health issues. These campaigns can include posters, flyers, and brochures distributed within the pharmacy and throughout the community. Campaigns can also be promoted through local media outlets, such as newspapers, radio stations, and community bulletins. Topics can range from seasonal health concerns, such as flu prevention, to ongoing issues like smoking cessation and chronic disease management.

Facilitating Support Groups

Establishing support groups for individuals with chronic conditions, such as diabetes, hypertension, or asthma, can provide a sense of community and mutual support. Pharmacists can facilitate these groups, offering education, encouragement, and resources to help members manage their conditions. Support groups can meet regularly at the pharmacy or virtually, providing a platform for sharing experiences, discussing challenges, and celebrating successes.

Offering Personalized Health Consultations

Providing personalized health consultations can enhance community engagement by addressing individual health needs and concerns. Pharmacists can offer medication reviews, lifestyle counseling, and health assessments tailored to each patient. These consultations can help build strong, trust-based relationships and encourage patients to take an active role in their health.

Participating in Community Events

Involvement in local events, such as fairs, festivals, and sports activities, allows pharmacists to connect with the community in informal settings. Setting up informational booths, conducting health screenings, and distributing educational materials can promote health awareness and encourage community members to visit the pharmacy for further services.

Engaging Youth and Families

Focusing on youth and families can have a lasting impact on community health. Pharmacists can visit schools to provide health education, participate in parent-teacher meetings, and offer family health workshops. Engaging children and their parents in health activities can foster lifelong healthy habits and create a ripple effect throughout the community.

Feedback and Community Involvement

Encouraging feedback from the community on health promotion efforts can provide valuable insights and foster a sense of ownership. Pharmacists can conduct surveys, hold focus groups, and invite suggestions to understand community needs and preferences better. Involving community members in planning and implementing health initiatives can enhance their relevance and effectiveness.

By employing these techniques, pharmacists can effectively engage with the community, promote health awareness, and foster a healthier population. Community engagement not only enhances the impact of health promotion activities but also strengthens the relationship between the pharmacy and the community it serves.

9.2 Family Planning and Health Screening Services

9.2.1 Providing Essential Services to the Community

9.2.1.1 Family Planning Services

Pharmacists play a crucial role in providing family planning services to the community, offering valuable contraceptive advice and services. Their accessibility and trust within the community position them as key healthcare providers in promoting reproductive health and family planning.

Role of Pharmacists in Providing Contraceptive Advice and Services

Contraceptive Counseling: Pharmacists are well-placed to offer counseling on various contraceptive methods, including oral contraceptives, condoms, intrauterine devices (IUDs), implants, patches, and emergency contraception. They can explain the efficacy, usage, side effects, and benefits of each method, helping individuals and couples make informed decisions based on their health, lifestyle, and reproductive goals. Counseling sessions should be private and conducted in a non-judgmental manner, ensuring confidentiality and comfort for the patient.

Over-the-Counter Contraceptives: Pharmacists can provide over-the-counter contraceptives, such as condoms, spermicides, and emergency contraception (e.g., morning-after pills). They can educate patients on proper usage, effectiveness, and the importance of consistent use to prevent unintended pregnancies. By offering these products conveniently, pharmacists can increase access to contraception, especially for individuals who may feel uncomfortable seeking these services elsewhere.

Prescription Contraceptives: In some regions, pharmacists are authorized to prescribe certain contraceptives, such as birth control pills or patches. This expanded role allows pharmacists to initiate and manage contraceptive therapy, providing a valuable service to individuals who may have limited access to other healthcare providers. Pharmacists can also assist in prescription refills and address any concerns or side effects that patients may experience.

Education and Awareness: Pharmacists can play an educational role by organizing workshops, seminars, and health talks on family planning and reproductive health. These events can raise awareness about the importance of family planning, the various contraceptive options available, and how to access these services. Educational materials, such as brochures and posters, can be displayed in the pharmacy to provide additional information.

Collaborative Care: Working collaboratively with other healthcare providers, such as doctors, nurses, and reproductive health specialists, pharmacists can ensure comprehensive care for patients. This collaboration can involve referring patients to other healthcare professionals for services beyond the pharmacist's scope, such as IUD insertions or implants. Effective communication and coordination among healthcare providers enhance the overall quality of care and ensure that patients receive appropriate and timely interventions.

Confidentiality and Privacy: Maintaining patient confidentiality and privacy is paramount when providing family planning services. Pharmacists should create a welcoming and private environment for consultations, ensuring that patients feel comfortable discussing sensitive topics. This trust is essential for encouraging individuals to seek advice and services related to contraception and reproductive health.

Follow-Up and Support: Providing ongoing support and follow-up is crucial for successful family planning. Pharmacists can schedule follow-up appointments or check-ins to monitor the patient's adherence to their chosen contraceptive method, address any side effects, and provide additional counseling if needed. Continuous support helps patients stay informed and confident in managing their reproductive health.

Emergency Contraception: Pharmacists can educate patients about emergency contraception options, such as levonorgestrel (Plan B) and ulipristal acetate (Ella), and their appropriate use. They can inform patients about the time-sensitive nature of these medications and provide guidance on how and when to use them effectively to prevent unintended pregnancies.

Community Outreach: Engaging in community outreach programs can extend the reach of family planning services. Pharmacists can collaborate with local organizations, schools, and community centers to provide education and resources on family planning and contraception. Outreach efforts can help address barriers to access and promote reproductive health awareness among diverse populations.

By offering comprehensive family planning services and contraceptive advice, pharmacists play a vital role in supporting the reproductive health of their communities. Their efforts contribute to improved health outcomes, reduced unintended pregnancies, and empowered individuals who can make informed decisions about their reproductive lives.

9.2.1.2 Health Screening Programs

Health screening programs are an essential service provided by community pharmacies, offering early detection and management of various health conditions. By conducting regular screenings, pharmacists can identify risk factors, monitor chronic diseases, and promote preventive health measures. Here are some common types of health screenings and their importance:

Blood Pressure Screening

Importance: High blood pressure (hypertension) is a major risk factor for cardiovascular diseases, including heart attack and stroke. Early detection and management of hypertension can significantly reduce the risk of these complications.

Screening Process: Blood pressure screenings involve measuring the systolic and diastolic pressures using a sphygmomanometer or automated blood pressure monitor. Pharmacists can provide immediate results and offer counseling on lifestyle modifications, such as dietary changes, exercise, and stress management, to help manage blood pressure. They can also refer patients to healthcare providers for further evaluation and treatment if necessary.

Cholesterol Screening

Importance: Elevated cholesterol levels are associated with an increased risk of cardiovascular diseases. Regular cholesterol screenings can help identify individuals at risk and guide interventions to lower cholesterol levels.

Screening Process: Cholesterol screenings typically involve a blood test to measure total cholesterol, low-density lipoprotein (LDL) cholesterol, high-density lipoprotein (HDL) cholesterol, and triglycerides. Pharmacists can perform these tests using fingerstick blood samples and provide immediate feedback. Counseling on diet, exercise, and medication adherence can help patients manage their cholesterol levels effectively.

Blood Glucose Screening

Importance: Monitoring blood glucose levels is crucial for the early detection and management of diabetes. Uncontrolled diabetes can lead to serious complications, including cardiovascular disease, kidney failure, and neuropathy.

Screening Process: Blood glucose screenings involve testing a small blood sample, usually obtained from a fingerstick, to measure blood sugar levels. Pharmacists can use this information to identify individuals with high blood sugar and provide counseling on diet, exercise, and medication adherence. Patients with abnormal results can be referred to healthcare providers for further evaluation and diagnosis.

Body Mass Index (BMI) Screening

Importance: BMI is a measure of body fat based on height and weight. High BMI is associated with an increased risk of various health conditions, including heart disease, diabetes, and certain cancers.

Screening Process: BMI screenings involve measuring height and weight and calculating the BMI using a standard formula. Pharmacists can provide counseling on healthy eating, physical activity, and weight management strategies to help patients achieve and maintain a healthy BMI.

Osteoporosis Screening

Importance: Osteoporosis is a condition characterized by weakened bones, increasing the risk of fractures. Early detection can help prevent fractures and improve bone health through appropriate interventions.

Screening Process: Osteoporosis screenings often involve using a bone densitometer to measure bone density, particularly in postmenopausal women and older adults. Pharmacists can provide education on calcium and vitamin D intake, weight-bearing exercises, and medications that can help strengthen bones.

Lipid Panel Screening

Importance: A comprehensive lipid panel provides detailed information about lipid levels in the blood, including total cholesterol, LDL, HDL, and triglycerides. This screening is crucial for assessing cardiovascular risk.

Screening Process: Lipid panel screenings involve a blood test, typically a fingerstick or venipuncture, to measure lipid levels. Pharmacists can interpret the results and offer counseling on lifestyle modifications and medication management to help patients maintain healthy lipid levels.

Smoking Cessation Screening

Importance: Smoking is a leading cause of preventable diseases, including lung cancer, heart disease, and chronic obstructive pulmonary disease (COPD). Identifying smokers and providing cessation support can significantly improve health outcomes.

Screening Process: Pharmacists can screen for smoking status during routine consultations and offer smoking cessation programs. These programs may include counseling, nicotine replacement therapy, and prescription medications to help individuals quit smoking.

Hepatitis and HIV Screening

Importance: Early detection of hepatitis and HIV can lead to timely treatment and reduce the spread of these infections. Regular screenings are particularly important for high-risk populations.

Screening Process: Hepatitis and HIV screenings involve blood tests or oral swabs to detect the presence of the virus. Pharmacists can provide pre- and post-test counseling, offer support services, and refer patients to specialized care if necessary.

Cancer Screening

Importance: Early detection of certain cancers, such as colorectal, breast, and prostate cancer, can significantly improve treatment outcomes and survival rates.

Screening Process: Pharmacists can offer information on available cancer screenings, such as fecal occult blood tests for colorectal cancer, mammograms for breast cancer, and prostate-specific antigen (PSA) tests for prostate cancer. They can guide patients on when and where to get these screenings and provide education on cancer prevention strategies.

By offering a variety of health screening programs, pharmacists can play a crucial role in early detection and prevention of chronic diseases. These screenings provide valuable opportunities to educate patients, promote healthy behaviors, and refer individuals to appropriate healthcare providers for further evaluation and management. Regular health screenings contribute to better health outcomes and enhance the overall well-being of the community.

9.2.1.3 Counseling and Support

Offering counseling services and support to patients during health screenings is a critical component of the pharmacist's role in promoting health and preventing disease. Through personalized counseling and continuous support, pharmacists can help patients understand their health status, make informed decisions, and adopt healthier lifestyles. Here are key aspects of providing effective counseling and support during health screenings:

Personalized Health Counseling

Understanding Results: Pharmacists should take the time to explain the results of health screenings in a clear and understandable manner. This includes interpreting numbers, such as blood pressure readings, cholesterol levels, and blood glucose levels, and explaining what these numbers mean in terms of the patient's health. Using visual aids or comparison charts can help patients grasp the significance of their results more easily.

Providing Recommendations: Based on the screening results, pharmacists can offer personalized recommendations for improving or maintaining health. This might include lifestyle modifications, such as dietary changes, increased physical activity, weight management, smoking cessation, and stress reduction techniques. For instance, if a patient has high blood pressure, the pharmacist might suggest reducing sodium intake, increasing physical activity, and monitoring blood pressure regularly.

Addressing Concerns: Patients may have concerns or questions about their health screening results and the implications for their overall health. Pharmacists should create a supportive environment where patients feel comfortable discussing their worries. Active listening, empathy, and reassurance are key elements of effective counseling. Pharmacists should provide accurate information and clarify any misconceptions the patient may have.

Medication Counseling

Explaining Medications: For patients who require medication based on their screening results, pharmacists should provide comprehensive information about the prescribed medications. This includes how the medication works, how to take it correctly, potential side effects, interactions with other drugs or foods, and the importance of adherence. Providing written materials or medication guides can reinforce verbal instructions.

Adherence Support: Pharmacists can offer strategies to improve medication adherence, such as setting up medication reminders, using pill organizers, and explaining the benefits of taking medications as prescribed. For patients with chronic conditions, ongoing support and follow-up can help ensure they continue to take their medications correctly and manage their conditions effectively.

Lifestyle and Behavioral Counseling

Setting Goals: Collaborating with patients to set realistic and achievable health goals can motivate them to make positive changes. Pharmacists can help patients identify specific, measurable, attainable, relevant, and time-bound (SMART) goals related to their health, such as losing a certain amount of weight, reducing blood pressure, or quitting smoking within a set timeframe.

Providing Resources: Pharmacists can connect patients with additional resources and support services, such as dietitians, exercise programs, smoking cessation programs, and mental health services. Providing information about community resources, support groups, and online tools can help patients access the support they need to achieve their health goals.

Follow-Up and Continuous Support

Regular Check-Ins: Scheduling regular follow-up appointments or check-ins allows pharmacists to monitor the patient's progress, address any new concerns, and adjust recommendations as needed. Continuous support and encouragement can help patients stay motivated and committed to their health goals.

Tracking Progress: Keeping a record of the patient's health screening results, medication history, and progress towards health goals can provide valuable insights and facilitate ongoing care. Pharmacists can use this information to tailor their counseling and support to the patient's evolving needs.

Encouraging Self-Monitoring: Teaching patients how to self-monitor their health, such as checking their blood pressure or blood glucose at home, can empower them to take an active role in managing their health. Pharmacists can provide guidance on how to use home monitoring devices and interpret the results.

By offering personalized counseling and continuous support during health screenings, pharmacists can significantly impact patient outcomes. Effective counseling helps patients understand their health, make informed decisions, and adopt healthier behaviors, ultimately leading to improved health and well-being.

9.3 First Aid and Disease Prevention
9.3.1 Basic First Aid and Preventive Measures
9.3.1.1 First Aid Training

Pharmacists, due to their accessibility and trusted role within the community, are often the first point of contact in medical emergencies. Therefore, having basic first aid training is essential for pharmacists to provide immediate and effective assistance until professional medical help arrives. Key first aid skills every pharmacist should know include:

Cardiopulmonary Resuscitation (CPR): CPR is a lifesaving technique that is critical in emergencies such as cardiac arrest or drowning. Pharmacists should be trained in both adult and pediatric CPR, including chest compressions and rescue breaths. Knowledge of how to use an automated external defibrillator (AED) is also essential, as it can significantly increase the chances of survival in cases of sudden cardiac arrest.

Managing Choking: Knowing how to perform the Heimlich maneuver to relieve choking in adults, children, and infants is an essential first aid skill. Pharmacists should be familiar with the different techniques used based on the age and size of the person choking.

Controlling Bleeding: Pharmacists should be able to manage both minor and severe bleeding. This includes applying pressure to wounds, using sterile dressings or bandages, and knowing when and how to use a tourniquet for severe arterial bleeding.

Treating Burns: First aid for burns involves cooling the burn with running water, covering it with a sterile dressing, and avoiding the application of ice or ointments directly on severe burns. Pharmacists should understand how to differentiate between first-degree, second-degree, and third-degree burns and provide appropriate care for each.

Managing Fractures and Sprains: Immobilizing the affected area, using splints, and applying cold packs to reduce swelling are key skills in managing fractures and sprains. Pharmacists should be able to recognize the signs of fractures and sprains and advise patients on seeking further medical evaluation.

Handling Allergic Reactions: Pharmacists should be able to recognize the signs of severe allergic reactions (anaphylaxis) and know how to administer an epinephrine auto-injector (e.g., EpiPen). They should also provide guidance on managing mild allergic reactions with antihistamines.

Providing Basic Wound Care: Cleaning wounds, applying antiseptics, and dressing wounds properly to prevent infection are fundamental first aid skills. Pharmacists should educate patients on the importance of keeping wounds clean and monitoring for signs of infection.

Responding to Poisoning: Pharmacists should know the basics of poisoning management, including identifying the source of poisoning, avoiding inducing vomiting unless directed by poison control, and providing appropriate first aid based on the type of poison. They should also have the contact information for local poison control centers readily available.

Recognizing and Managing Shock: Understanding the signs of shock (e.g., pale, clammy skin, rapid pulse, and shallow breathing) and knowing how to provide first aid (e.g., keeping the person lying down, elevating their legs, and covering them with a blanket) are critical in emergency situations.

Dealing with Heat and Cold-Related Illnesses: Pharmacists should know how to provide first aid for heat exhaustion, heatstroke, hypothermia, and frostbite. This includes recognizing symptoms and taking appropriate measures, such as moving the person to a cooler or warmer environment, providing hydration, and using gradual rewarming techniques.

Mental Health First Aid: Pharmacists should be aware of basic mental health first aid principles, including how to recognize signs of mental health crises, such as panic attacks, suicidal thoughts, or acute psychosis, and how to provide initial support and referral to appropriate mental health services.

Pharmacists should undergo formal first aid training through certified courses to acquire these skills and stay updated with regular refresher courses. Being prepared with these essential first aid skills enables pharmacists to respond effectively in emergencies, providing immediate care that can stabilize a patient and prevent further harm until professional medical help arrives. This training not only enhances the pharmacist's ability to serve their community but also builds confidence in managing a variety of medical emergencies.

9.3.1.2 Preventive Health Measures

Preventive health measures are essential for reducing the incidence of diseases and promoting overall health and well-being. Pharmacists play a vital role in educating and encouraging the community to adopt these measures, which include vaccinations, hygiene practices, and lifestyle changes.

Importance of Vaccines

Vaccinations are one of the most effective ways to prevent infectious diseases and their complications. Vaccines stimulate the immune system to recognize and combat pathogens, providing immunity against diseases such as influenza, measles, mumps, rubella, polio, hepatitis, and human papillomavirus (HPV). Pharmacists can promote the importance of vaccinations by:

- **Educating patients** about the benefits of vaccines and dispelling common myths and misconceptions.
- **Providing vaccination services** within the pharmacy, where permitted, to increase accessibility and convenience for patients.
- **Maintaining up-to-date knowledge** of vaccination schedules and guidelines to offer accurate advice and recommendations.
- **Organizing vaccination clinics** and collaborating with public health agencies to enhance community immunization rates.

By advocating for vaccines, pharmacists help protect individuals and communities from vaccine-preventable diseases, contributing to public health and reducing the burden on healthcare systems.

Hygiene Practices

Good hygiene practices are fundamental in preventing the spread of infections and maintaining overall health. Pharmacists can educate patients on the importance of personal and environmental hygiene, which includes:

- **Hand hygiene:** Washing hands regularly with soap and water for at least 20 seconds, especially before eating, after using the restroom, and after coughing or sneezing. Hand sanitizers with at least 60% alcohol can be used when soap and water are not available.
- **Respiratory hygiene:** Covering mouth and nose with a tissue or elbow when coughing or sneezing, and disposing of tissues properly to prevent the spread of respiratory infections.
- **Personal hygiene:** Regular bathing, oral hygiene, and keeping nails trimmed and clean to reduce the risk of infections.
- **Food hygiene:** Properly washing fruits and vegetables, cooking meat thoroughly, and avoiding cross-contamination in the kitchen to prevent foodborne illnesses.
- **Environmental hygiene:** Regular cleaning and disinfecting of frequently touched surfaces, such as doorknobs, light switches, and electronic devices, to reduce the spread of pathogens.

By emphasizing the importance of hygiene practices, pharmacists can help reduce the transmission of infectious diseases and promote a healthier environment.

Lifestyle Changes

Healthy lifestyle choices are crucial for preventing chronic diseases and enhancing overall well-being. Pharmacists can support patients in adopting and maintaining healthy habits through education and counseling on:

- **Balanced diet:** Encouraging the consumption of a variety of nutrient-rich foods, including fruits, vegetables, whole grains, lean proteins, and healthy fats. Educating patients on portion control and the benefits of reducing sugar, salt, and unhealthy fats in their diet.
- **Regular physical activity:** Advising patients to engage in at least 150 minutes of moderate-intensity aerobic exercise or 75 minutes of vigorous-intensity exercise per week, along with muscle-strengthening activities on two or more days per week. Promoting activities that patients enjoy to increase adherence.

- **Adequate sleep:** Emphasizing the importance of getting 7-9 hours of quality sleep per night for adults and maintaining a consistent sleep schedule.
- **Stress management:** Providing strategies for managing stress, such as mindfulness, meditation, deep breathing exercises, and engaging in hobbies and social activities.
- **Avoiding harmful behaviors:** Educating patients on the risks associated with smoking, excessive alcohol consumption, and drug abuse, and offering support and resources for cessation and rehabilitation.

By promoting these preventive health measures, pharmacists can empower patients to take proactive steps towards maintaining their health and preventing the onset of chronic diseases. These efforts contribute to a healthier community and reduce the long-term burden on healthcare systems.

9.3.1.3 Emergency Response

Responding to emergencies and providing immediate care are critical responsibilities for pharmacists, given their accessibility and trusted role in the community. Effective emergency response can stabilize a patient, prevent further injury, and potentially save lives. Pharmacists should be prepared with the knowledge and skills to handle a variety of medical emergencies. Here are key aspects of emergency response and immediate care:

Recognizing Emergencies

Identifying an emergency situation is the first step in providing effective care. Common emergencies that may occur in a pharmacy setting include:

- **Cardiac arrest:** Sudden loss of heart function, breathing, and consciousness.
- **Stroke:** Sudden numbness, confusion, trouble speaking, or difficulty walking.
- **Severe allergic reactions (anaphylaxis):** Symptoms include swelling, difficulty breathing, and hives.
- **Asthma attacks:** Severe shortness of breath, wheezing, and coughing.
- **Seizures:** Sudden, uncontrolled electrical disturbance in the brain.
- **Hypoglycemia:** Low blood sugar, causing shakiness, confusion, and sweating.

- **Injuries**: Cuts, burns, fractures, and head injuries.

Basic First Aid Skills

Pharmacists should be trained in basic first aid skills to provide immediate care during emergencies:

- **Cardiopulmonary Resuscitation (CPR)**: Perform chest compressions and rescue breaths to maintain circulation and breathing in a patient who is unresponsive and not breathing.
- **Use of Automated External Defibrillator (AED)**: Apply an AED to a patient in cardiac arrest to deliver an electric shock and restore a normal heart rhythm.
- **Heimlich Maneuver**: Perform abdominal thrusts to relieve choking in adults and children, and back blows and chest thrusts for infants.
- **Controlling Bleeding**: Apply direct pressure to wounds, use sterile dressings or bandages, and, if necessary, apply a tourniquet to control severe bleeding.
- **Treating Burns**: Cool the burn with running water, cover with a sterile dressing, and avoid applying ice or ointments directly on severe burns.
- **Managing Fractures and Sprains**: Immobilize the affected area with splints, apply cold packs to reduce swelling, and advise patients to seek medical evaluation.
- **Responding to Allergic Reactions**: Administer an epinephrine auto-injector for anaphylaxis, and provide antihistamines for mild allergic reactions.
- **Providing Basic Wound Care**: Clean wounds, apply antiseptics, and dress wounds properly to prevent infection.

Effective Communication in Emergencies

Clear and calm communication is essential during emergencies:

- **Calling for Help**: Dial emergency services (e.g., 911) immediately when an emergency is identified. Provide clear and concise information about the situation, including the patient's condition and the exact location.
- **Instructing Bystanders**: Direct bystanders to assist if necessary, such as fetching the AED, calling emergency services, or providing crowd control.

- **Reassuring the Patient**: Speak calmly and reassuringly to the patient, explaining what you are doing and why. This can help reduce their anxiety and make the situation more manageable.

Emergency Preparedness

Pharmacies should have a well-prepared emergency response plan:

- **Emergency Supplies**: Maintain a well-stocked first aid kit, AED, and other essential supplies such as sterile gloves, bandages, antiseptics, and emergency medications.
- **Staff Training**: Ensure all pharmacy staff are trained in basic first aid, CPR, and the use of AEDs. Regular training sessions and drills can help keep skills sharp and improve response times.
- **Clear Protocols**: Develop and display clear emergency response protocols for various scenarios, including step-by-step instructions on how to handle specific emergencies.
- **Emergency Contacts**: Keep an updated list of emergency contacts, including local emergency services, nearby hospitals, and poison control centers, readily accessible.

Post-Emergency Actions

After an emergency has been managed:

- **Documentation**: Record the details of the incident, including the patient's condition, the actions taken, and the outcome. This information is valuable for follow-up care and legal purposes.
- **Debriefing**: Conduct a debriefing session with staff to review the incident, discuss what went well, and identify areas for improvement.
- **Follow-Up Care**: Provide information to the patient about the next steps, including the need for further medical evaluation or treatment. Offer support and resources for their recovery.

By being well-prepared and equipped to handle emergencies, pharmacists can provide immediate and effective care that can stabilize patients and prevent further harm. This readiness enhances the pharmacy's role as a critical point of care in the community, ensuring the safety and well-being of its patients.

Chapter 9: Health Promotion in Community Pharmacy

9.4 Smoking Cessation Programs
9.4.1 Supporting Patients to Quit Smoking
9.4.1.1 Understanding Nicotine Addiction

Mechanisms of Nicotine Addiction and Withdrawal Symptoms

Nicotine addiction is a complex condition characterized by both physical and psychological dependence on nicotine, a substance found in tobacco products. Understanding the mechanisms behind nicotine addiction and the associated withdrawal symptoms is crucial for effectively supporting patients in smoking cessation efforts.

Mechanisms of Nicotine Addiction

1. Nicotine's Action on the Brain: When nicotine is inhaled through smoking or ingested via other tobacco products, it quickly enters the bloodstream and crosses the blood-brain barrier. In the brain, nicotine binds to nicotinic acetylcholine receptors, particularly in the mesolimbic dopamine system, which is associated with pleasure and reward. This binding stimulates the release of neurotransmitters, especially dopamine, in the nucleus accumbens, creating feelings of pleasure and reinforcing the behavior of smoking.

2. Dopamine Release: The release of dopamine creates a rewarding sensation that smokers often seek to replicate. This reward pathway is a critical component of addiction, as the brain becomes conditioned to associate nicotine intake with pleasurable feelings, leading to repeated use and dependence.

3. Neuroadaptation: Over time, the brain adapts to the presence of nicotine by increasing the number of nicotinic receptors and altering their sensitivity. This neuroadaptation contributes to tolerance, meaning that higher doses of nicotine are required to achieve the same pleasurable effects. It also plays a significant role in withdrawal symptoms when nicotine use is reduced or stopped.

Withdrawal Symptoms

1. Physical Symptoms: Nicotine withdrawal can lead to a range of physical symptoms, which typically begin within a few hours after the last cigarette and peak within the first few days. These symptoms can include:

- **Cravings**: Intense urges to smoke are a hallmark of nicotine withdrawal.
- **Irritability and Anxiety**: A common response to the absence of nicotine's calming effects.

- **Difficulty Concentrating**: Reduced levels of dopamine can impair cognitive function.
- **Increased Appetite and Weight Gain**: Nicotine suppresses appetite, so its absence can lead to increased hunger and subsequent weight gain.
- **Sleep Disturbances**: Nicotine affects sleep patterns, and withdrawal can lead to insomnia or disrupted sleep.

2. Psychological Symptoms: The psychological aspects of nicotine withdrawal can be just as challenging as the physical symptoms. These may include:

- **Depression**: The reduction in dopamine levels can cause feelings of sadness or depression.
- **Restlessness**: Smokers may feel antsy or restless without their usual nicotine fix.
- **Mood Swings**: Emotional instability is common as the brain adjusts to functioning without nicotine.

Managing Withdrawal Symptoms

1. Nicotine Replacement Therapy (NRT): Products such as nicotine patches, gum, lozenges, inhalers, and nasal sprays provide a controlled dose of nicotine to ease withdrawal symptoms and reduce cravings. NRT helps wean smokers off nicotine gradually, making the quitting process more manageable.

2. Prescription Medications: Medications like bupropion (Zyban) and varenicline (Chantix) can be prescribed to help reduce cravings and withdrawal symptoms. These medications work by targeting the brain's nicotine receptors and modulating neurotransmitter levels.

3. Behavioral Support: Counseling and behavioral therapies are integral to smoking cessation programs. These can include cognitive-behavioral therapy (CBT), motivational interviewing, and support groups, which help individuals develop coping strategies and address the psychological aspects of addiction.

4. Lifestyle Changes: Encouraging patients to adopt healthy lifestyle habits, such as regular physical activity, a balanced diet, and adequate sleep, can help mitigate withdrawal symptoms and support overall well-being.

5. Mindfulness and Stress Management: Techniques such as mindfulness meditation, deep breathing exercises, and yoga can help manage stress and anxiety, which are common triggers for smoking relapse.

Understanding nicotine addiction and the mechanisms of withdrawal is essential for pharmacists to effectively support patients in their journey to quit smoking. By providing a combination of pharmacological aids, behavioral support, and lifestyle recommendations, pharmacists can play a pivotal role in helping patients overcome nicotine dependence and achieve long-term smoking cessation.

9.4.1.2 Counseling Techniques for Smoking Cessation

Effective counseling is a key component of smoking cessation programs, providing patients with the support and strategies they need to quit smoking successfully. Here are some proven counseling techniques that pharmacists can use to help patients quit smoking:

Motivational Interviewing

Motivational interviewing is a patient-centered counseling technique that helps patients explore and resolve their ambivalence about quitting smoking. It involves the following principles:

1. **Express Empathy**: Show understanding and acceptance of the patient's feelings and struggles. Use reflective listening to convey empathy, such as saying, "It sounds like quitting smoking is something you really want to do, but you're not sure how to start."

2. **Develop Discrepancy**: Help the patient see the gap between their current behavior (smoking) and their broader goals and values (health, family, etc.). For example, "You mentioned wanting to be around for your grandchildren. How does smoking fit into that picture?"

3. **Roll with Resistance**: Avoid arguing or confronting the patient. Instead, acknowledge their resistance and explore it further. For instance, "I understand that quitting feels overwhelming right now. What do you think makes it feel so challenging?"

4. **Support Self-Efficacy**: Encourage the patient's belief in their ability to quit. Highlight their past successes in other areas as evidence of their capability. "You've managed to cut down your coffee intake before. That shows you have the strength to make changes when you set your mind to it."

The 5 A's Approach

The **5 A's** approach is a structured method for smoking cessation counseling that involves the following steps:

1. **Ask**: Systematically identify all tobacco users at every visit. "Do you currently smoke or use any other forms of tobacco?"
2. **Advise**: Strongly urge all tobacco users to quit in a clear, personalized, and non-judgmental manner. "Quitting smoking is the best thing you can do for your health. I believe you can do it, and I'm here to help."
3. **Assess**: Determine the patient's readiness to quit. "On a scale of 1 to 10, how ready do you feel to quit smoking in the next month?"
4. **Assist**: Help the patient develop a quit plan, provide counseling, and offer medication options if appropriate. "Let's talk about some strategies that can help you quit. Have you considered using nicotine replacement therapy or other medications?"
5. **Arrange**: Schedule follow-up contacts to provide ongoing support and prevent relapse. "I'd like to check in with you next week to see how things are going. How does that sound?"

Cognitive-Behavioral Therapy (CBT)

Cognitive-behavioral therapy (CBT) focuses on changing the thought patterns and behaviors that contribute to smoking. Techniques include:

1. **Identifying Triggers**: Help the patient recognize situations, emotions, or activities that trigger their urge to smoke. "What usually prompts you to light up a cigarette? Is it stress, boredom, or social situations?"
2. **Developing Coping Strategies**: Teach the patient alternative ways to cope with triggers and cravings. "Next time you feel the urge to smoke, try taking a short walk or practicing deep breathing exercises."
3. **Setting Realistic Goals**: Encourage the patient to set achievable goals and gradually reduce their smoking. "Let's start by cutting down the number of cigarettes you smoke each day. How about reducing by one cigarette per day for the first week?"
4. **Behavioral Substitution**: Suggest replacing smoking with healthier behaviors. "Whenever you feel like smoking, try chewing gum, sipping water, or using a stress ball."

Support Groups and Peer Support

Connecting patients with **support groups** or **peer support** can provide additional encouragement and accountability. These groups offer a sense of community and shared experience, which can be highly motivating. Pharmacists can refer patients to local or online support groups, where they can share their experiences and gain insights from others who are also trying to quit.

Use of Digital Tools and Resources

Leveraging digital tools, such as mobile apps, websites, and text messaging programs, can enhance smoking cessation efforts. These tools can provide reminders, motivational messages, tracking features, and access to educational resources. Pharmacists can recommend reliable digital tools that suit the patient's needs and preferences.

Positive Reinforcement

Using **positive reinforcement** to celebrate milestones and successes, no matter how small, can boost the patient's confidence and motivation. Acknowledge their efforts and progress regularly. "You've made it through your first smoke-free week – that's a fantastic achievement! Keep up the great work."

Providing Educational Materials

Giving patients **educational materials** about the benefits of quitting smoking, the health risks of continued smoking, and tips for managing cravings and withdrawal symptoms can reinforce counseling sessions. Brochures, handouts, and links to reputable online resources can be helpful.

Follow-Up and Continuous Support

Regular follow-up is crucial to provide ongoing encouragement and address any challenges the patient may face. Schedule follow-up appointments or calls to monitor progress, offer additional support, and adjust the quit plan as needed. Continuous support helps maintain the patient's commitment to quitting and prevents relapse.

By using these counseling techniques, pharmacists can effectively support patients in their journey to quit smoking, helping them overcome nicotine addiction and achieve a healthier, smoke-free life.

9.4.1.3 Pharmacological Aids for Quitting Smoking

Pharmacological aids play a crucial role in smoking cessation by reducing withdrawal symptoms and cravings, thereby increasing the chances of successful quitting. Pharmacists can guide patients in choosing the appropriate pharmacological aids, including nicotine replacement therapies (NRTs) and other medications.

Nicotine Replacement Therapies (NRTs)

NRTs provide a controlled dose of nicotine without the harmful chemicals found in tobacco smoke. They help to reduce withdrawal symptoms and cravings, making it easier for smokers to quit. The following are common forms of NRTs:

1. **Nicotine Patches**: Transdermal nicotine patches release a steady amount of nicotine through the skin over 16-24 hours. They are available in different strengths, allowing users to gradually reduce their nicotine intake.

   - **Usage**: Apply one patch to clean, dry, hairless skin on the upper body or upper outer arm. Rotate the application site to avoid skin irritation.
   - **Advantages**: Provides a consistent level of nicotine, easy to use.
   - **Considerations**: May cause skin irritation, sleep disturbances if worn overnight.

1. **Nicotine Gum**: Nicotine gum delivers nicotine through the oral mucosa. It is available in 2 mg and 4 mg strengths.

   - **Usage**: Chew the gum slowly until a tingling sensation is felt, then park it between the cheek and gum. Repeat this process for about 30 minutes.
   - **Advantages**: Provides quick relief from cravings, can be used as needed.
   - **Considerations**: May cause jaw discomfort, mouth irritation, and should not be used by individuals with dental issues or TMJ.

3. **Nicotine Lozenges**: Lozenges dissolve in the mouth, releasing nicotine gradually.

   - **Usage**: Allow the lozenge to dissolve slowly in the mouth without chewing or swallowing. Rotate it around the mouth to avoid irritation.
   - **Advantages**: Discreet, provides quick relief from cravings.
   - **Considerations**: May cause mouth or throat irritation, nausea if swallowed too quickly.

4. **Nicotine Inhalers**: These devices deliver nicotine vapor to the mouth and throat, mimicking the hand-to-mouth action of smoking.

   - **Usage**: Inhale through the mouthpiece, drawing the vapor into the mouth and holding it for a few seconds before exhaling.

- **Advantages**: Mimics the behavioral aspect of smoking, provides quick relief.
- **Considerations**: May cause throat irritation, coughing, and not suitable for individuals with respiratory issues.

5. **Nicotine Nasal Spray**: This spray delivers nicotine quickly through the nasal mucosa.

- **Usage**: Administer one spray in each nostril as needed for cravings.
- **Advantages**: Fast-acting, suitable for heavy smokers.
- **Considerations**: May cause nasal and throat irritation, not recommended for individuals with chronic nasal conditions.

Other Medications

In addition to NRTs, there are prescription medications that can help with smoking cessation:

1. **Bupropion (Zyban)**: Bupropion is an atypical antidepressant that helps reduce nicotine cravings and withdrawal symptoms. It affects the neurotransmitters dopamine and norepinephrine in the brain.

- **Usage**: Start taking bupropion one to two weeks before the quit date. The typical dosage is 150 mg once daily for the first three days, then increased to 150 mg twice daily.
- **Advantages**: Can be used in combination with NRTs, helps with depression and anxiety symptoms.
- **Considerations**: May cause insomnia, dry mouth, and should not be used by individuals with a history of seizures or eating disorders.

2. **Varenicline (Chantix)**: Varenicline is a partial agonist of the nicotinic acetylcholine receptors. It reduces cravings and withdrawal symptoms by stimulating these receptors and blocking nicotine's effects.

- **Usage**: Start taking varenicline one week before the quit date. The dosage is typically 0.5 mg once daily for the first three days, then 0.5 mg twice daily for the next four days, followed by 1 mg twice daily.
- **Advantages**: Reduces the rewarding effects of smoking, can be highly effective for many users.

- **Considerations**: May cause nausea, vivid dreams, and should be used cautiously in individuals with a history of psychiatric conditions.

Combination Therapy

Using a combination of NRTs or combining NRTs with prescription medications can enhance the effectiveness of smoking cessation efforts. For example, using a nicotine patch to provide a steady level of nicotine, along with nicotine gum or lozenges for breakthrough cravings, can be more effective than using a single form of NRT alone. Pharmacists can help patients develop a personalized cessation plan that may include combination therapy based on their smoking patterns and preferences.

Counseling and Support

In addition to pharmacological aids, behavioral support and counseling are critical for successful smoking cessation. Pharmacists should provide ongoing support, encourage patients to set a quit date, identify triggers, develop coping strategies, and offer follow-up consultations to monitor progress and adjust treatment as needed.

By offering a comprehensive approach that includes pharmacological aids, behavioral support, and continuous follow-up, pharmacists can significantly enhance patients' chances of quitting smoking and achieving long-term success.

9.4.1.4 Follow-Up and Support

Ongoing support and monitoring are crucial for patients attempting to quit smoking, as they significantly increase the chances of long-term success. Pharmacists play a vital role in providing continuous encouragement, addressing challenges, and ensuring patients stay on track with their cessation plans. Here are key elements of follow-up and support:

Regular Follow-Up Appointments

Scheduling Regular Check-Ins: Schedule follow-up appointments at regular intervals, such as one week, one month, and three months after the quit date. These check-ins can be in-person, over the phone, or through telehealth services. Regular follow-ups help to reinforce the patient's commitment to quitting and allow for timely interventions if challenges arise.

Assessing Progress: During follow-up appointments, assess the patient's progress in terms of adherence to their quit plan, use of pharmacological aids, and management of withdrawal symptoms. Ask about any smoking lapses or cravings and explore their triggers and coping strategies.

Providing Encouragement: Offer positive reinforcement for the patient's efforts and milestones achieved. Acknowledge even small successes, such as reducing the number of cigarettes smoked or managing a difficult situation without smoking. Positive reinforcement can boost the patient's confidence and motivation.

Addressing Challenges and Setbacks

Identifying Barriers: Discuss any challenges the patient is facing in their quit attempt, such as stress, weight gain, social situations, or emotional triggers. Understanding these barriers allows for the development of tailored strategies to overcome them.

Problem-Solving: Collaboratively develop solutions to address specific challenges. For example, if stress is a trigger, suggest stress management techniques such as deep breathing exercises, mindfulness, or engaging in physical activities. If social situations are challenging, discuss strategies for avoiding or managing these scenarios.

Managing Lapses: Reinforce that lapses are common and not a sign of failure. Encourage patients to view lapses as learning opportunities rather than setbacks. Help them analyze what led to the lapse and how to avoid similar situations in the future. Adjust the quit plan as needed to better support the patient's efforts.

Enhancing Motivation

Goal Setting: Help the patient set short-term and long-term goals related to their quit journey. Short-term goals might include staying smoke-free for a week or successfully navigating a social event without smoking. Long-term goals can focus on broader health and lifestyle improvements.

Visual Reminders: Encourage the use of visual reminders of the benefits of quitting, such as tracking money saved, days smoke-free, or health improvements (e.g., better lung function, reduced blood pressure). These reminders can be motivating and reinforce the positive impact of quitting.

Support Systems: Encourage patients to build a support network of family, friends, or support groups. Having a strong support system can provide additional encouragement and accountability. Suggest local or online smoking cessation support groups where they can share experiences and gain insights from others.

Continuous Education

Providing Resources: Offer educational materials and resources on smoking cessation, such as brochures, websites, mobile apps, and community programs. These resources can provide ongoing support and information outside of pharmacy visits.

Health Benefits: Continuously educate patients on the health benefits of quitting smoking, both immediate and long-term. Highlight improvements in cardiovascular health, respiratory function, and overall quality of life. Emphasizing these benefits can help maintain the patient's motivation and commitment.

Pharmacological Support

Adjusting Medications: Monitor the patient's response to pharmacological aids and adjust dosages or medications as needed. For example, if a patient is experiencing significant side effects from a nicotine patch, consider switching to a different form of NRT or adjusting the dosage.

Combining Therapies: If a single form of therapy is not effective, consider combining different pharmacological aids, such as using a nicotine patch with nicotine gum or lozenges for breakthrough cravings. Tailoring the medication regimen to the patient's needs can enhance their chances of success.

Relapse Prevention

Identifying High-Risk Situations: Work with the patient to identify high-risk situations that may lead to relapse, such as social gatherings, stress, or emotional distress. Develop strategies to manage these situations proactively.

Developing a Relapse Plan: Create a relapse prevention plan that includes specific steps to take if the patient experiences cravings or considers smoking. This plan can include reaching out to a support person, using a distraction technique, or referring to educational materials.

Encouraging Continuous Improvement: Remind patients that quitting smoking is a journey, and it's normal to face challenges along the way. Encourage them to focus on continuous improvement and to seek help whenever needed.

By providing ongoing follow-up and support, pharmacists can help patients navigate the challenges of quitting smoking, maintain their motivation, and achieve long-term success in their journey towards a smoke-free life. This continuous support is essential for helping patients overcome nicotine addiction and improve their overall health and well-being.

9.5 Child and Mother Care

9.5.1 Specialized Services for Women and Children

9.5.1.1 Maternal Health Services

Role of Pharmacists in Providing Prenatal and Postnatal Care

Pharmacists play a crucial role in supporting maternal health by providing essential services and guidance during both prenatal and postnatal periods. Their involvement can significantly impact the health outcomes of both mothers and their babies. Here are the key roles of pharmacists in maternal health care:

Prenatal Care:

1. **Medication Management:** Pharmacists help ensure that pregnant women are taking medications safely. They review prescriptions and over-the-counter (OTC) medications for potential risks to the fetus and advise on safer alternatives when necessary. This includes monitoring the use of prenatal vitamins and folic acid supplements, which are crucial for fetal development and preventing neural tube defects.

2. **Counseling on Lifestyle Modifications:** Pharmacists provide counseling on lifestyle changes that promote a healthy pregnancy. This includes advice on proper nutrition, exercise, avoiding harmful substances (such as tobacco, alcohol, and illicit drugs), and managing stress. Pharmacists can also educate pregnant women about the importance of staying hydrated and getting adequate rest.

3. **Managing Pregnancy-Related Conditions:** Pharmacists assist in managing common pregnancy-related conditions such as nausea and vomiting (morning sickness), constipation, heartburn, and gestational diabetes. They recommend appropriate treatments and lifestyle adjustments to alleviate these conditions while ensuring the safety of both mother and baby.

4. **Vaccinations:** Pharmacists ensure that pregnant women receive recommended vaccinations, such as the influenza vaccine and the Tdap vaccine (to protect against tetanus, diphtheria, and pertussis). These vaccinations help protect both the mother and the baby from serious infections.

5. **Prenatal Education:** Pharmacists provide education on various aspects of prenatal care, including the importance of regular prenatal visits, understanding prenatal tests and screenings, and recognizing signs of potential complications such as preeclampsia and preterm labor.

Postnatal Care:

1. **Medication Safety:** After childbirth, pharmacists continue to ensure that medications prescribed to new mothers are safe, especially if they are breastfeeding. They provide guidance on managing postpartum pain, depression, and other conditions while considering the safety of the infant.

2. **Breastfeeding Support:** Pharmacists offer advice and support to breastfeeding mothers, helping them address common issues such as sore nipples, mastitis, and milk supply concerns. They can also recommend appropriate lactation supplements and medications that are safe for breastfeeding.

3. **Postpartum Recovery:** Pharmacists assist new mothers in managing postpartum recovery, including wound care (for cesarean sections or episiotomies), managing postpartum bleeding, and addressing concerns such as urinary incontinence or hemorrhoids.

4. **Nutrition and Wellness:** Pharmacists provide guidance on maintaining a healthy diet and lifestyle during the postpartum period. This includes advice on nutrition to support breastfeeding, physical activity, and mental health.

5. **Contraceptive Counseling:** Pharmacists offer contraceptive counseling to new mothers, helping them choose appropriate postpartum contraceptive methods. They consider factors such as breastfeeding status, personal preferences, and health conditions in their recommendations.

9.5.1.2 Child Health Services

Immunizations, Nutrition, and Common Pediatric Issues

Pharmacists are also integral to child health services, providing essential care and guidance to ensure the well-being of children. Here are the key areas where pharmacists contribute to child health:

Immunizations:

1. **Vaccine Administration:** Pharmacists administer routine childhood vaccinations according to the recommended immunization schedule. This includes vaccines for diseases such as measles, mumps, rubella, polio, diphtheria, tetanus, pertussis, hepatitis B, influenza, and HPV (for older children and adolescents).

2. **Vaccine Education:** Pharmacists educate parents and caregivers about the importance of vaccinations, addressing concerns and dispelling

myths about vaccine safety and efficacy. They provide information on the diseases that vaccines prevent and the potential consequences of not vaccinating.

3. **Vaccine Record Keeping:** Pharmacists help maintain accurate immunization records for children, ensuring that they are up-to-date with their vaccines. They also provide reminders for upcoming vaccinations and booster doses.

Nutrition:

1. **Nutritional Counseling:** Pharmacists provide guidance on proper nutrition for infants, children, and adolescents. This includes advice on breastfeeding, formula feeding, introducing solid foods, and ensuring a balanced diet that supports growth and development.
2. **Supplements:** Pharmacists recommend appropriate nutritional supplements when necessary, such as vitamin D for infants, iron supplements for children at risk of deficiency, and multivitamins for picky eaters.
3. **Managing Dietary Restrictions:** For children with food allergies, intolerances, or specific dietary needs (such as celiac disease or lactose intolerance), pharmacists offer advice on managing these conditions and ensuring adequate nutrition.

Common Pediatric Issues:

1. **Acute Illnesses:** Pharmacists assist in managing common pediatric illnesses such as colds, flu, ear infections, and gastrointestinal issues. They recommend appropriate OTC medications and provide advice on symptom management and when to seek medical attention.
2. **Chronic Conditions:** For children with chronic conditions such as asthma, diabetes, or epilepsy, pharmacists provide ongoing support and education on medication management, adherence, and monitoring. They also offer tools and resources to help parents and caregivers manage these conditions effectively.
3. **Developmental Concerns:** Pharmacists identify and address developmental concerns, advising parents on appropriate interventions and referrals to specialists if needed. This includes guidance on speech and language development, motor skills, and behavioral issues.

4. **Safety and Injury Prevention:** Pharmacists educate parents and caregivers on safety measures to prevent injuries, such as childproofing the home, using car seats correctly, and ensuring safe sleep practices for infants.

By providing comprehensive maternal and child health services, pharmacists play a vital role in promoting the health and well-being of women and children. Their expertise and accessibility make them valuable resources for families, helping to ensure positive health outcomes and addressing the unique needs of this population.

9.5.1.3 Education and Support for Mothers

Providing comprehensive education and support for mothers is a critical component of maternal and child health services offered by pharmacists. By offering guidance on breastfeeding, nutrition, and childcare, pharmacists can help mothers make informed decisions, promote healthy practices, and ensure the well-being of both mother and child. Here are key areas of focus for educating and supporting mothers:

Breastfeeding Support and Education

1. Benefits of Breastfeeding: Educate mothers on the numerous benefits of breastfeeding for both the baby and the mother. Breastfeeding provides optimal nutrition, strengthens the baby's immune system, promotes bonding, and offers health benefits such as reduced risk of infections, allergies, and chronic conditions for the baby, and lower risk of breast and ovarian cancer for the mother.

2. Breastfeeding Techniques: Provide practical advice on breastfeeding techniques, including proper latch-on methods, positioning, and frequency of feeding. Pharmacists can offer tips to ensure a comfortable and effective breastfeeding experience, such as using pillows for support and finding a quiet, relaxing environment.

3. Managing Common Challenges: Help mothers address common breastfeeding challenges, such as sore nipples, engorgement, mastitis, and low milk supply. Offer solutions such as proper latch techniques, breast massage, warm compresses, and breastfeeding positions that can alleviate discomfort. Recommend consulting a lactation consultant for persistent issues.

4. Pumping and Storing Breast Milk: Guide mothers on how to use breast pumps, expressing and storing breast milk safely, and maintaining milk supply when returning to work or needing to be away from the baby.

Provide information on proper storage containers, refrigeration, and thawing techniques to preserve milk quality.

5. Supportive Products: Recommend supportive products such as nursing pads, nipple creams, breast pumps, and nursing bras that can enhance the breastfeeding experience and address common issues. Inform mothers about where to find these products and how to use them effectively.

Nutrition for Mothers and Infants

1. Nutritional Needs During Pregnancy and Lactation: Educate mothers about the importance of a balanced diet during pregnancy and lactation. Highlight the need for essential nutrients such as folic acid, iron, calcium, omega-3 fatty acids, and vitamins A, C, and D. Provide guidance on maintaining a nutritious diet that includes a variety of fruits, vegetables, whole grains, lean proteins, and dairy products.

2. Introducing Solid Foods: Advise mothers on when and how to introduce solid foods to their infants, typically around six months of age. Discuss the types of first foods, appropriate textures, and how to introduce new foods gradually to monitor for allergies or intolerances. Encourage the inclusion of iron-rich foods and a variety of fruits and vegetables.

3. Healthy Eating Habits: Promote the development of healthy eating habits for the entire family. Encourage regular family meals, limiting sugary and processed foods, and fostering a positive attitude towards food. Discuss portion sizes, meal planning, and the importance of hydration.

4. Addressing Nutritional Concerns: Help mothers manage specific nutritional concerns, such as food allergies, intolerances, and picky eating behaviors in children. Provide strategies for ensuring adequate nutrition despite these challenges and suggest appropriate dietary supplements if needed.

Childcare Education and Support

1. Childcare Basics: Offer guidance on essential childcare practices, including bathing, diapering, and dressing infants. Provide tips for maintaining a safe and hygienic environment, such as proper handwashing techniques and safe sleep practices to reduce the risk of sudden infant death syndrome (SIDS).

2. Developmental Milestones: Educate mothers on key developmental milestones for infants and young children, such as motor skills, language development, and social interactions. Discuss the typical timeline for these milestones and encourage regular check-ups with pediatricians to monitor progress.

3. Health and Safety: Provide information on childproofing the home, safe use of car seats, and first aid for common childhood injuries. Emphasize the importance of vaccinations and regular health screenings to ensure the child's well-being.

4. Emotional Support and Mental Health: Recognize the emotional and mental health needs of new mothers. Offer support and resources for managing postpartum depression, anxiety, and stress. Encourage mothers to seek help from healthcare providers or support groups if they experience overwhelming emotions or difficulties adjusting to motherhood.

Building a Supportive Community

1. Support Groups and Resources: Connect mothers with local support groups, online communities, and parenting resources. These platforms can provide valuable peer support, shared experiences, and practical advice. Inform mothers about available community programs, parenting classes, and workshops.

2. Follow-Up and Continuous Support: Schedule regular follow-up consultations to address ongoing concerns, provide additional guidance, and celebrate successes. Continuous support helps mothers feel confident and empowered in their parenting journey.

3. Customized Care: Tailor educational materials and counseling sessions to meet the specific needs of each mother and child. Consider cultural, social, and individual preferences when providing advice and support.

By offering comprehensive education and support on breastfeeding, nutrition, and childcare, pharmacists can significantly enhance the health and well-being of mothers and their children. This support fosters informed decision-making, promotes healthy practices, and ensures that mothers have the resources they need to navigate the challenges of motherhood successfully.

9.6 National Health Programs

9.6.1 Role of Community Pharmacists in Malaria and TB Control

9.6.1.1 Overview of National Health Programs

Introduction to Key National Health Programs and Their Objectives

National health programs are government-led initiatives aimed at addressing major public health challenges and improving the overall health of the population. These programs are designed to control, prevent, and eliminate diseases, enhance health outcomes, and promote health equity.

Community pharmacists play a crucial role in supporting these programs by providing education, screening, treatment, and referral services. Key national health programs in India include the National Vector Borne Disease Control Programme (NVBDCP) and the Revised National Tuberculosis Control Programme (RNTCP).

9.6.1.2 Malaria Control Initiatives

Malaria is a significant public health challenge in India, and the National Vector Borne Disease Control Programme (NVBDCP) is a comprehensive initiative aimed at reducing the incidence and mortality associated with malaria. Community pharmacists contribute to malaria control through various activities, including awareness, prevention, diagnosis, and treatment.

Awareness and Education

Public Education Campaigns: Pharmacists can participate in public education campaigns to raise awareness about malaria prevention and control. They can provide information on the transmission of malaria, symptoms, and the importance of early diagnosis and treatment. Pharmacists can distribute educational materials such as brochures, posters, and leaflets in the pharmacy and the community.

Personal Protective Measures: Educate the community about personal protective measures to prevent mosquito bites, such as using insecticide-treated bed nets (ITNs), wearing long-sleeved clothing, and applying insect repellent. Pharmacists can also demonstrate the proper use of these protective measures and encourage their consistent use.

Environmental Control: Advise the community on environmental control measures to reduce mosquito breeding sites. This includes eliminating standing water, covering water storage containers, and using larvicides. Pharmacists can collaborate with local health authorities to promote community-wide initiatives for vector control.

Prevention

Chemoprophylaxis: Provide information on chemoprophylaxis for travelers to malaria-endemic areas. Pharmacists can counsel travelers on the appropriate use of antimalarial medications, such as chloroquine, doxycycline, or atovaquone-proguanil, and the importance of completing the full course of prophylaxis.

Insecticide-Treated Nets (ITNs): Promote the use of ITNs, which are highly effective in preventing malaria. Pharmacists can distribute ITNs and educate the community on their proper use and maintenance.

Diagnosis and Treatment

Rapid Diagnostic Tests (RDTs): Pharmacists can use RDTs to facilitate the early diagnosis of malaria. RDTs provide quick results, enabling prompt treatment and reducing the risk of severe disease and transmission. Pharmacists should be trained in the proper use and interpretation of RDTs.

Antimalarial Medications: Dispense antimalarial medications according to national treatment guidelines. Pharmacists should ensure the availability of first-line antimalarials, such as artemisinin-based combination therapies (ACTs), and educate patients on the importance of adherence to the prescribed treatment regimen to achieve a complete cure and prevent drug resistance.

Management of Complications: Recognize the signs and symptoms of severe malaria and refer patients to appropriate healthcare facilities for advanced care. Pharmacists should educate the community about the importance of seeking medical attention for severe symptoms, such as high fever, convulsions, and altered consciousness.

Monitoring and Surveillance

Recording and Reporting: Pharmacists can assist in the monitoring and surveillance of malaria cases by maintaining accurate records of diagnosed cases and treatments provided. This data can be reported to local health authorities to support disease surveillance and control efforts.

Follow-Up: Conduct follow-up consultations to ensure that patients have completed their treatment and to monitor for any adverse reactions or complications. Pharmacists can also provide additional counseling on preventing future malaria infections.

Collaboration with Health Authorities

Integrated Vector Management (IVM): Collaborate with local health authorities to implement integrated vector management strategies, which combine multiple approaches to control mosquito populations and reduce malaria transmission.

Community Engagement: Engage with community leaders, schools, and organizations to promote malaria prevention and control initiatives. Pharmacists can participate in community meetings and health fairs to disseminate information and encourage community involvement.

By actively participating in malaria control initiatives, community pharmacists can significantly contribute to reducing the burden of malaria and improving public health outcomes. Their role in education, prevention, diagnosis, treatment, and collaboration with health authorities is essential for the success of national malaria control programs.

9.6 National Health Programs

9.6.1 Role of Community Pharmacists in Malaria and TB Control

9.6.1.1 Overview of National Health Programs

Introduction to Key National Health Programs and Their Objectives

National health programs are government-led initiatives aimed at addressing major public health challenges and improving the overall health of the population. These programs are designed to control, prevent, and eliminate diseases, enhance health outcomes, and promote health equity. Community pharmacists play a crucial role in supporting these programs by providing education, screening, treatment, and referral services. Key national health programs in India include the National Vector Borne Disease Control Programme (NVBDCP) and the Revised National Tuberculosis Control Programme (RNTCP).

9.6.1.2 Malaria Control Initiatives

Awareness and Education

Public Education Campaigns: Pharmacists can participate in public education campaigns to raise awareness about malaria prevention and control. They can provide information on the transmission of malaria, symptoms, and the importance of early diagnosis and treatment. Pharmacists can distribute educational materials such as brochures, posters, and leaflets in the pharmacy and the community.

Personal Protective Measures: Educate the community about personal protective measures to prevent mosquito bites, such as using insecticide-treated bed nets (ITNs), wearing long-sleeved clothing, and applying insect repellent. Pharmacists can also demonstrate the proper use of these protective measures and encourage their consistent use.

Environmental Control: Advise the community on environmental control measures to reduce mosquito breeding sites. This includes eliminating standing water, covering water storage containers, and using larvicides. Pharmacists can collaborate with local health authorities to promote community-wide initiatives for vector control.

Prevention

Chemoprophylaxis: Provide information on chemoprophylaxis for travelers to malaria-endemic areas. Pharmacists can counsel travelers on the appropriate use of antimalarial medications, such as chloroquine, doxycycline, or atovaquone-proguanil, and the importance of completing the full course of prophylaxis.

Insecticide-Treated Nets (ITNs): Promote the use of ITNs, which are highly effective in preventing malaria. Pharmacists can distribute ITNs and educate the community on their proper use and maintenance.

Diagnosis and Treatment

Rapid Diagnostic Tests (RDTs): Pharmacists can use RDTs to facilitate the early diagnosis of malaria. RDTs provide quick results, enabling prompt treatment and reducing the risk of severe disease and transmission. Pharmacists should be trained in the proper use and interpretation of RDTs.

Antimalarial Medications: Dispense antimalarial medications according to national treatment guidelines. Pharmacists should ensure the availability of first-line antimalarials, such as artemisinin-based combination therapies (ACTs), and educate patients on the importance of adherence to the prescribed treatment regimen to achieve a complete cure and prevent drug resistance.

Management of Complications: Recognize the signs and symptoms of severe malaria and refer patients to appropriate healthcare facilities for advanced care. Pharmacists should educate the community about the importance of seeking medical attention for severe symptoms, such as high fever, convulsions, and altered consciousness.

Monitoring and Surveillance

Recording and Reporting: Pharmacists can assist in the monitoring and surveillance of malaria cases by maintaining accurate records of diagnosed cases and treatments provided. This data can be reported to local health authorities to support disease surveillance and control efforts.

Follow-Up: Conduct follow-up consultations to ensure that patients have completed their treatment and to monitor for any adverse reactions or complications. Pharmacists can also provide additional counseling on preventing future malaria infections.

Collaboration with Health Authorities

Integrated Vector Management (IVM): Collaborate with local health authorities to implement integrated vector management strategies, which combine multiple approaches to control mosquito populations and reduce malaria transmission.

Community Engagement: Engage with community leaders, schools, and organizations to promote malaria prevention and control initiatives. Pharmacists can participate in community meetings and health fairs to disseminate information and encourage community involvement.

9.6.1.3 TB Control Programs

Contribution of Community Pharmacists in the Detection, Treatment, and Management of Tuberculosis

Tuberculosis (TB) remains a major public health challenge in India, and the Revised National Tuberculosis Control Programme (RNTCP) is a critical initiative aimed at reducing the incidence and mortality associated with TB. Community pharmacists play an essential role in supporting TB control programs through various activities, including early detection, treatment adherence, patient education, and monitoring.

Early Detection

Symptom Recognition: Pharmacists can be trained to recognize the symptoms of TB, such as a persistent cough lasting more than two weeks, weight loss, fever, and night sweats. Early detection is crucial for prompt treatment and reducing the spread of TB.

Screening Programs: Participate in community-based screening programs to identify suspected TB cases. Pharmacists can refer patients with symptoms suggestive of TB to designated TB diagnostic centers for further evaluation and testing.

Patient Education: Educate the community about TB symptoms, transmission, and the importance of seeking medical attention for prolonged respiratory symptoms. Pharmacists can distribute educational materials and engage in discussions with patients to raise awareness about TB.

Treatment Adherence

Directly Observed Treatment, Short-course (DOTS): Support the implementation of the DOTS strategy by ensuring that patients adhere to their TB treatment regimen. Pharmacists can supervise the intake of medication, monitor side effects, and provide encouragement to patients throughout the treatment course.

Medication Management: Dispense anti-TB medications according to national treatment guidelines. Pharmacists should ensure the availability of first-line anti-TB drugs and provide counseling on the importance of completing the full course of treatment to achieve a cure and prevent drug resistance.

Adherence Support: Implement adherence support strategies, such as reminder systems, follow-up calls, and pill organizers, to help patients maintain their treatment regimen. Pharmacists can also engage family members and caregivers in supporting the patient's adherence to treatment.

Patient Education and Counseling

Understanding TB Treatment: Provide patients with clear information about their TB treatment plan, including the duration of treatment, possible side effects, and the importance of adherence. Pharmacists should use simple language and visual aids to enhance understanding.

Managing Side Effects: Educate patients about common side effects of anti-TB medications and how to manage them. Pharmacists can offer advice on minimizing side effects and when to seek medical attention for severe reactions.

Reducing Stigma: Address the stigma associated with TB by educating patients and the community about the disease. Pharmacists can promote a supportive environment that encourages patients to seek treatment and adhere to their medication regimen without fear of discrimination.

Monitoring and Follow-Up

Adverse Drug Reactions: Monitor patients for adverse drug reactions (ADRs) to anti-TB medications and report any significant reactions to the appropriate health authorities. Pharmacists should provide guidance on managing mild ADRs and refer patients for further evaluation if needed.

Treatment Outcomes: Track the progress of patients undergoing TB treatment and document treatment outcomes. Pharmacists can collaborate with healthcare providers to ensure that patients receive appropriate follow-up care and support throughout their treatment journey.

9.6.1.4 Collaboration with Health Authorities

Working with Public Health Authorities to Implement and Support Health Programs

Collaboration between community pharmacists and public health authorities is essential for the successful implementation and support of national health programs. By working together, pharmacists and health authorities can enhance the effectiveness of disease control initiatives, improve patient outcomes, and strengthen public health systems.

Integrated Health Services

Coordination: Establish effective communication channels between community pharmacists and public health authorities to coordinate health services and activities. Pharmacists can participate in regular meetings, workshops, and training sessions organized by health authorities to stay informed about the latest guidelines and best practices.

Referral Systems: Develop and maintain efficient referral systems to ensure that patients receive timely and appropriate care. Pharmacists can refer patients to designated health facilities for diagnostic testing, specialized treatment, and follow-up care as needed.

Health Campaigns: Collaborate on health campaigns and outreach programs to raise awareness about key public health issues. Pharmacists can support vaccination drives, health screening events, and educational campaigns by providing information, resources, and services to the community.

Data Sharing and Surveillance

Reporting Systems: Contribute to public health surveillance by accurately recording and reporting cases of infectious diseases, adverse drug reactions, and other health events. Pharmacists can use standardized reporting systems to share data with health authorities, supporting disease monitoring and control efforts.

Data Analysis: Participate in data analysis and feedback sessions organized by health authorities. Pharmacists can provide valuable insights based on their interactions with patients and community members, helping to identify trends, challenges, and opportunities for improvement.

Capacity Building and Training

Training Programs: Engage in continuous professional development through training programs offered by public health authorities. Pharmacists can enhance their knowledge and skills in areas such as disease prevention, patient counseling, and medication management.

Resource Sharing: Access and utilize resources provided by health authorities, such as educational materials, guidelines, and toolkits. Pharmacists can also share their expertise and best practices with other healthcare providers, contributing to the overall capacity building of the healthcare system.

By actively collaborating with public health authorities, community pharmacists can play a pivotal role in advancing national health programs and improving the health and well-being of the communities they serve. Their contributions to disease prevention, patient education, treatment adherence, and public health surveillance are integral to the success of these initiatives.

CHAPTER TEN

Research and Home Medicines Review Programs

10.1 Home Medicines Review Program

10.1.1 Definition, Objectives, and Guidelines
10.1.1.1 Definition of Home Medicines Review (HMR)
Explanation of the HMR Program and Its Purpose

The **Home Medicines Review (HMR)** program is a collaborative healthcare initiative aimed at optimizing medication management and improving health outcomes for patients, particularly those with complex medication regimens or chronic conditions. This program involves a comprehensive assessment of a patient's medications conducted in their home environment by a qualified healthcare professional, typically a pharmacist. The primary objectives of the HMR program are to enhance the safe and effective use of medicines, identify and resolve medication-related problems, and promote adherence to prescribed therapies.

The HMR process begins with a referral from a general practitioner (GP) or another healthcare provider who identifies a patient that could benefit from a thorough medication review. Once the referral is made, a pharmacist visits the patient's home to conduct a detailed evaluation of all medications the patient is taking, including prescription drugs, over-the-counter (OTC) products, herbal remedies, and supplements. During the visit, the pharmacist reviews the patient's medication regimen, assesses their understanding of their medications, checks for potential drug interactions, evaluates adherence, and identifies any issues that may affect the patient's health outcomes.

The findings from the home visit are documented in a comprehensive report, which is then shared with the referring GP. The GP reviews the pharmacist's recommendations and collaborates with the patient to implement any necessary changes to their medication regimen. This collaborative approach ensures that the patient receives a tailored medication management plan that addresses their specific needs and concerns.

The purpose of the HMR program is multi-faceted:

- **Improving Medication Safety:** By identifying and mitigating medication-related risks, the HMR program aims to prevent adverse drug reactions, medication errors, and potential hospitalizations.
- **Enhancing Medication Adherence:** Through personalized education and support, the program helps patients better understand their medications and the importance of adhering to their prescribed treatment plans.
- **Optimizing Therapeutic Outcomes:** The program seeks to ensure that patients achieve the maximum therapeutic benefit from their medications by addressing any issues that may impede their effectiveness.
- **Supporting Self-Management:** By empowering patients with knowledge and resources, the HMR program promotes self-management of chronic conditions and overall health.

10.1 Home Medicines Review Program
10.1.1 Definition, Objectives, and Guidelines
10.1.1.2 Objectives of HMR

Goals of Improving Medication Management and Patient Outcomes

The **Home Medicines Review (HMR)** program is designed to achieve several key objectives aimed at improving medication management and enhancing patient outcomes. The goals of the HMR program are as follows:

1. Enhance Medication Safety

Preventing Adverse Drug Reactions: One of the primary objectives of the HMR program is to identify and mitigate potential adverse drug reactions (ADRs). By thoroughly reviewing all medications a patient is taking, including prescription drugs, over-the-counter (OTC) products, herbal remedies, and supplements, pharmacists can spot potential interactions and contraindications that may lead to harmful effects.

Reducing Medication Errors: The HMR program aims to reduce medication errors, such as incorrect dosages, improper administration, and duplicate therapies. By evaluating the patient's medication regimen in their home environment, pharmacists can ensure that medications are taken correctly and safely.

2. Improve Medication Adherence

Educating Patients: Providing patients with personalized education about their medications is a key objective of the HMR program. Pharmacists explain the purpose of each medication, proper dosing schedules, and potential side effects, helping patients understand the importance of adherence to their prescribed treatments.

Addressing Barriers to Adherence: The HMR program seeks to identify and address barriers that may prevent patients from adhering to their medication regimens. These barriers may include forgetfulness, complex dosing schedules, side effects, and financial constraints. Pharmacists work with patients to develop strategies to overcome these obstacles, such as using pill organizers, setting reminders, or discussing cost-effective alternatives with their healthcare provider.

3. Optimize Therapeutic Outcomes

Personalized Medication Management: The HMR program aims to optimize therapeutic outcomes by ensuring that each patient's medication regimen is tailored to their specific health needs. Pharmacists assess the effectiveness of current therapies and make recommendations for adjustments, such as changing dosages, adding or discontinuing medications, or considering alternative treatments.

Monitoring Chronic Conditions: By regularly reviewing and monitoring medications, the HMR program helps manage chronic conditions more effectively. Pharmacists can identify suboptimal treatment regimens and collaborate with healthcare providers to make necessary adjustments, ensuring better control of conditions such as diabetes, hypertension, and asthma.

4. Promote Patient Empowerment and Self-Management

Encouraging Self-Management: The HMR program empowers patients by providing them with the knowledge and tools they need to manage their health independently. By understanding their medications and how to use them correctly, patients are better equipped to take an active role in their healthcare.

Supporting Health Literacy: Improving health literacy is a key goal of the HMR program. Pharmacists provide clear, understandable information about medications and health conditions, helping patients make informed decisions about their care.

5. Strengthen Collaborative Care

Facilitating Communication: The HMR program promotes collaboration and communication between patients, pharmacists, and other healthcare providers. By sharing detailed medication review reports and recommendations with the referring GP, pharmacists ensure that all members of the healthcare team are informed and can work together to optimize patient care.

Coordinating Care: The HMR program helps coordinate care by ensuring that all aspects of a patient's medication regimen are considered. This includes addressing potential drug interactions, aligning medication schedules with the patient's daily routine, and ensuring that treatments from multiple healthcare providers are harmonized.

6. Reduce Healthcare Costs

Preventing Hospitalizations: By identifying and addressing medication-related issues early, the HMR program can prevent complications that may lead to hospitalizations. This not only improves patient outcomes but also reduces the overall burden on the healthcare system.

Optimizing Resource Use: The HMR program helps optimize the use of healthcare resources by ensuring that medications are used effectively and efficiently. This includes avoiding unnecessary or duplicate therapies and promoting cost-effective treatment options.

In summary, the objectives of the HMR program are centered on improving medication management, enhancing patient outcomes, promoting patient empowerment, strengthening collaborative care, and reducing healthcare costs. By achieving these goals, the HMR program plays a vital role in ensuring safe, effective, and personalized medication management for patients, particularly those with complex health needs.

10.1 Home Medicines Reviewa Program

10.1.1 Definition, Objectives, and Guidelines

10.1.1.3 Guidelines for Conducting HMR

Step-by-Step Procedures and Protocols for Implementing HMR

Conducting a Home Medicines Review (HMR) involves a systematic process that ensures thorough evaluation and management of a patient's medication regimen. Here are the step-by-step procedures and protocols for implementing an effective HMR:

1. Referral and Initial Contact

Identification of Eligible Patients: Healthcare providers, typically general practitioners (GPs), identify patients who may benefit from an HMR. These patients often have complex medication regimens, multiple chronic conditions, recent hospitalizations, or evidence of medication-related problems.

Referral Process: The GP formally refers the patient for an HMR by completing a referral form that includes relevant medical and medication history. This form is then sent to a qualified pharmacist trained in conducting HMRs.

Initial Contact: The pharmacist contacts the patient to explain the purpose and benefits of the HMR, obtain consent, and schedule a convenient time for the home visit.

2. Preparation for the Home Visit

Review of Patient Information: Before the home visit, the pharmacist reviews the patient's medical history, current medications, and any specific concerns noted by the GP. This preparation helps the pharmacist identify potential areas of focus during the review.

Gathering Tools and Materials: The pharmacist ensures they have all necessary tools and materials for the visit, such as medication review forms, educational materials, and any diagnostic tools (e.g., blood pressure monitor).

3. Conducting the Home Visit

Medication Reconciliation: During the home visit, the pharmacist performs a thorough medication reconciliation. This involves reviewing all medications the patient is taking, including prescription drugs, over-the-counter (OTC) products, herbal remedies, and supplements. The pharmacist verifies that the patient is taking the medications as prescribed and checks for expired or unused medications.

Assessment of Medication Use: The pharmacist assesses how the patient uses their medications, including dosage, frequency, timing, and any issues with administration. They also evaluate the patient's understanding of their medications and adherence to the prescribed regimen.

Identification of Medication-Related Problems: The pharmacist identifies any medication-related problems, such as drug interactions, side effects, duplicate therapies, incorrect dosages, and barriers to adherence. They also assess the appropriateness of each medication for the patient's current health status.

Patient Education and Counseling: The pharmacist provides education and counseling to the patient, addressing any questions or concerns they have about their medications. They offer guidance on proper medication use, potential side effects, and strategies for improving adherence.

Documentation: The pharmacist documents all findings from the home visit, including a detailed list of the patient's medications, identified issues, and recommendations for resolving medication-related problems.

4. Development of the Medication Management Plan

Collaborative Recommendations: Based on the assessment, the pharmacist develops a set of recommendations to optimize the patient's medication regimen. These recommendations may include changes to medication dosages, discontinuation of unnecessary medications, addition of new therapies, and strategies to address adherence issues.

Report Preparation: The pharmacist prepares a comprehensive report summarizing the findings and recommendations from the HMR. This report is shared with the referring GP and any other relevant healthcare providers involved in the patient's care.

5. Follow-Up and Monitoring

Review by GP: The GP reviews the pharmacist's report and recommendations, discusses them with the patient, and makes any necessary changes to the medication regimen. The GP may also schedule follow-up appointments to monitor the patient's progress.

Patient Follow-Up: The pharmacist conducts follow-up calls or visits to ensure that the patient understands and is following the updated medication plan. They address any new concerns or questions and continue to provide support for medication adherence.

Ongoing Monitoring: The pharmacist and GP work together to monitor the patient's medication regimen over time. This may include periodic reviews to assess the effectiveness of the treatment plan, identify any new issues, and make further adjustments as needed.

6. Continuous Improvement

Feedback and Evaluation: The pharmacist seeks feedback from the patient and GP on the HMR process and its outcomes. This feedback helps identify areas for improvement and enhances the quality of future reviews.

Professional Development: The pharmacist engages in ongoing professional development to stay updated on best practices, new medications, and guidelines for medication management. This ensures that they can provide the highest standard of care during HMRs.

By following these step-by-step procedures and protocols, pharmacists can conduct effective Home Medicines Reviews that improve medication management, enhance patient outcomes, and promote safe and effective use of medications.

10.1 Home Medicines Review Program

10.1.2 Methods and Expected Outcomes

10.1.2.1 Methods of Conducting HMR

Techniques for Reviewing and Assessing Patient Medications in a Home Setting

Conducting a Home Medicines Review (HMR) in a home setting involves various techniques to ensure a comprehensive assessment of a patient's medication regimen. These methods aim to identify medication-related problems, enhance medication adherence, and optimize therapeutic outcomes. Here are the key techniques for reviewing and assessing patient medications during an HMR:

1. Comprehensive Medication Reconciliation

Gathering Medication Information: Begin by collecting all medications the patient is currently taking. This includes prescription drugs, over-the-counter (OTC) medications, herbal remedies, vitamins, and dietary supplements. Ask the patient to gather all their medications, including those stored in different locations within the home.

Verification with Patient Records: Cross-check the gathered medications with the patient's medical records and the referral information provided by the GP. This helps ensure that all medications are accounted for and provides context for the review.

Documentation: Create a detailed list of all medications, including the name, dosage, frequency, route of administration, and indication for each medication. Note any discrepancies between what the patient is taking and what is prescribed.

2. Patient Interview and Assessment

Medical and Medication History: Conduct a thorough interview to gather information about the patient's medical history, current health status, and past experiences with medications. This includes discussing any allergies, adverse reactions, and hospitalizations.

Medication Use and Adherence: Assess how the patient takes their medications, including the timing, dosage, and any missed doses. Inquire about the patient's understanding of their medications and reasons for non-adherence, if applicable.

Symptom and Side Effect Evaluation: Ask the patient about any symptoms or side effects they are experiencing. Assess whether these could be related to their medications or underlying health conditions.

3. Assessment of Medication Management Practices

Storage and Organization: Evaluate how the patient stores and organizes their medications. Check for proper storage conditions, such as keeping medications away from heat and moisture, and assess the use of pill organizers or other tools to aid adherence.

Administration Techniques: Observe the patient's technique for administering medications, especially for those requiring specific methods, such as inhalers, injections, or eye drops. Provide guidance on correct techniques if needed.

Use of Assistive Devices: Assess the patient's use of assistive devices, such as pill dispensers, medication reminders, or mobility aids, that can support medication management.

4. Identification of Medication-Related Problems

Drug Interactions: Review the patient's medications for potential drug-drug interactions, drug-food interactions, and interactions with herbal supplements. Use clinical decision support tools and drug interaction databases to aid in this process.

Duplication of Therapy: Check for duplicate therapies where the patient may be taking multiple medications with the same therapeutic effect. This can occur with both prescription and OTC medications.

Appropriateness of Therapy: Evaluate whether each medication is appropriate for the patient's current health status and conditions. Consider the effectiveness, necessity, and potential risks of each medication.

Adverse Drug Reactions: Identify any adverse drug reactions the patient may be experiencing and assess the severity and impact on the patient's health.

5. Personalized Patient Education and Counseling

Medication Education: Provide the patient with detailed information about each medication, including its purpose, expected benefits, potential side effects, and proper administration. Use simple language and visual aids to enhance understanding.

Addressing Concerns: Address any concerns or misconceptions the patient has about their medications. Encourage open communication and provide reassurance to build trust and confidence in their treatment plan.

Adherence Strategies: Develop personalized strategies to improve medication adherence, such as setting up a medication schedule, using reminders, or simplifying the regimen where possible. Collaborate with the patient to find solutions that fit their lifestyle.

6. Collaboration and Reporting

Collaborative Recommendations: After completing the assessment, develop a set of recommendations to optimize the patient's medication regimen. These may include changes to dosages, discontinuation of unnecessary medications, initiation of new therapies, or addressing adherence issues.

Comprehensive Report: Prepare a detailed report summarizing the findings of the HMR, including the medication list, identified issues, and recommended actions. Share this report with the referring GP and other relevant healthcare providers involved in the patient's care.

Follow-Up and Support: Schedule follow-up visits or calls to monitor the patient's progress, provide ongoing support, and address any new issues that arise. Ensure continuous communication with the healthcare team to coordinate care.

By employing these techniques, pharmacists can conduct thorough and effective Home Medicines Reviews, leading to improved medication management, enhanced patient outcomes, and a higher quality of care in the community.

10.1 Home Medicines Review Program

10.1.2 Methods and Expected Outcomes

10.1.2.2 Expected Outcomes of HMR

Benefits such as Improved Medication Adherence, Reduced Hospital Admissions, and Enhanced Patient Safety

The Home Medicines Review (HMR) program is designed to optimize medication management and improve health outcomes for patients. By conducting comprehensive medication reviews in a home setting, HMR aims to identify and resolve medication-related issues, educate patients, and enhance the overall quality of care. The expected outcomes of HMR are multifaceted, encompassing clinical, economic, and patient-centered benefits. Here are the key expected outcomes of the HMR program:

1. Improved Medication Adherence

Enhanced Understanding: Through patient education and counseling, HMR helps patients understand the importance of their medications, how to take them correctly, and the expected benefits. This increased understanding leads to better adherence to prescribed regimens.

Personalized Strategies: By identifying barriers to adherence, such as complex regimens, side effects, or forgetfulness, pharmacists can develop personalized strategies to help patients take their medications as prescribed. These strategies may include simplifying medication schedules, using reminders, or employing pill organizers.

Patient Engagement: Engaging patients in their medication management through active participation and empowerment fosters a sense of responsibility and commitment to adhering to their treatment plans.

2. Reduced Hospital Admissions

Early Identification of Issues: HMR enables the early detection of medication-related problems, such as potential drug interactions, adverse drug reactions, or inappropriate therapies. Addressing these issues promptly can prevent complications that might otherwise lead to hospital admissions.

Prevention of Adverse Events: By closely monitoring patients and providing timely interventions, HMR reduces the risk of adverse drug events (ADEs) that could necessitate hospital visits. This includes managing chronic conditions more effectively and preventing acute exacerbations.

Continuity of Care: HMR promotes continuity of care by ensuring that medication changes and management plans are communicated effectively among healthcare providers. This coordination helps prevent gaps in care that could lead to hospitalizations.

3. Enhanced Patient Safety

Comprehensive Medication Review: Conducting thorough medication reviews allows pharmacists to identify and mitigate risks associated with polypharmacy, inappropriate prescribing, and potential medication errors. This comprehensive approach enhances patient safety.

Education on Adverse Drug Reactions: Educating patients about the potential side effects of their medications and what to do if they experience an adverse reaction ensures that they can respond appropriately and seek timely medical attention.

Proper Medication Use: Ensuring that patients use their medications correctly, including proper administration techniques and adherence to dosing schedules, reduces the risk of medication errors and enhances therapeutic outcomes.

4. Improved Health Outcomes

Optimized Therapy: By tailoring medication regimens to the individual needs of patients, HMR ensures that therapies are both effective and safe. This optimization leads to better management of chronic conditions and overall health improvement.

Patient Satisfaction: Personalized care and attention during HMR visits increase patient satisfaction and trust in the healthcare system. Satisfied patients are more likely to engage in their care and adhere to treatment plans.

Quality of Life: Addressing medication-related issues, reducing side effects, and improving adherence contribute to enhanced quality of life for patients. They experience fewer symptoms, better disease control, and improved overall well-being.

5. Cost-Effectiveness

Reduced Healthcare Costs: By preventing hospital admissions and minimizing adverse drug events, HMR contributes to significant cost savings for the healthcare system. This includes lower emergency room visits, reduced hospital stays, and decreased need for additional medical interventions.

Efficient Resource Utilization: Effective medication management through HMR ensures that healthcare resources are used efficiently. Patients receive appropriate therapies, avoiding unnecessary treatments and reducing wastage of medications.

6. Strengthened Healthcare Relationships

Collaboration with Healthcare Providers: HMR fosters strong collaborative relationships between pharmacists, GPs, and other healthcare providers. This collaboration ensures coordinated care and a holistic approach to patient management.

Patient-Provider Trust: Building rapport and trust with patients through regular home visits and personalized care strengthens the patient-provider relationship. Patients feel more comfortable discussing their concerns and following medical advice.

In summary, the Home Medicines Review program offers numerous benefits that collectively enhance patient care, improve medication adherence, reduce hospital admissions, and ensure patient safety. By addressing medication-related issues and providing tailored education and support, HMR plays a crucial role in optimizing health outcomes and improving the quality of life for patients in the community.

10.1 Home Medicines Review Program

10.1.2 Methods and Expected Outcomes

10.1.2.3 Documentation and Follow-Up

Importance of Accurate Documentation and Continuous Follow-Up with Patients

Accurate Documentation

Comprehensive Records: Accurate documentation is essential in the Home Medicines Review (HMR) process. It involves maintaining detailed records of all medications the patient is taking, including prescription drugs, over-the-counter (OTC) medications, herbal remedies, vitamins, and supplements. This comprehensive record ensures that all aspects of the patient's medication regimen are considered during the review.

Medication History: Documenting the patient's medication history, including any changes made to their regimen over time, helps track the effectiveness and safety of treatments. It also provides a clear timeline of medication use, which is crucial for identifying patterns and potential issues.

Identification of Issues: Detailed documentation of identified medication-related problems, such as drug interactions, adverse drug reactions, inappropriate therapies, and barriers to adherence, allows for precise tracking and follow-up. Recording these issues ensures that they are addressed and resolved promptly.

Recommendations: The pharmacist's recommendations for optimizing the patient's medication regimen should be clearly documented. This includes suggested changes to dosages, discontinuation of unnecessary medications, initiation of new therapies, and strategies to improve adherence. Clear documentation of these recommendations facilitates effective communication with other healthcare providers.

Patient Education and Counseling: Notes on the education and counseling provided to the patient during the HMR visit are important for continuity of care. Documenting what was discussed, the patient's understanding and concerns, and any agreed-upon strategies for adherence helps ensure that subsequent follow-ups are consistent and effective.

Communication with Healthcare Providers: Documentation serves as a formal record that can be shared with the referring GP and other relevant healthcare providers. This communication ensures that all members of the healthcare team are informed about the patient's medication management plan and can collaborate effectively.

Continuous Follow-Up

Monitoring Progress: Continuous follow-up is critical to monitor the patient's progress and ensure that the recommendations made during the HMR are being implemented effectively. Regular follow-ups allow the pharmacist to assess the patient's adherence to their medication regimen, address any new issues that arise, and provide ongoing support.

Addressing New Concerns: Patients may experience new symptoms, side effects, or changes in their health status after the initial HMR visit. Continuous follow-up provides an opportunity to address these concerns promptly and make necessary adjustments to the medication regimen.

Reinforcing Education: Follow-up visits or calls reinforce the education and counseling provided during the initial HMR. Repetition and reinforcement help ensure that the patient retains important information about their medications and understands how to manage their health effectively.

Adjusting Treatment Plans: As the patient's condition evolves, their medication needs may change. Continuous follow-up allows the pharmacist to work with the GP and other healthcare providers to adjust the treatment plan as needed. This dynamic approach ensures that the patient receives the most appropriate and effective therapies over time.

Building Patient-Provider Relationships: Regular follow-up helps build strong, trusting relationships between the patient and the healthcare team. Patients are more likely to feel supported and engaged in their care when they have consistent, ongoing contact with their healthcare providers.

Ensuring Compliance with Guidelines: Continuous follow-up ensures that the HMR process adheres to established guidelines and protocols. Regular reviews and updates of the patient's medication regimen help maintain compliance with best practices and standards of care.

Evaluation of Outcomes: Follow-up allows for the evaluation of the outcomes of the HMR. Assessing improvements in medication adherence, reduction in hospital admissions, enhanced patient safety, and overall health outcomes provides valuable feedback on the effectiveness of the program.

Feedback and Improvement: Gathering feedback from patients and healthcare providers during follow-up helps identify areas for improvement in the HMR process. This feedback can be used to refine techniques, enhance communication, and improve the overall quality of care.

In summary, accurate documentation and continuous follow-up are integral components of the Home Medicines Review program. They ensure that all aspects of the patient's medication regimen are thoroughly assessed, addressed, and monitored over time. By maintaining detailed records and providing ongoing support, pharmacists can optimize medication management, enhance patient outcomes, and promote safe and effective use of medications.

10.2 Research in Community Pharmacy Practice

10.2.1 Identifying Research Opportunities

10.2.1.1 Areas for Research in Community Pharmacy

Potential Research Topics Such as Medication Adherence, Patient Counseling, and Health Outcomes

Research in community pharmacy practice is essential for advancing the profession, improving patient care, and optimizing health outcomes. By identifying and exploring key areas for research, community pharmacists can contribute to evidence-based practice and the development of innovative solutions to healthcare challenges. Here are some potential research topics in community pharmacy:

1. Medication Adherence

Factors Influencing Adherence: Investigate the various factors that affect medication adherence, such as patient beliefs, socioeconomic status, health literacy, and the complexity of medication regimens. Understanding these factors can help develop targeted interventions to improve adherence.

Interventions to Improve Adherence: Evaluate the effectiveness of different interventions designed to enhance medication adherence, including medication synchronization, pill organizers, reminder systems, and pharmacist-led counseling. Research can compare the impact of these interventions on adherence rates and health outcomes.

Adherence in Chronic Conditions: Focus on adherence in patients with chronic conditions such as diabetes, hypertension, and asthma. Research can explore the barriers specific to these populations and identify strategies to support long-term adherence to prescribed therapies.

2. Patient Counseling

Counseling Techniques: Study the effectiveness of various patient counseling techniques, such as motivational interviewing, cognitive-behavioral therapy, and educational sessions. Research can assess how these techniques influence patient understanding, behavior change, and medication adherence.

Impact of Counseling on Health Outcomes: Investigate the impact of pharmacist-led patient counseling on health outcomes, such as improved disease management, reduced hospital admissions, and enhanced quality of life. This research can provide evidence for the value of pharmacist interventions in patient care.

Cultural Competency in Counseling: Examine the role of cultural competency in patient counseling. Research can explore how pharmacists can tailor their counseling approaches to meet the cultural, linguistic, and social needs of diverse patient populations, leading to better health outcomes.

3. Health Outcomes

Pharmacist-Driven Health Interventions: Evaluate the impact of pharmacist-driven health interventions on patient outcomes. This can include disease management programs, medication therapy management (MTM) services, and preventive health initiatives such as immunization programs.

Cost-Effectiveness of Pharmacy Services: Conduct cost-effectiveness analyses of community pharmacy services. Research can compare the costs and benefits of pharmacist interventions to traditional healthcare models, demonstrating the economic value of integrating pharmacists into the healthcare team.

Management of Chronic Diseases: Investigate the role of community pharmacists in managing chronic diseases. Research can assess the effectiveness of pharmacist-led disease management programs in improving clinical outcomes, patient satisfaction, and reducing healthcare costs.

4. Technology and Innovation

Digital Health Tools: Explore the use of digital health tools in community pharmacy practice, such as mobile health apps, telepharmacy, and electronic health records (EHRs). Research can assess how these technologies enhance patient care, improve medication management, and facilitate communication between healthcare providers.

Artificial Intelligence (AI) in Pharmacy: Investigate the potential applications of AI in community pharmacy, such as predictive analytics for medication adherence, automated drug interaction checks, and personalized medication recommendations. Research can evaluate the feasibility, accuracy, and impact of AI-driven tools on pharmacy practice.

5. Patient Safety and Quality Improvement

Medication Error Prevention: Study the strategies for preventing medication errors in community pharmacy settings. Research can focus on the effectiveness of safety protocols, staff training programs, and technology solutions in reducing medication errors and enhancing patient safety.

Quality Improvement Initiatives: Evaluate the impact of quality improvement initiatives on pharmacy practice. Research can assess how continuous quality improvement processes, such as medication reconciliation and audit-feedback cycles, contribute to safer and more effective patient care.

6. Public Health and Preventive Care

Role of Pharmacists in Public Health: Investigate the role of community pharmacists in public health initiatives, such as smoking cessation programs, weight management, and screenings for chronic diseases. Research can explore the reach and effectiveness of these programs in improving community health.

Vaccine Uptake and Immunization Programs: Study the factors influencing vaccine uptake in community settings and the impact of pharmacist-led immunization programs on vaccination rates. Research can identify best practices for increasing vaccine coverage and addressing vaccine hesitancy.

7. Health Disparities and Access to Care

Addressing Health Disparities: Examine the role of community pharmacists in addressing health disparities and improving access to care for underserved populations. Research can explore how pharmacists can contribute to reducing health inequities through targeted interventions and outreach programs.

Telepharmacy and Rural Health: Investigate the impact of telepharmacy services on access to care in rural and underserved areas. Research can assess how telepharmacy improves medication access, patient outcomes, and satisfaction in these communities.

By focusing on these research areas, community pharmacists can contribute valuable insights and evidence to the field of pharmacy practice. This research not only enhances the quality of care provided to patients but also supports the ongoing development and recognition of the community pharmacy profession as an integral part of the healthcare system.

10.2 Research in Community Pharmacy Practice

10.2.1 Identifying Research Opportunities

10.2.1.1 Areas for Research in Community Pharmacy

Potential Research Topics Such as Medication Adherence, Patient Counseling, and Health Outcomes

Research in community pharmacy practice is essential for advancing the profession, improving patient care, and optimizing health outcomes. By identifying and exploring key areas for research, community pharmacists can contribute to evidence-based practice and the development of innovative solutions to healthcare challenges. Here are some potential research topics in community pharmacy:

1. Medication Adherence

Factors Influencing Adherence: Investigate the various factors that affect medication adherence, such as patient beliefs, socioeconomic status, health literacy, and the complexity of medication regimens. Understanding these factors can help develop targeted interventions to improve adherence.

Interventions to Improve Adherence: Evaluate the effectiveness of different interventions designed to enhance medication adherence, including medication synchronization, pill organizers, reminder systems, and pharmacist-led counseling. Research can compare the impact of these interventions on adherence rates and health outcomes.

Adherence in Chronic Conditions: Focus on adherence in patients with chronic conditions such as diabetes, hypertension, and asthma. Research can explore the barriers specific to these populations and identify strategies to support long-term adherence to prescribed therapies.

2. Patient Counseling

Counseling Techniques: Study the effectiveness of various patient counseling techniques, such as motivational interviewing, cognitive-behavioral therapy, and educational sessions. Research can assess how these techniques influence patient understanding, behavior change, and medication adherence.

Impact of Counseling on Health Outcomes: Investigate the impact of pharmacist-led patient counseling on health outcomes, such as improved disease management, reduced hospital admissions, and enhanced quality of life. This research can provide evidence for the value of pharmacist interventions in patient care.

Cultural Competency in Counseling: Examine the role of cultural competency in patient counseling. Research can explore how pharmacists can tailor their counseling approaches to meet the cultural, linguistic, and social needs of diverse patient populations, leading to better health outcomes.

3. Health Outcomes

Pharmacist-Driven Health Interventions: Evaluate the impact of pharmacist-driven health interventions on patient outcomes. This can include disease management programs, medication therapy management (MTM) services, and preventive health initiatives such as immunization programs.

Cost-Effectiveness of Pharmacy Services: Conduct cost-effectiveness analyses of community pharmacy services. Research can compare the costs and benefits of pharmacist interventions to traditional healthcare models, demonstrating the economic value of integrating pharmacists into the healthcare team.

Management of Chronic Diseases: Investigate the role of community pharmacists in managing chronic diseases. Research can assess the effectiveness of pharmacist-led disease management programs in improving clinical outcomes, patient satisfaction, and reducing healthcare costs.

4. Technology and Innovation

Digital Health Tools: Explore the use of digital health tools in community pharmacy practice, such as mobile health apps, telepharmacy, and electronic health records (EHRs). Research can assess how these technologies enhance patient care, improve medication management, and facilitate communication between healthcare providers.

Artificial Intelligence (AI) in Pharmacy: Investigate the potential applications of AI in community pharmacy, such as predictive analytics for medication adherence, automated drug interaction checks, and personalized medication recommendations. Research can evaluate the feasibility, accuracy, and impact of AI-driven tools on pharmacy practice.

5. Patient Safety and Quality Improvement

Medication Error Prevention: Study the strategies for preventing medication errors in community pharmacy settings. Research can focus on the effectiveness of safety protocols, staff training programs, and technology solutions in reducing medication errors and enhancing patient safety.

Quality Improvement Initiatives: Evaluate the impact of quality improvement initiatives on pharmacy practice. Research can assess how continuous quality improvement processes, such as medication reconciliation and audit-feedback cycles, contribute to safer and more effective patient care.

6. Public Health and Preventive Care

Role of Pharmacists in Public Health: Investigate the role of community pharmacists in public health initiatives, such as smoking cessation programs, weight management, and screenings for chronic diseases. Research can explore the reach and effectiveness of these programs in improving community health.

Vaccine Uptake and Immunization Programs: Study the factors influencing vaccine uptake in community settings and the impact of pharmacist-led immunization programs on vaccination rates. Research can identify best practices for increasing vaccine coverage and addressing vaccine hesitancy.

7. Health Disparities and Access to Care

Addressing Health Disparities: Examine the role of community pharmacists in addressing health disparities and improving access to care for underserved populations. Research can explore how pharmacists can contribute to reducing health inequities through targeted interventions and outreach programs.

Telepharmacy and Rural Health: Investigate the impact of telepharmacy services on access to care in rural and underserved areas. Research can assess how telepharmacy improves medication access, patient outcomes, and satisfaction in these communities.

By focusing on these research areas, community pharmacists can contribute valuable insights and evidence to the field of pharmacy practice. This research not only enhances the quality of care provided to patients but also supports the ongoing development and recognition of the community pharmacy profession as an integral part of the healthcare system.

10.2.1.2 Formulating Research Questions

Developing Clear and Focused Research Questions and Hypotheses

Formulating research questions is a critical step in the research process, as it defines the scope, direction, and purpose of the study. Well-developed research questions guide the research design, data collection, and analysis, ensuring that the study addresses specific issues and contributes valuable knowledge to the field. Here are some key considerations for developing clear and focused research questions and hypotheses:

Identifying the Research Problem: Start by identifying the broad research problem or area of interest. This could be based on gaps in existing literature, clinical observations, or emerging trends in community pharmacy practice. Narrow down the broad problem to a specific, manageable issue that can be addressed through research.

Literature Review: Conduct a thorough literature review to understand the current state of knowledge on the topic. This helps identify gaps, controversies, and unanswered questions in the field. Reviewing previous studies also provides insights into potential research methods and theoretical frameworks.

Defining the Research Question: A well-defined research question should be specific, measurable, achievable, relevant, and time-bound (SMART). It should clearly state what the researcher aims to investigate and the expected outcomes. For example, instead of a vague question like "How can medication adherence be improved?" a more focused question would be "What is the impact of pharmacist-led counseling on medication adherence rates among diabetic patients over six months?"

Formulating Hypotheses: A hypothesis is a testable statement that predicts the relationship between variables. It provides a basis for data collection and analysis. Hypotheses can be directional (predicting a specific direction of the relationship) or non-directional (not specifying the direction). For example, a directional hypothesis could be "Pharmacist-led counseling will significantly improve medication adherence rates among diabetic patients."

Operationalizing Variables: Clearly define the variables involved in the research question and hypothesis. This includes independent variables (e.g., pharmacist-led counseling) and dependent variables (e.g., medication adherence rates). Operational definitions specify how these variables will be measured and observed.

Ensuring Feasibility: Consider the feasibility of the research question and hypothesis in terms of available resources, time, and access to data. Ensure that the research can be realistically conducted within the constraints of the study setting.

Ethical Considerations: Ensure that the research question and hypothesis align with ethical standards. Consider potential ethical issues related to patient consent, confidentiality, and potential risks or benefits to participants.

Examples of Research Questions and Hypotheses:

Medication Adherence: Research Question: "What factors influence medication adherence among elderly patients in a community pharmacy setting?" Hypothesis: "Patients with higher health literacy will show better medication adherence compared to those with lower health literacy."

Patient Counseling: Research Question: "How does the use of motivational interviewing techniques by pharmacists affect smoking cessation rates?" Hypothesis: "Patients who receive motivational interviewing from pharmacists will have higher smoking cessation rates compared to those who receive standard counseling."

Health Outcomes: Research Question: "What is the impact of pharmacist-led disease management programs on blood pressure control in hypertensive patients?" Hypothesis: "Hypertensive patients enrolled in pharmacist-led disease management programs will achieve better blood pressure control compared to those receiving usual care."

Technology in Pharmacy: Research Question: "How does the use of a mobile health app for medication reminders affect adherence in patients with chronic illnesses?" Hypothesis: "Patients using a mobile health app for medication reminders will show higher adherence rates compared to those not using the app."

By formulating clear and focused research questions and hypotheses, researchers can ensure that their studies are well-designed and yield meaningful and actionable insights. This contributes to the advancement of community pharmacy practice and the improvement of patient care and health outcomes.

10.2 Research in Community Pharmacy Practice

10.2.1 Identifying Research Opportunities

10.2.1.1 Areas for Research in Community Pharmacy

Potential Research Topics Such as Medication Adherence, Patient Counseling, and Health Outcomes

Research in community pharmacy practice is essential for advancing the profession, improving patient care, and optimizing health outcomes. By identifying and exploring key areas for research, community pharmacists can contribute to evidence-based practice and the development of innovative solutions to healthcare challenges. Here are some potential research topics in community pharmacy:

1. Medication Adherence

Factors Influencing Adherence: Investigate the various factors that affect medication adherence, such as patient beliefs, socioeconomic status, health literacy, and the complexity of medication regimens. Understanding these factors can help develop targeted interventions to improve adherence.

Interventions to Improve Adherence: Evaluate the effectiveness of different interventions designed to enhance medication adherence, including medication synchronization, pill organizers, reminder systems, and pharmacist-led counseling. Research can compare the impact of these interventions on adherence rates and health outcomes.

Adherence in Chronic Conditions: Focus on adherence in patients with chronic conditions such as diabetes, hypertension, and asthma. Research can explore the barriers specific to these populations and identify strategies to support long-term adherence to prescribed therapies.

2. Patient Counseling

Counseling Techniques: Study the effectiveness of various patient counseling techniques, such as motivational interviewing, cognitive-behavioral therapy, and educational sessions. Research can assess how these techniques influence patient understanding, behavior change, and medication adherence.

Impact of Counseling on Health Outcomes: Investigate the impact of pharmacist-led patient counseling on health outcomes, such as improved disease management, reduced hospital admissions, and enhanced quality of life. This research can provide evidence for the value of pharmacist interventions in patient care.

Cultural Competency in Counseling: Examine the role of cultural competency in patient counseling. Research can explore how pharmacists can tailor their counseling approaches to meet the cultural, linguistic, and social needs of diverse patient populations, leading to better health outcomes.

3. Health Outcomes

Pharmacist-Driven Health Interventions: Evaluate the impact of pharmacist-driven health interventions on patient outcomes. This can include disease management programs, medication therapy management (MTM) services, and preventive health initiatives such as immunization programs.

Cost-Effectiveness of Pharmacy Services: Conduct cost-effectiveness analyses of community pharmacy services. Research can compare the costs and benefits of pharmacist interventions to traditional healthcare models, demonstrating the economic value of integrating pharmacists into the healthcare team.

Management of Chronic Diseases: Investigate the role of community pharmacists in managing chronic diseases. Research can assess the effectiveness of pharmacist-led disease management programs in improving clinical outcomes, patient satisfaction, and reducing healthcare costs.

4. Technology and Innovation

Digital Health Tools: Explore the use of digital health tools in community pharmacy practice, such as mobile health apps, telepharmacy, and electronic health records (EHRs). Research can assess how these technologies enhance patient care, improve medication management, and facilitate communication between healthcare providers.

Artificial Intelligence (AI) in Pharmacy: Investigate the potential applications of AI in community pharmacy, such as predictive analytics for medication adherence, automated drug interaction checks, and personalized medication recommendations. Research can evaluate the feasibility, accuracy, and impact of AI-driven tools on pharmacy practice.

5. Patient Safety and Quality Improvement

Medication Error Prevention: Study the strategies for preventing medication errors in community pharmacy settings. Research can focus on the effectiveness of safety protocols, staff training programs, and technology solutions in reducing medication errors and enhancing patient safety.

Quality Improvement Initiatives: Evaluate the impact of quality improvement initiatives on pharmacy practice. Research can assess how continuous quality improvement processes, such as medication reconciliation and audit-feedback cycles, contribute to safer and more effective patient care.

6. Public Health and Preventive Care

Role of Pharmacists in Public Health: Investigate the role of community pharmacists in public health initiatives, such as smoking cessation programs, weight management, and screenings for chronic diseases. Research can explore the reach and effectiveness of these programs in improving community health.

Vaccine Uptake and Immunization Programs: Study the factors influencing vaccine uptake in community settings and the impact of pharmacist-led immunization programs on vaccination rates. Research can identify best practices for increasing vaccine coverage and addressing vaccine hesitancy.

7. Health Disparities and Access to Care

Addressing Health Disparities: Examine the role of community pharmacists in addressing health disparities and improving access to care for underserved populations. Research can explore how pharmacists can contribute to reducing health inequities through targeted interventions and outreach programs.

Telepharmacy and Rural Health: Investigate the impact of telepharmacy services on access to care in rural and underserved areas. Research can assess how telepharmacy improves medication access, patient outcomes, and satisfaction in these communities.

By focusing on these research areas, community pharmacists can contribute valuable insights and evidence to the field of pharmacy practice. This research not only enhances the quality of care provided to patients but also supports the ongoing development and recognition of the community pharmacy profession as an integral part of the healthcare system.

10.2.1.2 Formulating Research Questions

Developing Clear and Focused Research Questions and Hypotheses

Formulating research questions is a critical step in the research process, as it defines the scope, direction, and purpose of the study. Well-developed research questions guide the research design, data collection, and analysis, ensuring that the study addresses specific issues and contributes valuable knowledge to the field. Here are some key considerations for developing clear and focused research questions and hypotheses:

Identifying the Research Problem: Start by identifying the broad research problem or area of interest. This could be based on gaps in existing literature, clinical observations, or emerging trends in community pharmacy practice. Narrow down the broad problem to a specific, manageable issue that can be addressed through research.

Literature Review: Conduct a thorough literature review to understand the current state of knowledge on the topic. This helps identify gaps, controversies, and unanswered questions in the field. Reviewing previous studies also provides insights into potential research methods and theoretical frameworks.

Defining the Research Question: A well-defined research question should be specific, measurable, achievable, relevant, and time-bound (SMART). It should clearly state what the researcher aims to investigate and the expected outcomes. For example, instead of a vague question like "How can medication adherence be improved?" a more focused question would be "What is the impact of pharmacist-led counseling on medication adherence rates among diabetic patients over six months?"

Formulating Hypotheses: A hypothesis is a testable statement that predicts the relationship between variables. It provides a basis for data collection and analysis. Hypotheses can be directional (predicting a specific direction of the relationship) or non-directional (not specifying the direction). For example, a directional hypothesis could be "Pharmacist-led counseling will significantly improve medication adherence rates among diabetic patients."

Operationalizing Variables: Clearly define the variables involved in the research question and hypothesis. This includes independent variables (e.g., pharmacist-led counseling) and dependent variables (e.g., medication adherence rates). Operational definitions specify how these variables will be measured and observed.

Ensuring Feasibility: Consider the feasibility of the research question and hypothesis in terms of available resources, time, and access to data. Ensure that the research can be realistically conducted within the constraints of the study setting.

Ethical Considerations: Ensure that the research question and hypothesis align with ethical standards. Consider potential ethical issues related to patient consent, confidentiality, and potential risks or benefits to participants.

Examples of Research Questions and Hypotheses:

Medication Adherence: Research Question: "What factors influence medication adherence among elderly patients in a community pharmacy setting?" Hypothesis: "Patients with higher health literacy will show better medication adherence compared to those with lower health literacy."

Patient Counseling: Research Question: "How does the use of motivational interviewing techniques by pharmacists affect smoking cessation rates?" Hypothesis: "Patients who receive motivational interviewing from pharmacists will have higher smoking cessation rates compared to those who receive standard counseling."

Health Outcomes: Research Question: "What is the impact of pharmacist-led disease management programs on blood pressure control in hypertensive patients?" Hypothesis: "Hypertensive patients enrolled in pharmacist-led disease management programs will achieve better blood pressure control compared to those receiving usual care."

Technology in Pharmacy: Research Question: "How does the use of a mobile health app for medication reminders affect adherence in patients with chronic illnesses?" Hypothesis: "Patients using a mobile health app for medication reminders will show higher adherence rates compared to those not using the app."

By formulating clear and focused research questions and hypotheses, researchers can ensure that their studies are well-designed and yield meaningful and actionable insights. This contributes to the advancement of community pharmacy practice and the improvement of patient care and health outcomes.

10.2.1.3 Reviewing Existing Literature

Conducting Literature Reviews to Identify Gaps and Support Research Initiatives

Conducting a literature review is a fundamental step in the research process that involves systematically searching, evaluating, and synthesizing existing research on a particular topic. A thorough literature review helps researchers understand the current state of knowledge, identify gaps, and provide a strong foundation for new research initiatives. Here are the key steps and considerations for conducting a literature review:

Defining the Scope and Objectives: Clearly define the scope and objectives of the literature review. Determine the specific research questions or topics that the review will address. This helps focus the search and ensures that the review is comprehensive and relevant.

Searching for Relevant Literature: Use various sources to search for relevant literature, including academic databases (e.g., PubMed, Scopus, Web of Science), library catalogs, and online repositories. Use specific keywords and search terms related to the research topic to retrieve relevant articles, books, and reports.

Evaluating the Quality of Sources: Assess the quality and credibility of the sources retrieved. Prioritize peer-reviewed journal articles, authoritative books, and reputable reports.

10.2.2 Conducting Research in Community Pharmacy

10.2.2.1 Designing Research Studies

Choosing Appropriate Research Designs for Community Pharmacy Research

Designing a robust research study is crucial for obtaining reliable and valid results that can inform and improve community pharmacy practice. The choice of research design depends on the research questions, objectives, and available resources. Here are some common research designs used in community pharmacy research:

1. Descriptive Studies: Descriptive studies aim to describe the characteristics of a population or phenomenon. These studies often use surveys, interviews, or observational methods to gather data. For example, a survey might be conducted to assess patient satisfaction with pharmacy services or to describe the demographic characteristics of a pharmacy's clientele.

2. Cross-Sectional Studies: Cross-sectional studies involve collecting data at a single point in time from a specific population. These studies are useful for examining the prevalence of certain conditions or behaviors. For example, a cross-sectional study might investigate the prevalence of medication non-adherence among patients with chronic illnesses in a community pharmacy setting.

3. Cohort Studies: Cohort studies follow a group of individuals over time to observe the development of outcomes. These studies can be prospective (following participants into the future) or retrospective (looking back at past data). For example, a prospective cohort study might track patients who receive pharmacist-led counseling to monitor their medication adherence over six months.

4. Randomized Controlled Trials (RCTs): RCTs are considered the gold standard for evaluating the effectiveness of interventions. Participants are randomly assigned to either the intervention group or the control group, and outcomes are compared between the groups. For example, an RCT might evaluate the impact of a mobile health app on medication adherence by randomly assigning patients to use the app or to receive usual care.

5. Qualitative Studies: Qualitative studies explore participants' experiences, perceptions, and attitudes through methods such as interviews, focus groups, and content analysis. These studies provide in-depth insights that quantitative methods might not capture. For example, a qualitative study might explore patients' experiences with pharmacist-led smoking cessation programs.

6. Mixed-Methods Studies: Mixed-methods studies combine quantitative and qualitative approaches to provide a comprehensive understanding of the research problem. For example, a mixed-methods study might use surveys to quantify medication adherence rates and interviews to explore the reasons behind non-adherence.

Choosing the appropriate research design involves considering the research questions, the nature of the data, and the practical constraints. A well-chosen research design ensures that the study can effectively address the research objectives and produce meaningful and actionable findings.

10.2.2.2 Data Collection and Analysis

Techniques for Gathering and Analyzing Data Effectively

Effective data collection and analysis are critical components of the research process. They ensure that the data gathered are reliable, valid, and useful for answering the research questions. Here are some key techniques for data collection and analysis in community pharmacy research:

1. Data Collection Techniques:

Surveys and Questionnaires: Surveys and questionnaires are commonly used to collect data from large groups of participants. They can be administered in person, by mail, online, or through mobile apps. It's important to design clear and concise questions to avoid bias and ensure accurate responses.

Interviews: Interviews provide in-depth information about participants' experiences, perceptions, and attitudes. They can be structured (with a fixed set of questions), semi-structured (with a flexible guide), or unstructured (open-ended and conversational). Recording and transcribing interviews help in the accurate analysis of the data.

Observations: Observational methods involve systematically watching and recording behaviors and events. This technique is useful for studying interactions and behaviors in their natural context, such as observing patient-pharmacist interactions in a pharmacy.

Focus Groups: Focus groups gather a small group of participants to discuss a specific topic. This method helps generate rich qualitative data and diverse perspectives. Facilitators guide the discussion to ensure all relevant topics are covered.

Medical Records and Databases: Analyzing existing medical records and pharmacy databases can provide valuable information on medication use, health outcomes, and patient demographics. Access to accurate and comprehensive records is essential for reliable data.

2. Data Analysis Techniques:

Descriptive Statistics: Descriptive statistics summarize and describe the main features of a dataset. Measures such as mean, median, mode, standard deviation, and frequency distributions help understand the basic characteristics of the data.

Inferential Statistics: Inferential statistics allow researchers to make generalizations from a sample to a population. Techniques such as hypothesis testing, confidence intervals, and regression analysis help determine the relationships between variables and the significance of findings.

Thematic Analysis: Thematic analysis is used in qualitative research to identify, analyze, and report patterns (themes) within data. It involves coding the data, identifying themes, and interpreting their meaning and relevance to the research questions.

Content Analysis: Content analysis systematically categorizes textual or visual data to identify patterns, themes, and trends. It is useful for analyzing qualitative data from interviews, focus groups, and open-ended survey responses.

Statistical Software: Various statistical software programs, such as SPSS, SAS, R, and NVivo, assist in data analysis. These tools help manage data, perform complex statistical analyses, and visualize results.

Effective data collection and analysis require careful planning, appropriate tools, and adherence to ethical standards. Ensuring data accuracy, reliability, and validity is essential for producing credible and actionable research findings.

10.2.2.3 Implementing Research Findings

Translating Research Outcomes into Practical Applications to Enhance Pharmacy Practice

Implementing research findings into community pharmacy practice is essential for translating evidence into action and improving patient care. Here are some strategies for effectively implementing research outcomes:

1. Dissemination of Findings:

Publishing in Peer-Reviewed Journals: Sharing research findings through peer-reviewed journals ensures that the results are rigorously evaluated and accessible to the academic and professional community. This enhances the credibility and impact of the research.

Presenting at Conferences: Presenting research at professional conferences allows researchers to share their findings with peers, engage in discussions, and receive feedback. Conferences provide a platform for networking and collaboration.

Workshops and Training Sessions: Conducting workshops and training sessions helps disseminate research findings to practitioners. These sessions can provide practical guidance on how to implement evidence-based practices in community pharmacies.

2. Developing Practice Guidelines:

Evidence-Based Guidelines: Using research findings to develop or update practice guidelines ensures that community pharmacy practices are based on the best available evidence. Guidelines provide standardized recommendations for patient care and help improve consistency and quality.

Implementation Toolkits: Creating toolkits that include practical tools, checklists, and resources helps pharmacists implement research-based practices. These toolkits can provide step-by-step instructions and support for integrating new practices into daily workflows.

3. Collaborating with Stakeholders:

Engaging Healthcare Providers: Collaborating with other healthcare providers, such as physicians, nurses, and public health professionals, facilitates the integration of research findings into broader healthcare practices. Interdisciplinary collaboration enhances patient care and outcomes.

Involving Patients and Communities: Involving patients and communities in the research implementation process ensures that the practices are patient-centered and address their needs. Patient feedback and participation can help refine and optimize interventions.

4. Evaluating Implementation Outcomes:

Monitoring and Evaluation: Continuously monitoring and evaluating the implementation of research findings helps assess the effectiveness and impact of new practices. This process can identify challenges, successes, and areas for improvement.

Quality Improvement Initiatives: Using research findings to inform quality improvement initiatives helps drive ongoing enhancements in pharmacy practice. These initiatives can focus on specific areas such as medication safety, patient counseling, and health outcomes.

5. Policy Advocacy:

Advocating for Policy Changes: Using research findings to advocate for policy changes at the local, state, or national level can help create an enabling environment for evidence-based practices. Policymakers can use research evidence to make informed decisions that support public health and pharmacy practice.

Educating Policymakers: Educating policymakers about the importance and impact of research findings helps garner support for necessary changes. Providing clear, concise, and evidence-based information can influence policy decisions and resource allocation.

By effectively implementing research findings, community pharmacists can enhance their practice, improve patient care, and contribute to the advancement of the profession. Translating research

into action ensures that the benefits of research are realized in real-world settings, leading to better health outcomes for patients and communities.

10.2.2 Conducting Research in Community Pharmacy

10.2.2.1 Designing Research Studies

Choosing Appropriate Research Designs for Community Pharmacy Research

Designing a robust research study is crucial for obtaining reliable and valid results that can inform and improve community pharmacy practice. The choice of research design depends on the research questions, objectives, and available resources. Here are some common research designs used in community pharmacy research:

1. Descriptive Studies: Descriptive studies aim to describe the characteristics of a population or phenomenon. These studies often use surveys, interviews, or observational methods to gather data. For example, a survey might be conducted to assess patient satisfaction with pharmacy services or to describe the demographic characteristics of a pharmacy's clientele.

2. Cross-Sectional Studies: Cross-sectional studies involve collecting data at a single point in time from a specific population. These studies are useful for examining the prevalence of certain conditions or behaviors. For example, a cross-sectional study might investigate the prevalence of medication non-adherence among patients with chronic illnesses in a community pharmacy setting.

3. Cohort Studies: Cohort studies follow a group of individuals over time to observe the development of outcomes. These studies can be prospective (following participants into the future) or retrospective (looking back at past data). For example, a prospective cohort study might track patients who receive pharmacist-led counseling to monitor their medication adherence over six months.

4. Randomized Controlled Trials (RCTs): RCTs are considered the gold standard for evaluating the effectiveness of interventions. Participants are randomly assigned to either the intervention group or the control group, and outcomes are compared between the groups. For example, an RCT might evaluate the impact of a mobile health app on medication adherence by randomly assigning patients to use the app or to receive usual care.

5. Qualitative Studies: Qualitative studies explore participants' experiences, perceptions, and attitudes through methods such as interviews, focus groups, and content analysis. These studies provide in-depth insights that quantitative methods might not capture. For example, a qualitative study might explore patients' experiences with pharmacist-led smoking cessation programs.

6. Mixed-Methods Studies: Mixed-methods studies combine quantitative and qualitative approaches to provide a comprehensive understanding of the research problem. For example, a mixed-methods study might use surveys to quantify medication adherence rates and interviews to explore the reasons behind non-adherence.

Choosing the appropriate research design involves considering the research questions, the nature of the data, and the practical constraints. A well-chosen research design ensures that the study can effectively address the research objectives and produce meaningful and actionable findings.

10.2.2.2 Data Collection and Analysis
Techniques for Gathering and Analyzing Data Effectively

Effective data collection and analysis are critical components of the research process. They ensure that the data gathered are reliable, valid, and useful for answering the research questions. Here are some key techniques for data collection and analysis in community pharmacy research:

1. Data Collection Techniques:

Surveys and Questionnaires: Surveys and questionnaires are commonly used to collect data from large groups of participants. They can be administered in person, by mail, online, or through mobile apps. It's important to design clear and concise questions to avoid bias and ensure accurate responses.

Interviews: Interviews provide in-depth information about participants' experiences, perceptions, and attitudes. They can be structured (with a fixed set of questions), semi-structured (with a flexible guide), or unstructured (open-ended and conversational). Recording and transcribing interviews help in the accurate analysis of the data.

Observations: Observational methods involve systematically watching and recording behaviors and events. This technique is useful for studying interactions and behaviors in their natural context, such as observing patient-pharmacist interactions in a pharmacy.

Focus Groups: Focus groups gather a small group of participants to discuss a specific topic. This method helps generate rich qualitative data and diverse perspectives. Facilitators guide the discussion to ensure all relevant topics are covered.

Medical Records and Databases: Analyzing existing medical records and pharmacy databases can provide valuable information on medication use, health outcomes, and patient demographics. Access to accurate and comprehensive records is essential for reliable data.

2. Data Analysis Techniques:

Descriptive Statistics: Descriptive statistics summarize and describe the main features of a dataset. Measures such as mean, median, mode, standard deviation, and frequency distributions help understand the basic characteristics of the data.

Inferential Statistics: Inferential statistics allow researchers to make generalizations from a sample to a population. Techniques such as hypothesis testing, confidence intervals, and regression analysis help determine the relationships between variables and the significance of findings.

Thematic Analysis: Thematic analysis is used in qualitative research to identify, analyze, and report patterns (themes) within data. It involves coding the data, identifying themes, and interpreting their meaning and relevance to the research questions.

Content Analysis: Content analysis systematically categorizes textual or visual data to identify patterns, themes, and trends. It is useful for analyzing qualitative data from interviews, focus groups, and open-ended survey responses.

Statistical Software: Various statistical software programs, such as SPSS, SAS, R, and NVivo, assist in data analysis. These tools help manage data, perform complex statistical analyses, and visualize results.

Effective data collection and analysis require careful planning, appropriate tools, and adherence to ethical standards. Ensuring data accuracy, reliability, and validity is essential for producing credible and actionable research findings.

10.2.2.3 Implementing Research Findings

Translating Research Outcomes into Practical Applications to Enhance Pharmacy Practice

Implementing research findings into community pharmacy practice is essential for translating evidence into action and improving patient care. Here are some strategies for effectively implementing research outcomes:

1. Dissemination of Findings:

Publishing in Peer-Reviewed Journals: Sharing research findings through peer-reviewed journals ensures that the results are rigorously evaluated and accessible to the academic and professional community. This enhances the credibility and impact of the research.

Presenting at Conferences: Presenting research at professional conferences allows researchers to share their findings with peers, engage in discussions, and receive feedback. Conferences provide a platform for networking and collaboration.

Workshops and Training Sessions: Conducting workshops and training sessions helps disseminate research findings to practitioners. These sessions can provide practical guidance on how to implement evidence-based practices in community pharmacies.

2. Developing Practice Guidelines:

Evidence-Based Guidelines: Using research findings to develop or update practice guidelines ensures that community pharmacy practices are based on the best available evidence. Guidelines provide standardized recommendations for patient care and help improve consistency and quality.

Implementation Toolkits: Creating toolkits that include practical tools, checklists, and resources helps pharmacists implement research-based practices. These toolkits can provide step-by-step instructions and support for integrating new practices into daily workflows.

3. Collaborating with Stakeholders:

Engaging Healthcare Providers: Collaborating with other healthcare providers, such as physicians, nurses, and public health professionals, facilitates the integration of research findings into broader healthcare practices. Interdisciplinary collaboration enhances patient care and outcomes.

Involving Patients and Communities: Involving patients and communities in the research implementation process ensures that the practices are patient-centered and address their needs. Patient feedback and participation can help refine and optimize interventions.

4. Evaluating Implementation Outcomes:

Monitoring and Evaluation: Continuously monitoring and evaluating the implementation of research findings helps assess the effectiveness and impact of new practices. This process can identify challenges, successes, and areas for improvement.

Quality Improvement Initiatives: Using research findings to inform quality improvement initiatives helps drive ongoing enhancements in pharmacy practice. These initiatives can focus on specific areas such as medication safety, patient counseling, and health outcomes.

5. Policy Advocacy:

Advocating for Policy Changes: Using research findings to advocate for policy changes at the local, state, or national level can help create an enabling environment for evidence-based practices. Policymakers can use research evidence to make informed decisions that support public health and pharmacy practice.

Educating Policymakers: Educating policymakers about the importance and impact of research findings helps garner support for necessary changes. Providing clear, concise, and evidence-based information can influence policy decisions and resource allocation.

By effectively implementing research findings, community pharmacists can enhance their practice, improve patient care, and contribute to the advancement of the profession. Translating research into action ensures that the benefits of research are realized in real-world settings, leading to better health outcomes for patients and communities.

10.2.2.4 Collaboration with Academic and Health Institutions

Building Partnerships with Academic Researchers and Healthcare Organizations to Support and Disseminate Research

Collaborating with academic and health institutions is vital for advancing community pharmacy research and ensuring that findings are effectively translated into practice. Here are strategies for building productive partnerships:

1. Establishing Collaborative Research Projects:

Joint Research Initiatives: Partnering with academic researchers and healthcare organizations to design and conduct joint research projects can pool resources, expertise, and perspectives. This collaboration enhances the scope and quality of the research.

Interdisciplinary Teams: Forming interdisciplinary research teams that include pharmacists, physicians, nurses, and researchers from various fields ensures a comprehensive approach to addressing research questions and developing practical solutions.

2. Leveraging Institutional Resources:

Access to Research Facilities: Collaborating with academic institutions provides access to advanced research facilities, laboratories, and equipment that may not be available in community pharmacies. This access can enhance the rigor and capabilities of the research.

Utilizing Academic Expertise: Engaging with academic researchers brings specialized knowledge and expertise in research methodologies, data analysis, and theoretical frameworks. This expertise can strengthen the design and execution of research studies.

3. Engaging in Knowledge Exchange:

Workshops and Seminars: Participating in and organizing workshops, seminars, and symposiums with academic and healthcare partners facilitates knowledge exchange and keeps practitioners updated on the latest research developments and best practices.

Guest Lectures and Training: Inviting academic experts to provide guest lectures and training sessions for community pharmacists fosters continuous professional development and integrates new research findings into practice.

4. Enhancing Research Funding and Support:

Grant Applications: Collaborating with academic institutions can improve the chances of securing research grants and funding. Joint grant applications demonstrate a commitment to rigorous and impactful research, increasing the likelihood of funding approval.

Institutional Support: Academic and healthcare institutions often provide administrative and logistical support for research projects, including assistance with ethics approvals, data management, and publication processes.

5. Disseminating Research Findings:

Co-Authorship of Publications: Co-authoring research papers with academic and healthcare partners ensures that findings are disseminated through reputable and widely-read journals, reaching a broader audience and enhancing the impact of the research.

Conference Presentations: Presenting collaborative research at national and international conferences showcases the partnership's achievements and promotes the translation of research into practice across different settings.

6. Developing Community-Based Research Programs:

Community Engagement: Collaborating with academic and healthcare institutions to develop community-based research programs ensures that research addresses the specific needs and challenges of the local population. Engaging the community in the research process enhances relevance and impact.

Patient-Centered Research: Focusing on patient-centered research that involves patients and caregivers in the study design, implementation, and dissemination ensures that research outcomes are directly applicable and beneficial to patient care.

By building strong partnerships with academic and health institutions, community pharmacists can enhance the quality and impact of their research, ensure the effective translation of findings into practice, and contribute to the advancement of the pharmacy profession. Collaborative efforts foster innovation, improve patient care, and promote the continuous development of evidence-based practices in community pharmacy.